LIVES OF WIVES

Laura (Riding) Jackson

Lives of Wives

with a Foreword and Afterword
by the author

SUN &
MOON
CLASSICS
71

LOS ANGELES
SUN & MOON PRESS
1995

Sun & Moon Press
A Program of The Contemporary Arts Educational Project, Inc.
a nonprofit corporation
6026 Wilshire Boulevard, Los Angeles, California 90036

This edition first published by Sun & Moon Press in 1995
10 9 8 7 6 5 4 3 2 1
FIRST SUN & MOON EDITION
©1988, 1939 by Laura (Riding) Jackson
Reprinted by permission
Biographical material ©1995 by Sun & Moon Press
All rights reserved

This book was made possible, in part, through an operational grant from
the Andrew W. Mellon Foundation and through contributions to
The Contemporary Arts Educational Project, Inc.,
a nonprofit corporation

Cover: Stephen McKenna, *Clio Observing the Fifth Style*, 1985
Design: Katie Messborn
Typography: Guy Bennett

LIBRARY OF CONGRESS CATALOGING IN PUBLICATION DATA
Jackson, Laura (Riding) [1901–1991]
Lives of Wives
p. cm — (Sun & Moon Classics: 71)
ISBN: 1-55713-182-1
I. Title. II. Series.
811'.54—dc20

Printed in the United States of America on acid-free paper.

FOREWORD

MODERN history really begins with the founding of the Persian Empire. The first emphatic punctuation in history after this is the time of Alexander and Aristotle; and the next after that is the time of Herod the Great.

In the language of Daniel: ancient times were of gold and silver; the age of Cyrus the Persian was of brass; the age of Alexander, of iron, later mixed with clay. And then came the stone which broke into pieces this image of many metals: unhewn stone, like that of the altar of burnt-offerings at Jerusalem.

I have called my version of these three crucial ages preceding the Christian era 'Lives of Wives' because the principal male characters are here written of as husbands rather than as heroes. L. R.

CONTENTS

I

A PERSIAN LADY, AND HER CONTEMPORARIES

II

MACEDONIAN TIMES

III

NEW WAYS IN JERUSALEM

I

A PERSIAN LADY
AND HER CONTEMPORARIES

THE MEDES AND THE PERSIANS

EAST of the River Tigris and Assyria lay Media, the country of the Medes; and south of Media, towards the Great Gulf, lay a country inhabited by a people closely related to the Medes, called Persians. The Medes and the Persians were descended from a horde of wandering tribes that had come down from the north, conquering the native population, then settling down and making these regions their home. They seem to have had no very distinct genius of their own, but to have absorbed the ways and achievements of others, though never more than they could absorb gracefully and sensibly. This has remained a striking characteristic of the Persians— the common name for Medes and Persians after Cyrus, a petty king of old Persia, conquered Media. They early became a civilized, if not great, people.

To the Persians belongs the honour of having been the first gentlemen and ladies in the world.

The Medes became civilized before the Persians, from being more exposed to contact with foreigners; an important Assyrian route to the East led through Media. While suffering from repeated invasions by the Assyrians and constant exactions of tribute, the early Medes were gradually absorbing as much of Mesopotamian culture as they could easily impose upon their simple mountain life. The Persians to the south also came under foreign influence, but less directly; and they took a correspondingly longer time to achieve unity and self-confidence. Nevertheless the Medes kept more strictly than did the Persians to the native religion of the land—a religion of fire-worship and nature-worship. When, shortly before the time of Cyrus, there arose in Bactria to the east of Media a prophet called Zoroaster, his teachings—which were coloured with Indian religious ideas—spread faster among the Persians than among the Medes. Zoroaster condemned the old forms of nature-worship, but the fire-altars continued to be ritualistically important; and the Magi, the fire-priests of native stock, maintained the old religion alongside the new.

In the centre of the Zagros mountains the Medes grew into a strong federation of tribes. Dwarf oaks mark this region as of a kindlier nature than the rest of the Iranian land, in which large tracts of desert abound—except for that part bordering on the Caspian Sea, where vines grow luxuriously and which was not improbably the mother-place of vines and wines. The cultivation of the vine and the making of wine represent two important elements of the gentlemanly life; and the handsome horse a third. In Media were to be found the famous Nisean horses, of which the white were held sacred—and which were indeed the best.

By about the seventh century B.C. the Medes had entirely conquered the Persians and their kings had become supreme over the whole land. The first king was democratically chosen; but severe rules were laid down to make the person of the king reverenced. Very few people were permitted to see him face to face, all petitions being delivered to him through messengers. This custom continued into later times; and most of the life of a Persian king, but for the seasons devoted to war, was thus lived in the private quarters of his palace, among the women and eunuchs of the royal household.

The capital of the Median kingdom was Ecbatana, which lay at the foot of a huge granite range rising above it to a height of six thousand feet. This beautiful city was built in seven successive levels on a low hill of the range; and for each level a different colour was used in the masonry and architectural decorations. Instead of being overshadowed by the severe granite background, the city cast a gentle iridescent glow upon it.

With their racial kinsmen the Persians now in their power, the Medes set out from Ecbatana to revenge themselves on the Assyrians, from whom they had over a long period suffered many humiliations. The king who led them was Cyaxares. His army was strong and confident; his horsemen, who used both the bow and the javelin, fought with a deadly accuracy of aim. The siege of the great Assyrian city of Nineveh was begun, and then abandoned when Cyaxares had news that the wild Scythians had descended upon his country and were dealing cruelly with his people. After he had driven out the Scythians, Cyaxares went into Assyria again and renewed the siege of Nineveh; which this time fell to him. And now Babylon, to the south of Nineveh, at last was able, with the help of Cyaxares, to shake off the Assyrian yoke. The stern Assyrian Empire collapsed; and a new kingdom of Babylon was formed, with Nabopolassar at its head—who had been governor of Babylon under the Assyrians.

This Nabopolassar was the father of Nebuchadnezzar, of Biblical fame, who succeeded him as king. To Nebuchadnezzar succeeded in turn his son; who was dethroned by the priestly party, however, for his partiality to the Jews. Then a son-in-law of Nebuchadnezzar's was King of Babylon—the husband of his elder daughter; and then the son of this son-in-law. And then Nabonidus was King, which brings us into the time of our story. For he began to reign in 556; and Cyrus, whose wife Amytis we shall learn of, became king of the Persian province of Anshan in 558.

The wife of Nabonidus was Nitocris, Nebuchadnezzar's youngest daughter. Nitocris ruled as regent in Babylon during her husband's long absence in Arabia. Messages passed occasionally between Nitocris and Amytis, of a more intimate kind

than the customary official exchanges; for wives could speak
to one another as queens might not. But the story of Nitocris,
and how it happened that Nabonidus was so many years away
from home, will be told when we come to the war that
Cyrus made on Babylonia.

2

THE RISE OF CYRUS, HUSBAND OF AMYTIS

WHEN the Medes conquered their kinsmen the Persians, certain Median families moved into Persia—military and civil governors, tax-collectors, merchants. As the danger of rebellion against Median rule decreased and the Persians began to take their unity with the Medes for granted, the relations between these two parts of the Median Empire became more easy-going: never altogether friendly, since the Medes looked down upon the Persians, but at any rate free on either side of fear of active hostility from the other. The Median rule was a light one; fewer Median officials were sent to Persia than at first, and fewer soldiers to keep order. In many parts of Persia no Medes were to be seen at all, and yet the sovereignty of Media was generally acknowledged. Those Median families that had settled in Persia soon after its conquest married into the noble Persian families; and thus it was that Cyrus had in him a strain of Median blood.

One of these noble families, that to which Cyrus belonged and which was the least of the seven leading families of Persia, kept up a private tradition of resentment against Median rule —partly from being somewhat ashamed of its blood-connexion with the Medians, partly because its elders envied the more ancient families and nourished the ambition that, by bringing about the liberation of Persia, one of their line would advance the family to first rank. As a boy Cyrus had secretly designated himself for this rôle. In the village-capital where his family had set its seat he trained his playmates to address him as Great King. One of his war-like games was to make an expedition against the sheep that grazed on the outskirts of the village, scattering them in all directions: the sheep were always 'the Medes'. After the battle Cyrus would be declared Great King of the Medes and the Persians.

Cyrus was a young man when he succeeded to the king-ship of Anshan. Gradually he began to fire other princes with a sense of the lost dignity and freedom of Persia; not, for a long time, to the point of revolt, but with the result at least of persuading them to send envoys once a year to the city of Susa, to exchange greetings and discuss what matters they might have in common. In choosing Susa as a place of con-ference, he showed shrewd judgement. It was a hot, desolate city, a sun-baked ruin in the richly watered land of old Elam that lay south of Media, near the Persian Gulf. When the Medes first conquered Persia, some of the noble families had fled here, and remnants of them still survived—people who had not forgotten the great change in Persian fortunes. Moreover, apart from Pasargadae in central Persia, it was the only Persian city of historic dignity; and Pasargadae had been slowly de-clining in grandeur and prosperity. Susa had also declined, but it had had too long and ancient a history of power to be entirely a lost city. The importance of Susa as a rallying-point for a new Persia was, besides, chiefly in its position. It was already a step toward a more ambitious view of Persian fortunes that the envoys should come from the arid interior into this fertile plain, reminding of easier ways of life, the rich resources closed to them so long as they continued as they were.

It will help rather than delay our story to know something of old Elam where Susa stood, since it was with a sense of the antique magnificence of this land that Cyrus built up Susa again and made it, in the years of his prime, the southern capital of his empire. In early times Elam had been the home of a vigorous and thriving people. Chief among its achieve-ments was the development of the art of working metals: it was from Elam that the art first spread, in these regions.

16

Another thing to know of Elam is that its people were of two colours; in the plain dwelt black tribes, but the hill people were white. By Cyrus's time there had been much intermixture, but often the black strain came out strongly. When Cyrus became Great King, a certain number of his royal guard were always from this quarter of his empire, chosen for their dark faces and the fine effect of these among the white. From Elam came that Memnon of whom we hear as turning up at Troy during the Trojan War with a band of soldiers, among them Ethiopians. These Ethiopians were no doubt black Elamites; and Memnon himself was perhaps of this race. With the growth of the Assyrian Empire the Elamite Empire passed out of history; yet the city of Susa lingered on, lonely but never altogether dead—even after having been cruelly sacked by the Assyrians in the middle of the seventh century.

Such was the place that Cyrus later raised to imperial pride again, spending a part of every year here in the cool season—unless he was away at war. His wife Amytis always accompanied him on these visits, but she hated the place. She felt at home with him only when they were in Ecbatana, which was their hot-weather residence.

Rumours of these assemblages of Persians at Susa reached Astyages, the Median Emperor; and he began to be alarmed lest the young king of Anshan become a serious danger to peace in the south. Astyages was old and nervous and of uneven temper, and this worry for the southern part of his empire made him more difficult to live with than ever. So Amytis his daughter urged him to send the courtier Harpagus to Susa, to discover what was really going on there: Harpagus was a competent and cheerful person, not one to bring back a gloomy report. Besides, Amytis herself was now curious to know about this Cyrus. Amytis's gift of curiosity is one thing to remember about her; and her placidity of temper is another. These two gifts were, indeed, the chief elements of her character, and their combination made her a sensible woman. But she was not witty, or clever above the average. The Medes, on the whole, had far less humour in them than the Persians.

When Harpagus returned to Ecbatana from his visit of inspection to Susa, he reported only that Cyrus was a pleasant young man who laughed a great deal and was fond of fineries and ornaments and showing off before his fellow-satraps. Still nervous, somehow, Astyages again sent Harpagus to Susa with presents for Cyrus, delicately worked jewels and chains of Arabian gold. And all the time Harpagus was in Susa he was plotting with Cyrus against Astyages, perhaps for no other reason than that he was a cheerful man and Astyages an irritable one. The position that he held at court was one of high favour; the only person at court of equal favour with Harpagus was Astyages's son-in-law Spitamas, Amytis's rather elderly husband.

After this second visit to Susa, Harpagus reported that Cyrus was anxious to speak with Astyages in person; he did not, of course, say that Cyrus meant to come to Ecbatana with an army. Harpagus now busied himself in winning over the other courtiers and the army leaders to a plot to give the throne of Media to Cyrus. This was not difficult, since Astyages must die soon and there was none to succeed him but his son-in-law Spitamas, who was as irritable and gloomy as his father-in-law.

Meanwhile Cyrus in Susa had called an assembly of all the leading Persians and was working to engage their interest in an expedition to Media without revealing the real nature of his purpose. For if he had told them that he meant to seize the Median throne and establish Persian sovereignty over Media, they would have shrunk from the plan as wild and over-difficult and, besides, turned against him for his ambition. What he told them was that Astyages had made him a general and asked him to exhort his fellow-satraps to help the Medians in an expedition against the Bactrians, who dwelt to the east of Media, and against the Sacae, a group of powerful tribes to the north—both were indeed then causing Astyages trouble.

'If we thus assist the Median King,' Cyrus urged, 'our favour with him will be secure: and he has promised us great riches, and the freedom to make new settlements in Media if we choose.' When they could not reach a decision he said: 'Will you promise to do as I say for two days, so that I may show you how to decide?' And they consented; for a tempting prospect had been set before them, and they were anxious not to make a wrong decision.

On the first day he asked them to clear a plot of ground that was covered with rough stones and rubble, being close to an abandoned gravel pit; which they did. On the second day he had silken canopies brought there, under which he ordered them to recline. Then an elaborate feast was served, camels and donkeys constantly arriving laden with sacks of good things, and slaves with heavy platters of savoury meats. All day long they tasted as they pleased of this wonderful variety: dates, figs, melons and grapes, mulberry preserve, wine softened with juice of lime and orange and pomegranate, sweet cakes crisp with almonds and pistachio nuts, and enchanting manna from the tamarisk tree that grew in pleasant water-courses. Women were carried here in their litters, to peer out through the folds of their curtains at the lavish sight and listen to the songs and watch the stately dances of the soldiers—who moved their wicker shields with beautiful precision, making sharp, intricate patterns as they danced. (These dances of men later ceased to be a festival custom, all dancing being then done by a separate class of girls.)

The daintiest of the sweets were from time to time brought to the litters; and then silver basins—jewelled fingers were extended from the curtains and dipped softly into the water. In one of these litters was Cassandane, Cyrus's wife, whom he treated generously but could not love. She was not of sound mind, and had become a cruel trial to Cyrus after the birth of their son Cambyses. This boy was like his mother, subject to fits of dangerous anger that frequently ended in swooning and foaming. Cassandane, guessing what plans Cyrus nourished, watched the feast with sorrowful foreboding.

At sunset Cyrus spoke. 'You have given me the guidance of these two days,' he said, 'and fulfilled your pledge honourably, especially in lending yourselves to the work of the second day. Now I would ask you: which of these two days do you prefer?'

To this all replied: 'The latter.'

'If you will follow me,' Cyrus told them, 'your life shall be full of such days.'

A deep shout of approval greeted his words; but it was broken by a shriek from the litter of Cassandane, who knew that if Cyrus set off for Media she would never see him again. Which is indeed how it happened. The boy Cambyses, however, Cyrus took with him. He made fitting provision for Cassandane before he left, but she did not long survive.

As Cyrus neared Ecbatana with his men (it was in the year 550) he sent a herald forward with a message to Astyages: a message not of greeting but challenge. It had been reported to Astyages a little time before that Cyrus's escort seemed like a small army rather than a courtly retinue; so that he was not unprepared for this turn of events. He had ordered his own powerful army to be in readiness to meet Cyrus in battle, and should have been in no alarm about this apparently ludicrous invasion. But it was in his nature to take a pessimistic view of any issue in which he himself was deeply concerned; and it often happens that people who seem unduly pessimistic are moved by a correct intuition that pleasant things will not come their way. Astyages did not suspect Harpagus's falsity, did not know that at least half the army was ready to betray him to Cyrus. Yet he directed the preparations for the coming battle in a desperate mood of resignation to defeat.

Harpagus had by this time confided in Astyages's son-in-law Spitamas, persuading him that the army was in any case on the point of revolt and he could take advantage of the confusion arising from Astyages's death (Harpagus expected Cyrus to kill Astyages) to make himself King. Amytis perhaps came to know of her husband's ambition; however it was, she withdrew from Ecbatana with her two boys to a near-by village to await events. She did not love Spitamas, and had a longing to see Cyrus. She was dutifully devoted to her father, but was very tired of his company. If she knew what was being plotted, her emotions must at this time have been greatly divided.

Three battles decided the fate of Media. In the first, half of the Median army went over to Cyrus. In the second, the other half was defeated by Cyrus and his new Median supporters. The third battle was in Ecbatana itself. Astyages made a frantic resistance, with the help of the young boys and old men that had been left behind. When the Magian priests interfered, urging that the city yield itself to Cyrus, Astyages and his weak band turned on them and beat them all to death; but the city fell.

When Cyrus entered lovely Ecbatana and entered into possession of the Palace and satisfied himself that it was a perfect realization of his dreams of splendour, his first thought was for the old King. But Spitamas had anticipated him—casting Astyages into prison; it was Spitamas's plan to put Astyages out of the way and then, with Harpagus's help, to arouse the Medes to drive out Cyrus and make himself king in succession to Astyages. Cyrus's sudden interest in the fate of Astyages spoiled Spitamas's design—in which, though he did not know it, he would certainly not have had the help of Harpagus. For when Cyrus learned how Spitamas had treated the old man, he was incensed, and ordered him to be freed and treated

with honour. Spitamas he ordered to be killed without delay
for his discourtesy to his king and father-in-law. Then Cyrus
said: 'And where is the wife of this man?'

Thus Amytis was brought to Ecbatana and received in her
own palace by a stranger. She knew that Cyrus had dealt
graciously with her father; she knew that her husband was
dead. She was going to meet the Persian prince about whom
she had so much curiosity. Would he have brought any of
his wives with him? Probably not. She was pretty, of an
amiable disposition. He would undoubtedly want to settle
in Media, in order to take full control of the empire. She
was quite happy about her future.

The Palace stood on the seventh and topmost level of the
mound on which Ecbatana was built, and everything here
was of roseate tone, skilfully brightened with gold. The walls
of the Palace were ruddy clay, but the foundations and door-
frames and steps, and the short, stout supporting columns,
were all of stone. The first part of the Palace was a large
reception-hall, where the king's councillors met those who
wished to make petitions to the king, and discussed among
themselves—as this public business allowed—the greater
matters of State. The king himself never came here, and
was rarely, indeed, seen by any of his subjects but the soldiers,
and by these only when he was away with the army on fighting expeditions. A chosen few of the court were permitted
to penetrate behind the reception-hall to speak to him. Here
was a little conference-chamber, where the king himself came
when some urgent matter arose; but for the most part it
was not the king but a favoured eunuch who came here—to
receive messages and deliver the king's opinion. Behind this
conference-chamber the women's quarters began. It might
be said that the king had no home of his own, and was rather
the guest of his family of women and eunuchs.

The reception-hall was of severe appearance, undecorated
except for the relief that ran along the lower half of the wall:

stone carvings of animals, with figures of men at intervals representing famed personages but all looking remarkably alike. Among the animal representations the lion of the far south and the tiger of the north were prominent, but all wore the same mild look; the wild boar seemed no fiercer than the gazelle, the wolf and the leopard stood like friends next the innocent wild ass of the salt-marshes; the eagle and the hawk flew with the charming hoopoe.

At one end of the reception-hall was a stone dais where the chief members of the council sat when receiving petitioners or envoys from distant provinces or states. At each end of the wall facing the entrance, curtain-hung arches led into passages between which stood the conference-chamber. At the end of each passage was a door into the region sacred to the women and eunuchs, and the king. When a king entered his palace the words used were: 'And the King disappeared into his palace.' Which was true, since he immediately then took his place among the women, with whom few from the outside world might treat besides himself. Thus it was that a king could be as two different men: the stern leader of wars, and the gracious person whom the women knew. And since much of his governing was done from within the women's quarters—where he deliberated the petitions and difficulties brought to his attention by messengers from the men of his council—it was in many respects a gracious government. But those decisions which the councillors were privileged to make by themselves were sometimes harsh ones.

When Amytis entered the reception-hall in her litter a splendid sight confronted her. A banquet had been spread, as for a thousand; and around the hall stood the royal guards in double number, as always on great occasions—bright turbans, gleaming bangles, yellow boots laced high. Harpagus came forward to receive her and attend her to the inner quarters. She spoke through the folds of her litter-curtains, in a friendly voice, not upbraiding him.

'And are you happy in this change of things, Harpagus?'

'My own happiness, Lady,' he answered, 'matters little. What most concerns me is that you be happy in it.'

This was not mere insincere flattery; for he knew that much depended on a good understanding between Amytis and Cyrus. The Medes would be the readier to accept Cyrus if Amytis became his wife.

Astyages received his daughter in the women's quarters.

'Show Cyrus no hate or contempt,' he whispered. 'He has so far dealt fairly with us.'

To which Amytis answered in a clear voice that Cyrus himself could hear: 'Let me first see the man.'

Cyrus stood at the far end of this softly lighted hall. The way in which Astyages took Cyrus's hand, in leading him to Amytis, told her that some intimate ceremony had been celebrated between them: either a ceremony of adoption, by which Cyrus had become the foster-son of her father, or a ceremony of marriage, by which he had become his son-in-law. From the eager bearing of Cyrus, and the nervous step with which he approached her, she knew it must be the second.

He was wearing the flowing Median royal robe of purple, with sleeves of double width, and the high, glittering royal tiara; and eunuchs waved the fly-fans around him in the sweeping stroke used only for a king, or his wives; and the chief eunuch carried before him the royal sceptre, surmounted by the golden apple. When he came near the litter he paused: much depended on the first words. A eunuch stood ready with wine-cups. Cyrus glanced at them for a moment.

'Lady Amytis, first of Median women: it is difficult for a stranger to find words, unless he tell something of his own land.'

'Speak of your own land then, Great Stranger.' Cyrus had chosen his words wisely, for all foreign subjects were interesting to Amytis.

The glance at the wine-cups had given Cyrus an idea. 'In my land, Lady Amytis, there is something better than wine: the water of the Choaspes River, by Susa.'

Now, this water was not very different from other pleasant drinking-waters; and Cyrus had only mentioned it by chance, thinking what to say. Amytis was not greatly interested in the subject of drinking-water. But she said: 'How wonderful it would be to taste of this water!'

'You shall, I swear, by the angels of this day.' And so it happened that during their life together a flask of the water of the Choaspes was always upon their table. Cyrus partook of it as little as did Amytis; it was a pleasantry about which neither of them ever laughed.

Then into Amytis's litter a cup of wine was handed, which she tasted and handed out again; and where her lips had wetted the cup Cyrus now drank. A fresh cup was given to Astyages; after he had drunk from it, it was handed round from woman to woman, each touching her lips to it. This was the confirmation of the marriage-ceremony that Astyages had previously celebrated with Cyrus. Amytis now emerged from her litter, smiling to herself. A eunuch approached her with the queenly tiara, which Cyrus took from him and set upon her head. Another approached her with the queenly staff of rule, which she touched lightly with her fingers. Then the chief steward came, bearing his wand of office, which she touched in acceptance of his submission. Then the Palace treasurer, bearing a golden salver on which lay a variety of jewels—emerald and sapphire and topaz and cornelian, and their own Median lapis lazuli from the Salt Desert: these were tokens of the Queen's wealth, that none but herself might claim. Then Amytis and Cyrus sat down upon a golden couch, and the acts of homage to the new Queen continued: the chief chamberlain in the name of all the chamberlains, the chief cook in the name of all the cooks; and the chief musician of the Palace, and the chief cup-bearer.

And where the chief man was not a eunuch, and so could not enter the Queen's presence, the message of homage was borne to her by one of her own eunuchs—in letters of gold upon ox-hide: from the chief musician of the King's court, and the chief musician of the army, and the chief herald, and the chief huntsman, and from the commander of the Median guard, and the commander of the Persian bodyguard.

As a courtesy to Amytis, Cyrus had not stood his bodyguard in the reception-hall, so that she should upon entering be greeted only by her own people. Those who were now banqueting in the hall were all Medes. In a huge dining-hall in a building at the back of the Palace there was a second feast for the Persian leaders and soldiers and the men of Cyrus's bodyguard, and all the rest of the Palace household besides—to the number of fifteen thousand. The costume of the Persian soldiers was still a strange sight to the Medes: their soft felt caps instead of turbans, their varicoloured tunics, scaled like fish, their trousers, their girdles from which daggers hung. But soon this was to become the costume of Median soldiers as well.

Food began to be served in the inner Palace also; and to this banquet Amytis's two young sons were brought in, and Cyrus's boy Cambyses as well. They did not make friends now, or ever, for Cambyses was no normal boy, nor did he grow into a normal man. But he came to have an impetuous love for Amytis, who for many years was the only one who could quiet him in his fits of fury.

They ate from gold and silver plate, and meats of many kinds were brought—sheep and goat, camel and ass, ostrich and goose; and many varieties of sweetmeats. Fragrant branches and flowers were from time to time strewn on the floor to freshen the air—jasmine and lilac and roses, and hawthorn from the hill valleys. Ecbatana was not without gardens, but these could never have yielded enough flowers for the Palace. The heaped baskets that the women carried

were filled from the royal parks that lay in the neighbourhood
of Ecbatana, hemmed in by poplars: so beautiful, all, and
heavily scented, that they were called 'paradises'. In these
parks also grew the strange flowering tree that was later
christened the Judas-tree—and provided the material from
which the baskets were woven.

While they ate they talked easily and happily, everyone
feeling pleasure in the occasion. At the other two banquets
that were going on at the same time, many of the men fell
to dice-playing; and some went off in parties to hunt. But
here in the inner Palace they enjoyed themselves quietly,
without much stirring. For a while there were gay exclama-
tions at the presents that the eunuchs kept bringing in: every
distinguished woman of Amytis's court was thus honoured
by Cyrus. It should be told, however, that none of these
ear-rings, bangles, chains, neck-bands and girdles matched
those that Cyrus himself wore. To Amytis no such presents
could be given. The saying was: 'One does not offer gifts
of water to the sea.'

Gradually the women and the eunuchs fell asleep; and old
Astyages was carried off to the palace that had been assigned
to him; and the children were removed. So Cyrus and
Amytis talked on undisturbed, with only Amytis's dear friend
Mandane to hear them. All this time Amytis had been
studying Cyrus. He was handsome, and a little vain. His
hair hung in four shiny locks, more beautifully arranged than
any man's head she had ever seen; and the fringe of his robe
was made to sweep the ground, and the band of rosettes above
it was studded with jewels in a manner that would have been
repugnant in another, but in him was altogether agreeable.
For, Amytis had decided, he meant no more than to do what
he did extremely well, and to be an engaging sight to others.
Moreover, he had the brightest smile she had ever seen, and
made many jokes—some of which she did not understand,
but which amused her nevertheless.

'And will not your wives in Persia be grieving over your absence?' she asked.

'The good countenance of one wife consoles a man for the weeping countenances of those he has left behind.'

'And in your land have you the same virtues as we have in ours: to speak the truth, and give hospitality to all who come fairly, and make no debts?'

'Rather we say in our land: "The most virtuous man is he who is beloved of others." My virtues are therefore yours to bestow.'

'And in your land are there women who work the elm plough along with men, as in ours?'

'In our land there are no such women as in yours.'

'In your land do women plot with eunuchs for the good conduct of affairs, as here?'

'My dear Lady Amytis, think not that I come to unteach the Medes their wisdom, and love of women.'

'And do you say, as we say, that to have many sons is to have great wealth, but to have many daughters is to have much delight? And do you say that the home is guarded by angels, but demons guide one when one goes abroad? And do you love the noble cock, and say a prayer for him when he cries at dawn? And do you know how to bury your nail-parings so that they may not be used evilly against you?'

'These are all grave questions, Lady, to which I dare not answer hastily—and the answers to which you had perhaps teach me yourself. But there is a question I should like to ask of you. Have you ever had a dream of me?'

'Now, it is strange that you should ask that,' said Amytis, clapping her hands with satisfaction. 'For a few nights ago I had a very marvellous dream indeed, which I took to signify something concerning you, but which one of our Magi to whom I sent for an interpretation believed to contain in it a prophecy of a great disaster. In my dream a wild-cat freely entered the Palace and sat down upon my couch. All fled

28

from it except myself, who stood at a distance watching it. It leapt this way and that upon the couch, and then suddenly a gentle fallow deer was there, such as we have in our mountains. And I was terrified for what the cat would do to the gentle deer, but as the cat leapt over the deer a vine seemed to rise all around, which, growing fast and thick, soon hid the deer from sight; and it seemed only that the cat was jumping playfully among the branches of the vine. And I was pleased. Then the vine spread to where I stood, and made a bower over me, until I saw no more.'

'The wild-cat,' Cyrus said, 'can be no other but myself. And the gentle deer is Media. And the growing vine is according as one sees the matter. Much will come to pass through my sitting upon the golden couch of the royal palace of Ecbatana. To those who like little events, and these few, it is a great disaster when great events, and these many, come to pass in their time. But to those who have a curiosity of things, that time is most desirable to live in which is marked by a busy coming and going of events.'

'That is my way of thinking,' Amytis replied. 'When a message comes from a far land, I cannot rest until I know how it reads. My father says that no message is good news, but I say that any news, however unpleasant, is better than none—for, if nothing happened, what would be the sense of being alive?'

'And that is also my way of thinking, Lady. And this was my purpose in coming to Media, to make many things happen for your interest, that you might have reasons for wanting to live.'

'Yes,' answered Amytis solemnly. 'At my age one is not ready to think of death. I am never ill, which is a sign that evil spirits have no power over me. So I am not afraid of events. What may be unhappy for others will perhaps befall happily for me.'

Cyrus was delighted by her health, and her belief in her

29

own fortunateness: with such a wife he could dare much. It was the duty of a king to brave dangers, but it was also his duty to spare his women needless apprehension. From this second duty Amytis's serene nature freed him.

Amytis went on: 'I was loth to think that a vine could be a thing of evil meaning. I have never seen a vine growing except in pictures, but there is surely no evil in wine, or in the grape. That is what I am most eager to see one day—the land of the snowdrops, where the vine grows.'

It so happened that Cyrus was planning to make an expedition into the vine country, against the troublesome Sacae; and he now formed the design of taking Amytis with him. He put faith in Astyages's word that he would not encourage the Medes to take advantage of this absence to rebel against the Persians.

The Sacae lived along the eastern shores of the Black Sea, and around the upper shores of the Caspian Sea. But a number of the tribes had moved south and joined forces to make raids from time to time into Media. Cyrus hoped to challenge them at some point along the southern shore of the Caspian, and thus Amytis would have the journey of her heart's wish. Harpagus was given the leadership of the army. Of the soldiers and their weapons we have already learned that they carried wicker shields; under these hung their quivers. Their arrows were of reed, their bows large, their spears short. The men of the royal guard were armed with bow and pike. And thousands of fine horses gave strength to the army: the Medes and the Persians being always most powerful in their cavalry. Numerous black soldiers went with them—besides those of Cyrus's bodyguard; for by the time he set out he had received large reinforcements from Persia, being unwilling to trust himself and his small band of Persians to the yet untried loyalty of the Medes. With Amytis, in litters mounted on camels, went her companion Mandane and a few other women. The journey was not arduous, and became more and more pleasant as they neared the sea. But the war with the Sacae did not turn out quite as Cyrus had expected.

His scouts located the Sacae easily, and the first battle ended with the capture of their king and so great a weakening of their forces that Cyrus had no further anxiety. He sent a large part of his army off under Harpagus to the east, to subdue the Bactrians, who had also been troublesome recently. His intention was to linger a little while yet near the sea, for Amytis's sake, and then return home in leisurely stages. But while he and Amytis were enjoying themselves in this manner, the Sacean Queen raised an army of ten thousand women, which descended unexpectedly on Cyrus and his reduced forces, taking both him and Amytis prisoner. This queen, Sparetha, was naturally disconcerted to find Cyrus's elegant wife among her prisoners: hesitating what to do with her, how to treat her. And disconcerted also by Amytis's evident delight at being captured and seeing so much more of the outer world than she had expected. But from being disconcerted Sparetha became good-humoured; for Amytis had a power of putting people in good-humour. An exchange of prisoners was arranged, and then a perpetual bond of peace sworn.

After this expedition Cyrus remained for a few years at home, working to bring about a harmony of relations between the Medes and the Persians; and to strengthen the religion of the prophet Zoroaster, and encourage the study of the Persian book of revelations, the Avesta. The old priesthood of the Magi continued, but their religion was now an affair of their own rather than a common religion for everyone. Yet they were held in great respect as wise men; and the fire-altars in lonely spots which they tended, their customs of sacrifice and their use of the sacred bundle of twigs and other ancient things, were all cherished as links between the old days and the new.

During this time a son was born to Amytis and Cyrus; and Cyrus had taken no new wife. There were now, with Amytis's two children by her first husband, four sons in the household. Since Croesus, the King of Lydia, had advanced his empire to the borders of Persia (as Media and Persia together must now be called), and in his pride committed many threatening acts against Cyrus's empire, Cyrus felt that a war against Croesus must soon be undertaken: the smaller the empire he would have to leave to his four sons, the more quarrelling there would be among them and misery for all. Amytis was of the same mind—and curious to hear news of those distant places, and excited at the thought of receiving occasional messages from Cyrus by which she could follow the course of distant events. Moreover, Cyrus was by now possessed of a strong desire to show himself abroad as the Great King of Persia, lord of a mighty army.

So, bidding Amytis and his boys good-bye, and stroking all the dogs of the household lovingly, Cyrus departed in a light-hearted mood for his important war. Outside the Palace the priests of Ahura Mazda, the heavenly Zoroastrian god of good things, were awaiting him, to pronounce incantations to ward off evil and lies from him on his long journey: in those days there were no temples in Persia. High up in the mountains, meanwhile, the fire-priests were sacrificing ibex, that the country might not come to harm in Cyrus's absence.

3

THE DEFEAT OF CROESUS

IT has not yet been told that the mother of Amytis was a sister of Croesus, so that Croesus was the uncle of Amytis and the brother-in-law of old Astyages her father; the marriage had been arranged in token of peace between the two kingdoms of Media and Lydia. Thus Amytis had some curiosity of Croesus as a relative; but no feeling of pain, however, that her own husband should be making war on her mother's own brother. Her mother had died young, and Amytis scarcely remembered her; and there had long been no communication between the two families except official messages. Besides, there were unpleasant rumours about Croesus's character: he was proud to foolishness, and had attained much of his power by sly methods, not meeting dangers honourably.

When Croesus was a young man, and his father still King at Sardis, the beautiful Lydian capital, Solon of Athens paid a visit to this court. Croesus had married shortly before this time, and his wife suffered from the weeping complaint, falling into fits of tears for hours on end. Anything that might possibly please her was tried: rare foods, rare jewels, celebrated minstrels, dazzling clothes. But the fits of tears continued, and her health declined until it seemed that nothing could save her. Having heard much of Solon's wisdom, Croesus appealed to him for advice about his wife's health. After speaking with the woman, Solon said: 'There are two kinds of illness—those which proceed from some fault in one's own constitution, and those which proceed from some fault in others. Your wife has the face of a person in whom there is no ill or evil of her own. Among the Medes they give

the urine of a cow to the sick, believing that it will drive out
the evil spirit that has entered into the sufferer's body. But
the evil spirit in this case is not in your wife.'

'In whom, then?' exclaimed Croesus. 'Name the person,
and I shall have him killed—or sent to a distance if it be a
woman.'

'I would not be the cause of punishing anyone for evil of
which he may not be aware. The best way, therefore, would
be to forbid all who now have converse with your wife to
keep away from her for a year. Give her a new retinue of
women, and keep away from her yourself, that the thing may
seem a freakish design for her cure rather than an accusation
against any who have been in her company.'

So it was that Solon brought about the tranquillity of
Croesus's wife. For after a year of complete separation from
him she was strong enough to endure his vanity, and a little
older, and Croesus himself a little older and a little less wild
in his vanity.

This Solon, now very old, was a fantastically good man
for his time. As he said, he had won support for his ideas
by their strangeness rather than by their worth. The people
of Attica, weary of harsh and confused laws and the incessant
conflict that went on between the leading families, were in a
condition, he said, to accept any ideas that were new ones;
and therefore incapable of judging for many years whether
the laws he had established for them were good ones, or
merely different. This was chiefly why, though so old, he
had left Athens to travel abroad; a second reason was his
desire to revisit the cities that he had known as a younger
man, when he was a foreign merchant. Solon came of a
noble family that had become impoverished, and he had
been able to redeem its fortunes in trade. Amasis, King of
Egypt, claimed that Solon had acquired many of his demo-
cratic ideas during his sojourn in Egypt. But it must not be
forgotten that Solon was a poet, never ceasing to write verses

all his life, and that it was therefore natural for him to think out ways for a better order of life. When his friends at Athens would have persuaded him to remain to see that his laws were closely obeyed, he said: 'It is not my work to impose my thoughts but to think them.'

We must be patient with these tales of places so far from Amytis, since they were the very things that most interested her; when Cyrus returned after defeating Croesus, it was such tales that he brought her. By that time Solon had been long dead, and Peisistratus was tyrant in Athens. Upon Solon's return from his journeys Peisistratus had invited him to share in the government of Attica, but Solon was unwilling, though ready to give advice when asked.

'And what kind of wife did this man of marvellous wisdom have?' Amytis asked, when she heard all these tales.

Cyrus could not answer. But Croesus, whom Cyrus had captured and brought home with him, said: 'What kind of wife she was I do not know, but he must have esteemed her greatly. For when Solon visited Thales the philosopher at Miletus, Thales's mother begged him to persuade her son to marry—since Thales had made a vow never to marry, which his mother considered unnatural. And Solon is said to have told him that he might be a clever philosopher without a wife, but never a sensible one.'

'I like what you tell me of this Solon,' commented Amytis.

'And Thales is said to have answered that, as he thanked fortune for not being a woman, he could not live with a woman without pitying her for what she was, and yet he had no pity for women in him.'

'What an idiot this Thales must be!' Amytis said.

'That is my own opinion of him,' Croesus replied. 'He believes that lifeless things have souls. And they say that he studies the stars for hours without pause, and is always falling into ditches or tripping over stones and getting himself bruised, or running into people and making them angry.'

'If he had a wife,' Amytis said, 'he would not behave so foolishly.'

Miletus, where Thales lived, was one of the cities of the western coast of Asia Minor that Croesus had subdued—indeed, he had subdued them all. When Croesus sent to these cities for assistance in the war that he was planning to make against Cyrus, Miletus alone dared to refuse, which was why Cyrus later spared it. Croesus also made an alliance against Cyrus with Amasis of Egypt; and with the coast islands, which had been importing horses and arms from Greece to defend themselves against Croesus, who had planned to reduce them—so that the island league and Croesus himself both gained by this truce. He could expect no help from Athens, but he sent Peisistratus a handsome present for his good-will. Sparta was in a position to help him, and gave him a promise of help, but in the end remained out of the war and sent him a somewhat mean present instead. However, Croesus was able, by rich offers, to tempt many foreign mercenaries into his army; and the favourable answers which the Oracle at Delphi gave to his envoys increased his confidence of victory. As was usually the way with oracular pronouncements, the answers that the envoys brought back to Croesus could be interpreted in two opposite senses: if it had not been thus, the Oracle would have lost much of its popularity, and received far fewer presents.

All these preparations lasted many months, during which Croesus sent small expeditions to disturb various outposts of the Persian Empire, in order to provoke Cyrus to come against him in battle. At last Croesus set out with his army, moving eastward. With him went Thales of Miletus. How this came about is interesting for the light it throws upon both their characters. It was Thales who first urged the Milesians not to send help to Croesus. 'Let me go to him and say that you think you can send him no greater help than your Thales. And I will accompany him on this campaign, and advise him, and thus all will be pleased.' When Thales delivered his message, Croesus was so amused by the vanity of the man that he could not be angry with the Milesians; and pleased in his own vanity at the thought of being attended even to the battle-field by a famous man of learning. Thales for his part was anxious to demonstrate his usefulness, but until they reached the River Halys there was little he could do except make weather-forecasts, which were of some help indeed to the army when they were correct. At the River Halys—on the other side of which lay Cappadocia, that Croesus was pledged not to molest—the army was held up by the depth of the water at the point where a crossing was intended. Therefore Croesus's generals went to work to divert half the river, to make it shallow for fording; and to this work Thales applied all his mathematical talents.

Now, the art of diverting rivers for military needs was well known in these times. Nebuchadnezzar had practised it in making the fortifications of Babylon, and his daughter Nitocris was soon to practise it herself in extending these fortifications to protect the city from Cyrus. And Cyrus did the same thing against her. Croesus and his generals could have managed very well without Thales's nice calculations; but there was no harm in damming the river and digging the necessary canal according to strict mathematical rules, though it took a little longer this way.

The two armies met not far from the port of Sinope on the Black Sea, after Croesus had done a good deal of damage in Cappadocia. Neither king was anxious for a decisive battle here. Croesus's forces were inferior to Cyrus's and, moreover, Croesus wished to lure Cyrus westward, confident that he could win more help from his allies if they saw Cyrus attempting to extend his empire to the very shores of the Aegean. Cyrus himself had set his heart on taking Croesus's famed capital of Sardis on this expedition, and did not wish to waste his forces in a Cappadocian war—which would mean having to return to Ecbatana to organize a fresh expedition. Amytis would expect him to have the work done when he returned, so that he could live with her in peace until it seemed proper to wage some new war of conquest for the advancement of the Empire. Therefore he arranged a three months' truce with Croesus; who returned to Sardis in triumph, advertising that he had defeated Cyrus in the East and making fresh treaties with his allies for a final crushing war against the Persians. Croesus idled away the winter, dismissing his foreign mercenaries; the three months of truce passed, and Cyrus was reported to be still lingering in Cappadocia.

In this winter Croesus lost a dear son, by boasting of his prowess in hunting: laying a wager that he could kill a wild boar though armed only with a dagger. The death of this young man so affected his mother that the old weeping fits returned. She had two more sons, but one was a mere boy and the other had been dumb and short-witted from birth.

Suddenly Cyrus appeared with his army before Sardis and besieged it. Croesus could get help from nowhere. Amasis was not ready to meet Cyrus in battle, and the Spartans were preparing for a war of their own. There were four steps in the capture of Sardis. First, Cyrus placed his pack-camels before his foot-soldiers, and the smell of these so offended the horses of Croesus's protecting forces that they ran off with their riders; and Cyrus came close to the city walls. Then, Cyrus had great wooden engines of war erected about the walls by night, which were covered with foliage and seemed an ominous apparition to the defenders, who fled from the ramparts. When Croesus ordered them back to their positions they found the wall damaged in many places, though not yet scaled: which increased their superstitious fear. Then, the walls were at last scaled at a point which was considered so strong that it had been left weakly guarded. Though many of his soldiers were now posted in the city, Cyrus did not yet enter it as a conqueror, for he believed it a more glorious victory to force his enemy to suggest acceptable peace terms than to impose humiliating terms upon him.

While the peace negotiations were going on, Cyrus had Croesus's youngest son for a hostage. When Cyrus learned that, under cover of the truce, Croesus had sent men out to poison the stream that the Persian soldiers drank from, he was very angry at this breach of faith; and his soldiers, for revenge, gave some of the poisoned water to Croesus's son. The boy's body was sent into the city, and upon seeing it his mother threw herself from the walls. Thus she saved herself from further years of unhappiness with Croesus. For if she had lived Cyrus would probably have brought her back to Ecbatana as well, since she was Amytis's aunt by marriage; and she would have been more closely tied to the company of Croesus than ever before. But it should be said that after Croesus was removed to Persia his character improved greatly.

Croesus had taken refuge in the Temple of Apollo when Cyrus entered the city; he was still unable to believe in his defeat, and the priests flattered him that the rainstorm beating outside was a sign that Apollo would intervene to drive off the Persians. Cyrus's soldiers found him there with his dumb son and brought them through the storm to the Palace, where Cyrus was. They were both so wet and bedraggled when they came into Cyrus's presence that he at first mistook the son for the father, since he seemed the more miserable and his infirmities gave him an old look.

Cyrus addressed the son severely: 'Had you dealt honourably with me, I should have had the pleasure of receiving you honourably—as an enemy who dealt fairly, and the near relative of my wife.'

The son shrank away, dazed and frightened. As Cyrus turned from him in contempt, Croesus stepped forward, his head high. 'I am Croesus, and that is my poor son.'

This so melted Cyrus that, instead of making further reproaches, he ordered them both to be taken away and reclothed and warmed. When Croesus was brought to him again Cyrus met him with a smile, encouraging him to speak.

'It is no easy thing, Nephew, for a proud man, a name of fear and wonder to the world, to see his power fall away like the walls of a house struck with earthquake. It was not as a king that I broke my truce-word, since I was no more a king, but as a proud man with no pride left. Therefore, whatever you choose to do with me, I shall not suffer humiliation, having already sunk as low with myself as a man may, and live.'

Cyrus could not resist this perhaps not altogether artless appeal to his magnanimity. He decided to send Croesus to Ecbatana immediately, trusting to Amytis to keep him from mischief.

'If you can love me after having been destroyed by me,' Cyrus said, 'I shall make you great again and have you for my closest counsellor. You shall live once more like a king.'

'A lion bearded is never a lion again. Rather let me be as a jackal, that serves the lion.'

Cyrus replied: 'I think you are more the lynx than the jackal, Uncle.'

And so Croesus went on to Ecbatana before Cyrus. But his dumb son was left behind.

Cyrus meanwhile busied himself with bringing the surrounding country under his rule. Against all the cities of the Aegean coast he sent expeditions, except Miletus, because it had refused Croesus help. Thales claimed the credit of this, boasting that a philosopher had done what an army could not. The other Ionian cities despised Miletus for breaking faith with them in submitting without resistance to Cyrus. They appealed to Sparta for help, but the Lacedaemonians were not anxious to intervene. However, they sent envoys to Cyrus, to entreat him to leave the cities in peace; which was in their interest, since much of their trade was with Ionia. Cyrus knew that they had no intention of helping the cities, and warned them sternly that if they attempted to interfere further he would reduce Sparta as he had reduced Sardis. This warning was delivered contemptuously; the Persians despised a nation that engaged widely in trade.

While Cyrus was at Sardis messages came to him that the Derbices in the far east had allied themselves with their Indian neighbours and were becoming insolent. Cyrus set out with Harpagus and his army to fight them, leaving behind a Persian, Tabalus, in control of the government of Lydia. The great treasure of Croesus he gave into the charge of a Lydian, Pactyas, who had been useful to him in his dealings with the Ionian cities, and whom he believed loyal. Pactyas was to proceed with the treasure to Ecbatana; for this journey Cyrus provided him with a sufficient escort of soldiers.

The expedition against the Derbices was unlucky; Cyrus was caught in an elephant ambush and wounded by an Indian arrow. They were eventually defeated, but the arrow was a poisoned one, and during the journey homewards Cyrus lay sick in his litter. Further, a rumour reached the Sacae that Cyrus had been killed, and they revolted. Cyrus sent his now weary army against them and directed the battle from his litter. They were overwhelmed; and at last Cyrus could think of home.

By the time Cyrus returned to Ecbatana, ailing from his wound, Croesus and his niece had become fast friends; many were their talks together, much did Amytis learn from Croesus about the ways of life in the West and the great people he knew. He told her the story of Ladice, the Greek wife of the Egyptian King—with whom she had exchanged greetings during Cyrus's absence, though relations between Persia and Egypt were strained because of various alliances that the Egyptian King had made against Cyrus.

'Why should Ladice have told me in her message,' Amytis asked, 'that she still continued in Aphrodite's favour, in spite of her husband's advanced age?'

'Ah, that is one of those domestic secrets which kings and queens share with the whole world. Amasis first saw Ladice at the Greek city of Cyrene in Libya—the Cyreneans helped him in the rebellion by which he became King. She was very beautiful; and, also, her being Greek engaged the sympathies of the Greeks across the seas and all the Greek colonists in Egypt. It would, moreover, have been difficult for him to win the hand of an Egyptian princess, since he was of not very high birth and the defeated ruling caste remained hostile to him. So they were married. But Amasis was a very nervous man, and for some time found himself unable to have marital connexion with his wife. This annoyed him greatly; the story spread and was the subject of much lewd mockery. At last Ladice made a vow to Aphrodite to devote a golden image to her if she took the spell from Amasis—which all the world can see at Cyrene and know the reason of. With Aphrodite's help Amasis was able to conduct himself like a man with his wife.'

'Oh, I am glad to hear that,' said Amytis. 'These things are most important, since had Amasis continued to fail with Ladice he would have taken another wife, and the whole course of his life and the fortunes of Egypt itself would have been different. He might have married a woman who would have brought about his ruin. Egypt prospers, does it not?'

'All too well for Cyrus's peace of mind!'

'Oh! Will my husband be making war on Egypt then? I should be sorry to hear that. I have heard that Amasis governs it well.'

'He does indeed,' Croesus replied. 'He has established a just system of taxes, and just laws, and built many beautiful temples. The most renowned is the temple at Karnak. I have seen it myself. The long path leading up to it is flanked with magnificent great sphinxes.'

'Sphinx—that is a strange woman like a lion, is it not? I have heard of her. They say she appears sometimes to men in dreams and tells them the deep secrets of life. When they awake they forget what she has told them, and become frantic to remember, and kill themselves. It seems very cruel, but perhaps there is some justice in it. For men forget too easily what women tell them, and it is very annoying.'

Amytis heard also of Pythagoras, whom she had seen as a girl: he had come to the court of her father, Astyages, to study the wisdom of the Magi. Croesus told her how Pythagoras had founded clubs of men and women for the study of his ideas, and how his followers were disliked everywhere for their wise airs.

'And what are these ideas he teaches?' Amytis asked.

As Pythagoras had visited Croesus at Sardis he was able to tell her a little about them. 'Well, many of them have to do with numbers, nonsensical to me. But some of them are quite simple, and seem reasonable enough. He teaches that by cultivating a quiet and virtuous habit of mind one can know the mysteries of life; and that there is a great "Something" which is more important than everything else that is.'

'Of course there is! One doesn't need a philosopher to tell one that. We call it Ahura Mazda. He calls it "Something". I call it Being Angry, for I only feel it when something angers me, which happens rarely.'

'Pythagoras teaches that anger is a sin and calm a virtue.'

'I seem to remember that he was a quarrelsome, ill-behaved man when he visited my father—always arguing. He must have learned that from us. What else does he teach?'

'That fire is the most sacred element.'

'He learned that from us too. To think that he should have become so famous!'

And she also heard of the fame of Aesop, who, like Pythagoras, had had the travelling habit and also visited the court of Astyages. When Croesus told Amytis some of Aesop's tales—for Aesop had visited him at Sardis—she exclaimed:

'Why, those are *our* Median tales!' And did not know whether to be pleased or not.

'But does he tell only tales of animals?' she asked.

'Only of animals,' Croesus said. 'You see, he tries to teach moral lessons with his tales, and by having animals for characters he makes them laughable, so that one is not too much bored.'

'That is well. We have many beautiful tales of men and women as well as droll tales of animals, and I should not like to think of those tales travelling the world as if they belonged to nobody in particular. Nor do I agree that a tale which carries a moral lesson need be made laughable in order to be interesting. The most charming tale I know has the deepest possible moral meaning, and is very serious, but not at all boring. I'll tell it to you one day. It is about the first woman and man, who lived in a beautiful paradise in the Babylonian Plain, called the Garden of Edin. We women make up these tales with our eunuchs. But I don't know who made up this one—perhaps my mother.'

And Amytis heard how Peisistratus the tyrant of Athens was once driven out of the city for refusing to let his wife have children, which incensed her family as an insult to its blood and made the woman very unhappy. 'I do not much believe in that story,' Amytis said. 'A woman who really wants children can manage these things.'

And she heard how, when Peisistratus secretly returned to Athens from his banishment, he brought with him a dwarf-woman whom he gave to the priests to represent the goddess Athene in their pageants; which so delighted them that they used their influence to get him the power again.

'These Greeks,' Amytis said, 'are a puzzling people. They do great and clever things, and at the same time low things—or so it seems to me, from all I hear of them.'

Croesus replied: 'You are quite right, my dear. I was much under their influence when I was King, and myself did great and clever things and low things. I think it comes of being unhappy. I have never in my life met a truly happy Greek.'

'And what of your wife?' Amytis asked. 'Could she not help to make you happy?'

'I made her too unhappy for that,' Croesus answered.

While Cyrus was still on his journey homewards a thing happened that grieved and angered Amytis; and the presence of Croesus was a strong consolation and support to her. Her father, Astyages, was in the south for his health, it being the cool season when it was pleasant there. (But during Cyrus's absence Amytis did not keep up her husband's custom of spending the cool season at Susa.) Being anxious that Astyages and Croesus should meet again, since they were brothers-in-law, she sent a trusted courtier with an escort to fetch her father home. But this man was afraid that Croesus and Astyages would conspire together against Cyrus in his absence, and was resolved not to bring Astyages back to Ecbatana. Shortly after the courtier had departed, Amytis had a dream about a lion prowling in the desert, and it seemed to her in her dream that the lion was looking for something that she did not want him to find. In the morning, on waking, instead of sending for a Mage to interpret it, she discussed the dream with Croesus, saying it gave her an uneasy feeling about her father. Croesus agreed that, if it signified that some evil work against her father was going on, it was best not to consult the Magi, who might be in the plot. So she sent a large body of Median soldiers after the courtier—those who had accompanied him being Persians.

The Medians learned that Astyages had been abandoned in the desert on the way home, to die of thirst. Scouring the desert, they found his body; and brought it to Amytis. On Croesus's advice she made the crime a public matter, having the culprit tried openly before the Palace, to discourage any further plotting: he was condemned to be blinded and then crucified. But Amytis was vexed by the popular commotion that the trial caused; for, she said, it made the punishment a greater event than the death of her father.

Astyages was buried with all the honours due to a king. His body was coated with wax and placed in a magnificent tomb, cut in the mountain-side, that he himself had constructed when he was undisputed ruler of the Medes and the Persians. At near-by altars beasts were cut up, the pieces boiled and then laid on the ground to be chanted over—to purify Astyages's body of any demons that might have entered into it since his death.

Soon after the burial of Astyages, Cyrus arrived at Ecbatana. He was a long time in recovering from his wound, but this did not displease him, since it was an excuse for spending his days entirely with Amytis, chatting with her and Croesus, and giving little thought to public affairs. His children, too, delighted him—his stepsons, and Tanyoxarces, his son by Amytis; but of Cambyses, his eldest son, he despaired.

It will be remembered that when Cyrus left Sardis he had given all of Croesus's treasure into the charge of one Pactyas, a Lydian, commanding him to carry it to Ecbatana. But the treasure had not arrived; and soon after his return rumours reached Ecbatana that Pactyas had organized a revolt among the Lydians against their Lydian governor. Cyrus asked Croesus to consult with Harpagus, the leader of his army, as to what should be done. Harpagus wanted to return with the army and destroy Sardis. But Croesus urged that it would be a loss to Cyrus to destroy this beautiful city. And Cyrus let Croesus have his way. The Lydians were now forbidden to carry weapons and ordered to learn to play the cithara. 'For, as Pythagoras counsels,' Croesus said, 'music has a wonderfully softening effect on the will.'

'I think he must have learned that from us,' Amytis said. 'We employ it upon unmanageable children—I often cure Cambyses's fits of rage with a song.'

For six years now Cyrus did no warring himself—leaving it to Harpagus to make punitive expeditions when trouble arose anywhere. Then certain Jews came to him secretly from Babylon, of the faction that wished the Jews to be allowed to return to Jerusalem (but there were many content with their life in Babylonia); and for various reasons Cyrus decided to act.

During this period at home with Amytis a daughter was born to them.

4

THE CAPTURE OF BABYLON

WE shall now see how it was that the Hebrew prophets
regarded the Persians, alone of all the stranger peoples, as
pleasing to God, although they believed differently—not
hating evil but merely holding aloof from it. Jehovah of the
Jews said of Cyrus: 'He is my shepherd, and shall perform
all my pleasure: even saying to Jerusalem, Thou shalt be
built; and to the Temple, Thy foundation shall be laid.'
These things, indeed, Cyrus made possible, and the Jews
called him their Lord's anointed, who fulfilled the prophecy
made by Jeremiah.

There were numerous colonies of Jews in Babylonia. In
the eighth century B.C. the Assyrian kings had attacked the
Israelites and brought home many captives; and Sennacherib
at the close of the century had added to the number of Babylonian Jews by bringing home some of the Judeans. But
it was not until the time of Nebuchadnezzar that Jerusalem
itself fell. The Jews were valued for their wisdom and industry
and their skill in many crafts; and, living for the most part
usefully and happily in Babylonia, they were well liked and
honoured. Those whom Nebuchadnezzar brought home and
settled in Babylon were especially esteemed; among them
were the Jewish king's soldiery, and all his learned men, and
the best craftsmen and smiths of the city; and the whole staff
of the palace of King Jehoiakim, which amounted to many
thousands; and all who sang or played in the Temple. For
some time Jerusalem had been under tribute to Egypt; now
it was freed from this tyranny, but the best things of the land
of Judaea were gone from it. Not only the people who were

its pride: even the treasures of the Temple and of the Palace. And when the king whom Nebuchadnezzar had put in Jehoiakim's place rebelled, the Babylonians once again made an expedition against Jerusalem. This time they burned the Temple of the Jews, and destroyed the city walls; and more captives were brought to Babylon.

Now, as has been told, when Cyrus became Great King of the Persians and the Medes, Emperor of a wide domain, Nabonidus ruled in Babylon, having married Nitocris, a younger daughter of Nebuchadnezzar. As King of Babylonia, he was a personage of dignity and importance, and many lesser kings looked to him for protection against the growing power of Cyrus. He had been a respected adviser at the court of Nebuchadnezzar, and won fame as a diplomat and arbitrator; it was he who brought about peace between the Medes and Lydians in 585. But a change came over Nabonidus when he assumed the kingship; or, rather, he was now free to follow his real inclinations. After Nebuchadnezzar's death the priestly party had become overweeningly powerful at the Babylonian court, making and unmaking kings, assassinating those that stood in their way. Nabonidus did not pay allegiance to the official Babylonian religion, the first god of which was Marduk; and this was the chief reason why, in the third year of his reign, he withdrew to Tema in Arabia, in the far west, leaving the management of things to Queen Nitocris and his son Belshazzar.

The ruling Babylonian caste, which included the priestly party, was of Chaldean origin. Nabonidus was of native Babylonian stock; his mother was a priestess of the moon-god at Ur, and he himself of this faith. Therefore he felt at ease in Arabia, a land of moon-worshippers. Between Nitocris and Nabonidus there were no difficulties in religious matters. Their son Belshazzar was brought up in the official religion, but their daughter became a moon-priestess like her paternal grandmother. There was good reason why

49

Nitocris should have been thus liberal in religious matters. Her mother had been an Egyptian princess, the daughter of Necho II of Egypt whom Nebuchadnezzar defeated in war; Nebuchadnezzar had allowed her mother to educate her in the worship of the Egyptian god Ammon. Then, as Nitocris grew older, she was obliged to pay formal service to harsh Babylonian Marduk; and marriage with Nabonidus brought her into contact with the pleasant ceremonial of moon-worship.

During the years that Nitocris ruled in Babylon while Nabonidus was absent in Arabia, she skilfully avoided the semblance of rule. The purposes and plans were hers, but their execution she left to her son Belshazzar, a man of much energy though little wit; in all official proclamations and prayers it was his name, and his father's, that appeared, never her own. When she wished to send a personal message to Persia or, it might be, to Egypt, she addressed herself to Amytis, not to her husband Cyrus—or to Ladice, the Greek Queen of Egypt, not to her husband King Amasis.

When Amytis sent messages to Nitocris she never failed to inquire after her husband, and indeed was more curious to hear news of him than to learn what new things Nitocris had accomplished in Babylon. Arabia, where Nabonidus lived, was a mystery-land. He conducted strange works of religion there; but devoted himself to trading activities as well, sending by camel to Babylon such precious Arabian products as frankincense, myrrh, cassia and cinnamon—which sometimes reached Persia.

Upon leaving Babylon, Nabonidus had first of all marched against Tema in Arabia and occupied it; then he settled here and began a pious rebuilding of ancient temples and a zealous strengthening of the moon-cult. Round Tema there lay underground the remains of earlier settlements. These Nabonidus excavated, at first in order to study ancient forms of moon-worship, but later with a scholar's passion to fit together and ponder any fragments whatever that his slaves found. Tales of this unkingly industry, and the never clearly understood manner of his departure from Babylon, caused people to wonder if he were mad. Nitocris was much pitied, as a deserted wife who had neither quarrelled with her husband nor yet been put away; and certainly she never seemed happy. Nabonidus's behaviour would have been more understandable if he had been a man who shrank from war. But he had imposed himself on Tema with resolute military action; and he had also made an expedition against the Syrians to ensure that he should not be troubled by them in his Arabian home. Then, toward the end of his life, he went bravely against Cyrus. But of this, presently.

Toward the end of Queen Nitocris's regency, certain Jews of Babylon banded themselves together to plot for the return of the Jews to their native land and the rebuilding of the Temple. Their whole hope was in Cyrus; for they knew that Cyrus took great interest in the ways in which other peoples worshipped. 'To worship a god,' Cyrus said, 'is to dream of the hidden truth.' And of the Jews he had said: 'It seems to me they dream with their eyes open.'

Now, it occasionally happened that embassies came from Babylon to Ecbatana, to confer upon frontier difficulties that arose between the two countries. The growing power of Cyrus was naturally a worry to Queen Nitocris; she was anxious for peace between them but unwilling to yield on any single point, believing that a small surrender of dignity would tempt Cyrus to press for a greater. All dealings with the Persians were conducted in Belshazzar's name, but the guiding hand was Nitocris's, and in her restraint of Belshazzar's more unguarded pride she had the support of the wise Jews at court. Of the wise men at court there were two parties: the Chaldean magicians who flattered and amused Belshazzar and his wives and concubines, and the learned Jews of Nitocris's retinue, chief among whom was one Daniel, who had enjoyed great favour with Nebuchadnezzar himself. Thus it was, Nitocris's power being the stronger, that the embassies sent from Babylon to Ecbatana were generally composed of Jews.

In 539 there arrived at Ecbatana an embassy from Babylon headed by a Jew called Sheshbazzar, who was the leader of the plot to engage the interest of Cyrus in the cause of the Jews. Nitocris was now alarmed about the relations of Babylonia with Persia. She was old, and found it less easy than once to restrain Belshazzar, whom the Chaldean army chiefs had already persuaded to make a hostile military demonstration against the Persians on the eastern border. She was also distressed by Belshazzar's growing hostility toward the Jews, who were a people of influence among them; only recently Belshazzar had dared to bring the sacred vessels of the old Temple at Jerusalem into the Palace and use them at a gay banquet. It had greatly incensed all the Jews, so that it was not without misgiving that she entrusted this embassy of conciliation to them—yet she felt that they were more to be relied on for discreet behaviour than the Chaldean functionaries.

When Sheshbazzar arrived at Ecbatana, Cyrus conducted him and the other members of the embassy to the near-by town of Barena, where Croesus lived. This town Cyrus had given to Croesus for his honourable residence, together with a garrison of cavalry and archers and javelin-throwers; and Amytis was often a visitor here, as she was at that moment. The Jews unfolded their tale, and all that related to Nitocris Amytis heard with great sympathy, for it seemed to her that she must be a lonely woman, working all these years without a husband and having to rely on a son of a different spirit from hers and on advisers of a different blood. Nitocris had sent this message to Amytis by the Jews: 'The Queen at Babylon sends an embrace of peace to the Queen at Ecbatana. Being near death, she asks for her sweet thoughts, despite what bitterness may arise between our two empires—for there should be a kindness among women above the events of men, and such love as perhaps, unknown to us, the gods have for one another.' When this was read to her, Amytis was moved to tears, though she only half-understood its meaning.

While the embassy of the Jews was in consultation with Cyrus and Croesus, a messenger came bearing greetings from Nabonidus. After fourteen years of absence in Arabia, he had at last returned to Babylon, to see his wife before she died. His arrival was an occasion of great joy, and for the first time since his departure Nitocris ordered the New Year Festival to be again publicly celebrated.

But it would seem that Nabonidus took his son Belshazzar's part against his wife, though it was by her wisdom that Babylonia had prospered during his long absence. For not long after the arrival of the first messenger there came another, to say that Belshazzar had taken courage to advance toward Media at the head of his army and make raids across the frontier. When Amytis heard this news she cried: 'Oh, poor Nitocris, scorned by the son whom she made a king and by the husband in whose place she ruled so well and loyally. They must indeed be punished for this unkindness to her.' And Cyrus and Croesus studied with the Jews, and with Harpagus the leader of the Persian army, how to punish them.

During this visit Sheshbazzar found time to tell of the glories of Jerusalem that the Babylonians had destroyed. Cyrus was most interested to hear how the Jews believed that they had in them a power to know the good from the evil at sight. 'There is a burning within us,' Sheshbazzar said, 'a flame that Jehovah has planted—which is a flame of love when we see good, but a flame of hate when we see evil.' To which Cyrus answered, 'We Persians are a cooler people, and fear the fiery passions lest we be too much controlled by them—which is perhaps why we hold fire sacred, to be

kept apart rather than allowed to burn in our hearts.' But
he admired the Jews for their love of virtue, and he saw
that in punishing the arrogance of Belshazzar and Nabonidus
he could also gain honour in the world for assisting these good
people. Further, as Croesus pointed out, to make the Jews
powerful at Jerusalem again would give more security against
Amasis of Egypt, who was a constant threat to Cyrus in
the West, always ready to ally himself with any enemy of
Persia's.

Amytis was curious about this power which the Jews
claimed of instantly knowing the good from the evil.
Sheshbazzar was very knowledgeable in the value of jewels,
and to make plain to her this power which the Jews claimed,
he said: 'Put all the jewels you are wearing in my lap.'
Which she did. Then, picking them up one by one very
quickly and returning them to her, he said: 'This is a rare
one, indeed'—'This is false'—'This is pleasant to look at,
but not so pure a jewel as this which is set like a poor piece
of glass.' And Amytis saw that he spoke truly. 'Thus can
a Jew,' Sheshbazzar said, 'pick and turn over in his mind
the people he meets, and measure their worth.' And Amytis
said: 'Perhaps we do the same, but do not own to it. For
instance, we hold all insects to be created by evil spirits, and
I myself often say, when someone gives me a feeling of evil,
"That person wears a sting." Is it something like that?'
To which Sheshbazzar replied: 'Exactly like that, I should
say, Lady.' And then Amytis told the Jews the Palace story
of the first woman and man, who lived in the Garden of
Edin. For she thought they would be interested to hear of
how the woman found a tree in the Garden the fruit of
which, if eaten, would give her this very power of which
the Jews spoke. But in her story it was a power that brought
much sorrow with it. 'As indeed it does, Lady,' Sheshbazzar
said. 'The sad fate of the Jews shows this. For it makes us
proud, so that we sometimes rejoice at our power to know

evil rather than lament that there should be evil. For which our God punishes us severely.'

Cyrus now enlisted the Jews in his cause, and he was also enlisted in theirs. Sheshbazzar could count on the Jews who belonged to the Jerusalem party to start a revolt in Babylon at the proper moment. Those who wished to return to Jerusalem and rebuild the Temple were in a minority, but they were a powerful minority, including the priests, the scholars, the aristocratic families and, most important of all, the military families. The greater part of the Jews had settled themselves comfortably and profitably in their new home, but in some the rancour of captivity continued to smoulder; of these Sheshbazzar was the guiding spirit. Cyrus promised him that, when he had conquered Babylon, all the precious vessels and ornaments and jewels of which Nebuchadnezzar had stripped the Temple would be delivered up to the Jews again to take back to Jerusalem; Sheshbazzar should be governor of Jerusalem, in return for his acknowledgement of Cyrus's suzerainty.

This is the proclamation that Sheshbazzar brought back with him from Ecbatana, and which he read out to the assembled Jews when Cyrus stood with his army outside the walls of Babylon:

> Thus saith Cyrus King of Persia: The Powers of Heaven have been given me, to do justice on earth, and relieve the oppressed peoples. Heaven has charged me to free the Jews from the bondage that the Assyrians first laid upon them, to let them go up to Jerusalem, which is in Judah, and build the house of the Lord God of Israel, which is in Jerusalem.

The city of Babylon was the most strongly fortified in the world, and it was protected by the Chaldean guards, the fiercest and cruellest soldiers in the world. Nebuchadnezzar had fortified the land round Babylon to the north and west—for in this reign there was peace with Media to the east and no danger from the south. Nitocris his daughter improved these fortifications. Great earthworks were constructed along the road to Media; and high up the Euphrates canals were dug to control the river and make it follow a winding course, so that an invader might be prevented from sweeping down on the city. Also, a long way above Babylon, she created an artificial lake. By these means the force of the water was broken and the city protected from attack by way of the river. On the shores of the river, at weak points, she built high embankments, as a further protection against invasion. Within the city itself she built a strong brick wall along the river's course, temporarily diverting it to do so; the new wall joined the walls surrounding the two parts of the city, which was cut in two by the Euphrates. Finally, she had a bridge built between the parts, all intercourse between them having been by ferry before this. But she made a rule that the planks of the bridge must be removed every night, to prevent robbers from crossing from one bank to the other.

Cyrus, marching with his army toward Babylon to the south-west, was delayed at the River Gyndes, which was in flood. An unlucky thing had happened. Harpagus had held the river impassable, but Cyrus laid a wager that he could cross it mounted—promising Harpagus a gift if he failed. The current at the spot where they were ran very strong. Cyrus rode his favourite horse—one of the sacred white breed; the horse was carried away by the force of the flood, and he himself rescued with great difficulty by his soldiers. The loss of this animal distressed him for its own sake, and also because the Persians held it to be an ill omen when a sacred horse died unnaturally.

While Cyrus was brooding over the death of his horse, wondering whether it would not be prudent to abandon the expedition, Croesus and Harpagus were consulting with a Mage that accompanied the army—to learn if there was not some way to lift the curse. There was a way, the Mage said: should a marriage be celebrated before the dawn of the next day, the omen could be changed to a fortunate one. This was not an impossible thing to bring about, for Cyrus had brought with him a girl of marriageable age.

Amytis herself was responsible for the presence of the girl in the Persian camp. Her name was Spaco, and she was a daughter of Mandane, formerly the first of Amytis's ladies, who had died while Cyrus was absent in Lydia. On his return he found that Amytis had adopted the child, and during his six years of leisurely Palace life he had grown very fond of her. But in the last year Spaco had ceased to be a child; she would no longer sit on Cyrus's lap and let him fondle her. When preparations for the expedition against Babylonia were being made, Amytis formed a plan, with Croesus, that Cyrus should take Spaco for a second wife. All this time Cyrus had wanted no other wife besides Amytis, which pleased her greatly. But, she argued, Cyrus might remain long in Babylon, since he wished to knit it to Persia in a closer way than was possible with remote Lydia; and he would need a wife near him in that event. She herself did not care to leave Ecbatana; why should he not have Spaco, whom she loved, instead of some strange Babylonian woman?

Cyrus took Spaco with him, but said he would only marry her if he found it necessary to remain in Babylon longer than a year. Croesus was delighted with the words of the Mage, for if Cyrus married Spaco now he would both lift the curse put upon the expedition by the unnatural death of the white horse and fulfil Amytis's plan, which he thought a wise one. But Cyrus did differently. He gave Spaco to Harpagus, as the gift he had promised him if he lost the wager about crossing the river—deciding that in any case he would remain in Babylon no longer than a year. He might have given Spaco to his son Cambyses, who was with the expedition and wanted her. But Cyrus, loving Spaco, preferred to give her to a kind and reasonable old man than to a cruel and unreasonable young man.

Cyrus did not get his army across the Gyndes until the spring of the next year, it being the end of the year 539 when he first came to it. By then nearly two hundred channels had been dug on either side of the river to distribute the water, which remained high even after the flood had subsided. Cyrus had paid a visit to Ecbatana—to see Amytis, and tell her what he had done with Spaco and how now he felt himself pledged not to remain long in Babylonia after conquering it. If he had married Spaco, Amytis would have felt that she had won a victory; but this was also a victory, and—she could not deny—an even more gratifying one.

Having crossed the Gyndes, the Persian forces met Belshazzar and his army at Opis, on the River Tigris, and defeated him: in this battle Belshazzar was killed. Hearing this, his father, Nabonidus, went out to meet Cyrus. But by quick marching and a division of his forces Cyrus evaded him, capturing all the towns on his way as he approached Babylon. The part of his army with Harpagus reached the city first: Babylon was already captured when he arrived. Harpagus had accomplished this by diverting the Euphrates into a marsh and sending his troops along the shrunken water-course into the city by night. The Jews had assisted Harpagus, overcoming the Chaldean guards on the wall, and hurling them into the moat.

As Cyrus was about to enter the city Queen Nitocris lay dying. Her son was killed, her husband taken captive by Cyrus. Amytis had thought that Cyrus would bring her back to Ecbatana, and had looked forward to receiving her. But when she heard of Nitocris's death in her own land, she felt that this was a more fitting end for her. 'She should never have allowed Nabonidus to leave her alone all those years,' Amytis said. 'If he had stayed at home this would never have happened.' Yet as her husband's wife she could not but be glad that it had happened so: Babylonia was a rich country to own, and now there would be much coming and going between Babylon and Ecbatana.

When Cyrus entered Babylon he found the people more grieved for the death of Nitocris than for their defeat by the Persians. He made no triumphal procession, but ordered the days of mourning to be respected by his men; and with Nabonidus attended the body of the Queen to the tomb she had prepared for herself above one of the city gates. Nabonidus was exiled to Carmania, in Persia; he died there in 525, a very old man, three years after the death of Cyrus.

What interested Amytis most, of all the tales that Cyrus and Croesus had to tell on their return, was their account of the departure of the Jews for Jerusalem. The Jews who stayed behind in Babylonia had all brought rich offerings to those about to depart; these were displayed in the streets, but the holy vessels that Cyrus had given into their possession were borne under a curtained canopy, the fringe of which was said to be of pure gold thread. At the head of the procession went Sheshbazzar and certain Jewish nobles; then came the priestly Levites, blowing their trumpets to celebrate the holiness of the occasion. Of the Jews who remained, many who watched wept at the sight of departing friends. Some wished that they could have laid sober sense aside and joined the exalted band, but others called it a foolish business. And, as the procession wound through the city on its way to the gate, groups of Jewish children ran along with it, calling and shouting, and darting into the ranks to be embraced by people whom they recognized. The Babylonians themselves were moved to tears by the spectacle: except the Chaldeans, who would have rejoiced to see all the Jews go—for they regarded the fall of the city as the work of the Jews.

Daniel, who had been Nitocris's chief counsellor, remained in Babylon. He had already begun to make himself useful to Harpagus, whom Cyrus had appointed permanent governor of the conquered land. Cyrus now named Gobryas, a Persian, leader of the army in Harpagus's place.

From time to time news reached Ecbatana of the troubles the Jews were having in the task of the rebuilding of the Temple. For the Samaritan Jews wished to join in the work, and the Jews of Jerusalem did not consider them holy enough. Indeed, the Temple was not to be rebuilt for twenty-two years yet. Nevertheless, in Cyrus's lifetime a ceremony of resanctification was held among the ruins and a proud report of it sent to him, that read as if the work were already finished:

'Once more the Lord hears our voices rise from hence in praise of him. The singing men and ·women fill the holy place with their sweet airs: the chosen choir of the Lord. And the dancing girls use their timbrels again; and the cymbals clash; and the priests try the strength of their trumpets, nor do the notes drop down in sorrow but depart joyfully, like birds flying after their song. Once more the sacred musical band, of the full number of eight score and six, challenges the enemies of the Lord to battle: our hymns are songs of victory, the splendours of the Lord go before us. The cythern and the psaltery and the harp: such are the weapons with which the Lord has armed us in the days of our re-establishment. May the knowledge of all this be pleasurable to Cyrus, for it is to his honour: the Lord loves him for his love for us.'

Amytis longed to hear some of this music; and Cyrus sent to Jerusalem to ask that a troupe of the musicians of Jerusalem travel to Ecbatana, to perform before her. Shesh-bazzar begged Cyrus not to press this demand, saying that they would have need of all musicians when the Temple was completed—a thing certain to come about before many months. 'In Babylon, moreover,' he added, 'there are those who can answer the wish of your Queen.' And he named certain Jewish musicians of Babylon whom he knew to be profoundly skilled. These Harpagus sought out, and sent to Ecbatana.

But Amytis was only half-pleased; for the music they played and the songs they sang were very sad ones, full of lamenting notes; while the music described in the message from Jerusalem she imagined as very joyous.

'We hung up our harps on the willows of Babylon,' the Babylonian musicians sang mournfully. This refrain, translated into Persian, became a familiar saying in the Palace. When one of Amytis's women sulked too long over a scolding, Amytis would remark to the others, 'She has hung up her harp in Babylon.'

THE DEATH OF CYRUS

ALONG the eastern shores of the Caspian Sea lived a strong group of tribes called the Massagetae, of Amazonian descent. The River Araxes was the southern border of their country; then came the River Oxus, the northern border of Persia in this region. As among the Sacae, women fought in their battles—for centuries trained in the use of the bow. Their queen was Tomyris: a young widow of grim courage, and shrewdness in dealing with strangers. For years the Massagetae had kept their pledge to Cyrus to go into the land between the two rivers on peaceful errands only, and never in large numbers; and to make no alliance with any neighbouring group of tribes. Particularly they were pledged not to join themselves with the Sacae, part of whom lived to the north of them—the Sacae having given Cyrus trouble early in his reign. The women of the Sacae played an active part in public affairs, as did the women of the Massagetae; and about fifty years before the time of Cyrus a Sacean queen, Zarina, had stirred ambitions of greatness in her people and led them far afield on expeditions of conquest. Together the Sacae and the Massagetae might seriously endanger his northern borders. Cyrus had been on the whole lucky in his wars against men; but he felt that where women were the enemy, fortune might take unexpected turns.

About ten years after the capture of Babylon rumours reached Cyrus that Tomyris was making visits to Chorasmia, across the River Oxus, and farther east where another group of the Sacae lived, and even southward to Bactria, the land of the prophet Zoroaster's birth. He was reluctant to take measures of war against her if she could be brought to a peaceful turn of mind by other means; he was now entering upon old age and desired to spend his remaining years in training his sons to the government of the empire, and in living composedly with Amytis.

Cambyses's education Cyrus had given into the charge of Croesus, for whom this unruly prince had some respect. But Cyrus hoped secretly that Cambyses would not live long—it was quite possible that he would die in one of his fits. All confidence of a prosperously conducted empire Cyrus placed in Tanyoxarces, his son by Amytis, a noble and gentle-mannered young man. He usually took Tanyoxarces with him on his journeys to various parts of the empire. They were often accompanied by young Mandane (named after Amytis's dead friend), Cyrus's daughter by Amytis—between her and Tanyoxarces there was a tender affection, and Cyrus himself doted on her. There was an uneasiness in the family because Cambyses had an unwholesome passion for his half-sister; Amytis feared for what would happen to Mandane, whom she loved in an unhappy way not natural to her, should Cyrus die and Cambyses succeed him in power. Although it pained Amytis to be so frequently parted from her daughter, she was only at peace when Mandane and Cambyses were separated. If Mandane was about the Palace, it was always a trial to Amytis to make excuses why Cambyses could not see her; for when he felt his will opposed he would fall into a dreadful rage.

Such was the state of Cyrus's domestic affairs when rumours of the activities of the Queen of the Massagetae became so alarming that he felt moved to send Croesus to her, as ambassador extraordinary. Never before had Cyrus shown so much honour either to king or queen. For with Croesus went Amytis, to use softness with her should Croesus fail: so much importance did Cyrus attach to the occasion that he sent his dearest friend, and his very dear wife. Croesus and

Amytis wondered at his anxiety; it seemed almost as if he feared Tomyris, and indeed he said that he had a wish to avoid war with her. Moreover, Gobryas was not Harpagus's equal as an army leader.

'There is a time in a man's career,' Croesus agreed, 'when he must be done with events, and study how to lead a quiet life, so that death does not come upon him suddenly, but as a natural end.'

When Croesus and Amytis had crossed the River Oxus and come to the River Araxes, Croesus sent messengers to Tomyris, asking for an audience in most flattering terms: to bring Cyrus's compliments to her and confirm the friendship of the Persians and the Massagetae in a closer alliance than that which then existed between them. Tomyris ordered that Croesus and his suite be well entertained, but refused him an audience, saying that she was perfectly content with the alliance that she had formed with Cyrus at the beginning of her reign; that she had not brought the Massagetae to a weaker state and therefore saw no reason for offering Cyrus more favourable terms of alliance; that if Cyrus's own power was weakening, it was her duty as a queen to take what advantage of this she could. Croesus smiled at her reply, but Amytis grew angry. Tomyris so far did not know that Cyrus's queen had accompanied Croesus, her presence having been kept a secret for her safety should the Massagetae prove hostile and attempt to take her captive. But now Amytis laid caution aside and announced herself to Tomyris; she knew that Tomyris would want to see her, for curiosity if for no other reason. And so they met.

Tomyris was dressed like a warrior when she received Amytis; and Amytis in her most magnificent court finery. They could not understand each other, and, as Amytis wished to see Tomyris face to face, no interpreter could be present: it was against Persian etiquette for a man to look freely at a woman unless they were bound by some close tie or he was a person of high honour or importance. Amytis and Tomyris spoke not a word, but only looked at each other and struck attitudes —each making the other turn round, to examine her garments, Amytis pushing Tomyris away when she touched her too roughly. Tomyris wore no ornament except, around her neck, a heavy golden chain. Amytis signed to Tomyris that she give her this, and held out a girdle set with emeralds to be taken by her in exchange; which Tomyris clasped upon herself, laughing at the effect, and then handed back to Amytis not very graciously.

'She is coarse and ugly,' Amytis thought to herself, 'and her eyes are like a pig's. And yet I can imagine a man loving her, for fear.'

Amytis, to show herself the better-mannered, took Tomyris's golden chain, and parted from her with disdainful courtesy. Tomyris stood grinning insolently as Amytis withdrew; and yet she could not help feeling that the Persian woman had somehow won the battle. She must have brooded over the matter and grown irritated, for when Croesus and Amytis had crossed the Araxes a messenger reached them from Tomyris, demanding that Amytis return the golden chain— which, Tomyris said, she had only meant to show her, not to give her. To this Amytis replied that Cyrus himself would return the chain in time, which Tomyris might then wear in token of submission. For Amytis had by now resolved that Cyrus must humble this stupid and insolent woman.

Croesus was against the expedition, and in his heart so was Cyrus. But Amytis wished it, and Cyrus would not have felt easy in opposing her.

'There is wisdom and unwisdom in this expedition,' he said. 'And perhaps more wisdom in leaving the woman alone, since she has as yet done us no great harm. But who am I, to have the right and the good sense to act only wisely?'

On this journey, because it was dangerous, he denied himself the company of Tanyoxarces, taking Cambyses instead. And with him he carried the golden chain that Amytis had taken from Tomyris. When he reached the banks of the Araxes he sent messengers to Tomyris to say that he had come to place the chain round her neck again. Her answer to the messengers was that, if he gave her back the chain in a fair way and went away peacefully, she would consider the matter closed; but otherwise she would fight him, leaving it to him to choose where the battle should take place, whether on the side of the river on which he had encamped or upon her own ground. Croesus advised Cyrus not to let Tomyris cross the river. For if they should be defeated, then she could easily cross the Oxus into Persia; whereas if they won a battle upon her ground they could then overrun the whole country and tame the Massagetae for always.

Cyrus crossed the river with part of his army, leaving Croesus and Cambyses behind with the rest. Here, during the night, he had a great banquet spread; then, before dawn came, he withdrew a little with his troops, leaving his camp open to the Massagetae. Confronted by so many strange delicacies and drinks, they fell upon them excitedly, not thinking that this might be a trap—judging that Cyrus had fled at their approach. After a few hours, when they all lay in a helpless stupor, from the unaccustomed wine, Cyrus surprised them. The men he killed, the women fighters he disarmed and sent back to Tomyris; her son he took captive. Then Tomyris swore that she would not rest until she had taken Cyrus himself captive, and sent a message to him to say that he must expect no mercy from her, since he had' played so vile a trick upon her soldiers.

'It was indeed not well done,' Cyrus told himself. 'I have come to the end of my wisdom, perhaps. No man has more than a just measure of it.'

Croesus wanted to be at Cyrus's side during the approaching battle, but Cyrus was anxious that, in the event of disaster, Croesus should survive him, to care for Amytis and control the wildness of Cambyses. So Croesus remained on the other bank of the river, but sent across half of the troops that were with him.

Cyrus lost the battle and was captured. Thereupon Cambyses regarded his father as dead and insisted upon setting out immediately for Ecbatana to be proclaimed King. Croesus was painfully uncertain what to do in these extreme circumstances—whether to stay to learn Cyrus's fate, or go after Cambyses to restrain him from the follies that he would now be tempted to commit. It was too late to think of rescuing Cyrus by force. Over half of the troops that had gone into battle with Cyrus were killed, and the remainder were in no condition to fight again. The troops that had stayed with Croesus were just sufficient to ensure a safe and orderly retreat into Persia, should the Massagetae attempt to pursue them. Tomyris refused to negotiate for the ransom of Cyrus : his one chance, therefore, was in his own power to persuade her to release him. But, for all Croesus knew, Tomyris might have already killed him.

Should he linger there for news of Cyrus, or should he follow Cambyses ? He had with him Tomyris's son, whom Cyrus had captured and sent across the river, but she apparently believed him dead. Should he send the boy back to his mother, in the hope that this would move her to release Cyrus ? But there was no assurance that she would exchange generosity for generosity—and what if Cyrus were dead ? Croesus therefore thought it best that the boy should be taken to Ecbatana; Tomyris would in time learn that he was alive, and thus be restrained from further impudences and outrages. He also sent messengers ahead to ask for a fresh army, under a responsible leader, to punish the Massagetae—not to rescue Cyrus, since by the time they arrived his fate would probably have been decided one way or the other. Croesus no longer opposed Cambyses's desire to lead the troops homewards; and at the last moment, with sorrowful reluctance, he made up his mind to go with Cambyses. One of Cambyses's first acts, after he had declared himself King, was to have Tomyris's son killed, in revenge for his father's death—which he took for a certainty. This occurred in the early days of their march homewards, and convinced Croesus that in choosing to accompany Cambyses, instead of waiting against hope to press for Cyrus's release, he had done wisely. There were anxious times ahead.

And what of Cyrus? Amytis said to Croesus: 'It was I who made him go, Uncle, and since I loved him it cannot have been altogether madness. Better that he should be killed honourably, by an enemy, than by his own son.' For she felt sure that her husband was dead. That Cambyses would have killed Cyrus is not improbable—he had long resented his father's partiality for Tanyoxarces.

Eventually the Massagetae were defeated, and Tomyris was forced to tell them the fate of Cyrus. Her story was that she had not at first killed him, but entertained him kindly, resolved to make him love her. In this, she claimed, she had succeeded: they had been married according to the custom of the Massagetae—by which the husband must swear to have no secrets from his wife. And then, because Cyrus refused to tell her various secrets of state she was curious to know, such as which tribes of the Sacae had pledged themselves against her in the event of a great war between the Persians and the Massagetae, she had him crucified, according to the custom of the Massagetae with regard to a husband who broke his marriage-oath.

The body of Cyrus was brought to Ecbatana, and as it entered the city Tomyris, in chains, followed behind. None jeered at her, and she was even treated with a certain terrible courtesy. Amytis only stared silently at her when she saw her, as one might stare at a captured tiger that had destroyed a dear friend or relative.

When Cyrus's body was prepared for burial, he was found

to be wearing the golden neck-chain that Amytis had given him to return to Tomyris. Whether Cyrus had worn it willingly or whether Tomyris had put it round his neck after he was dead, to taunt Amytis, she could not tell. When the chain was shown to her, Amytis had Tomyris brought into her presence again, and fastened it with a stony smile upon the dazed but still defiant queen. And then Amytis ordered that Tomyris be lodged in a house of suitable dignity, but severely guarded and left always in solitude—'to think again and again of her great crime, till it seem to her the greatest crime ever committed.' Amytis also ordered that the house of Tomyris be not far from Ecbatana, so that she might go to look at her when she wished.

In Tomyris's bedroom, where she must see it every morning when she awoke, there was hung an image of Cyrus crucified. 'If it is true that there was love between them,' Amytis said, 'the sight will slowly make her mad.' Tomyris did not go mad, but was killed a few months later by Cambyses. The explanation he gave was that Tomyris caused unnecessary expense, and that these strange visits to the house were not good for Amytis. But the real reason was that he loved killing.

Cyrus was buried in ancient Pasargadae, in a tomb that he had had built during the last few years of his reign. The architect was one concerned in the building of the Temple at Jerusalem—he was a Greek from Cyrene, the Egyptian Queen's birthplace. The tomb stood high, its narrow door-way being approached by steps, and was surrounded by a colonnade; the walls were made of huge blocks of stone clamped together. And the writing on the tomb told that this was Cyrus, who founded the Empire of Persia and was King of Asia. 'Grudge me not therefore this monument,' it said.

In the testament that Cyrus left he told his children to obey their mother and use Croesus as their counsellor. But

after Cyrus's death Cambyses avoided contact with Amytis,
lest her influence restrain his passions and make his life uncomfortable. His half-brother Tanyoxarces had been sent to
Bactria, to control from there the eastern portion of the
Empire. Cambyses now asked him to come to Ecbatana to
discuss affairs in the East with him; and at the public feast
of welcome, before Amytis saw him, poison was put in his
cup. Amytis was only told that Tanyoxarces had suddenly
sickened at the feast. But she knew well enough, as everyone
else knew, that Cambyses had brought her son from Bactria
on purpose to see him die before his eyes. She had also
guessed that Cambyses had violated Mandane, his half-
sister—though Mandane said nothing, for dread of him.
When Mandane told Cambyses that she was pregnant, he
pretended to disbelieve her and worked himself into a rage
—during which he kicked her so violently that she died.
No one saw this, but Amytis knew that Cambyses had killed
her.

Yet Cambyses was shrewd enough not to let his passions
lead him in the conduct of public affairs; he always listened
soberly to the counsels of Croesus, and rarely acted against
them. It was in part Croesus's sagacity that kept the Persians
from revolting against Cambyses; for they hated him and
were horrified that this should be a son of Cyrus. The
times were sad ones; and should have been happy. Cyrus
had made them a great and strong people, yet without corrupt-
ing their innate virtues and graces. Their name was everywhere respected, and even those whom they had conquered
spoke well of them. It was said: 'A Persian may become
your enemy, but he remains your friend.' The dark character
of Cambyses was known to every Persian. There were no
open complaints against him, but it was whispered from
mouth to mouth that the times were sad ones—and there
was never doubt what was meant, though no more than
this might be said. Croesus's power over Cambyses quieted

the anxiety of those who understood how dangerous he might be to the security of the land; and a general and characteristic fear ruled the tongues of all the Persians, lest scandalous rumours of Cambyses's abnormalities pervade the whole world.

Croesus often attempted to comfort Amytis. 'Yes,' she would reply, 'these are sad times, but would it be natural if they were happier ones? Do you think that I did not expect there to be so much difference between Cyrus alive and Cyrus dead? And suppose I had died first? Would not Cyrus perhaps have married one of those princesses whom they brought before him so persistently every time we went to Susa, because they were of ancient Persian blood—so that, if Cambyses died, one of the Persian race should succeed to the throne and not Tanyoxarces, who was very much of a Mede? And surely this would have made a sad difference— since I cannot imagine that any other woman could have been so good a wife to Cyrus and so loving a queen of Persia as myself. Let it be, dear Uncle, and do not think that I grieve excessively. As proud families nurse their troubles gently, as if the troubles of others were all worse than theirs, so we must regard these times. And very likely in other countries more horrible things are suffered than we know among ourselves.'

By the year 525, three years after the death of Cyrus, it became necessary to make war on Egypt, for the security of the empire. Croesus accompanied Cambyses on this expedition, and helped him to conduct the war successfully. Cambyses would have killed King Amasis and taken his wife Ladice captive, to bring back to Ecbatana for his mother to see.

'She has long been interested in this Greek woman, and they have frequently exchanged messages. It might please her, and make her hate me a little less.'

'It would please her better,' Croesus answered, 'to learn that you had sent Ladice to her people in Cyrene. Foreigners do not interest her so much as formerly.' So Cambyses did this. Amasis was sent to Susa, where he soon died.

Cambyses remained in the West, while Croesus returned to Ecbatana, regarding Egypt as pacified. But Cambyses suspected Amasis's son of new plots against Persia, and killed him with his own hands in the palace at Sais. Then Cambyses went to Nubia on an expedition of conquest, but accomplished nothing; after which he sent troops into the desert, to attempt other conquests in Africa, but the army utterly disappeared, never being heard of again. Ashamed to return to Persia with so little glory, and perhaps afraid to face reproach from Croesus, Cambyses retired into Syria; where he died not long afterwards. He left a wife, Atossa, whom some writers have described as the daughter of Cyrus. However, Cyrus had only one daughter; and according to other writers she died after having been mistreated by Cambyses, and was called Mandane. Let us say that she was a relative of Cyrus, though not his daughter.

Croesus took charge of affairs in Ecbatana during Cambyses's absence, but he was fast weakening from age and at last told the notables in council that they must choose another to take Cambyses's place until he returned. But Croesus died during their deliberations. His death was a signal for an outbreak of despair and conspiracy—during which Amytis left the capital and set out for India, across the borders of Bactria, where her two sons by her first husband now lived in exile. Representatives of the opposing parties at Ecbatana came to her respectfully and urged her not to depart.

'We shall soon be at ease again,' they assured her. 'You shall see!'

'I wish to see no more,' she told them. 'It has already been a little too much for one lifetime.'

Nevertheless she was soon looking forward to life in a new country, and thus her women were not sorely pressed to keep her in good spirits, as they had expected. Indeed, she exerted herself to cheer them, rather: many were distressed to be going so far from home, though for her sake they tried to hide it.

'To live in exile,' she told them, 'must certainly pain the heart, and yet I think that we shall find it entertaining.'

This is how we now expect a lady of charm to behave under trouble—it is no new thing. And it is part of her charm that we are unable to judge from appearances what she is privately feeling.

Cyrus had been as good a husband to Amytis as his position in the world allowed. He would have been a still better husband if he had not died horribly, but it cannot be said that Amytis did not play a part in bringing about his death. Every wife shares her husband with the world, which is his grave—and for the immortal trifle that may be left to her should not be ungrateful, considering how much necessary waste there is in the life of any man.

II

MACEDONIAN TIMES

PERSIA IN DECLINE

AFTER Cambyses, son of Cyrus, Darius was King of the Persians; he strengthened the frontiers of the Empire and drew the whole East within the Persian political scheme. For about two hundred years from the time of Cyrus the rule of the Persians hung over the East like an ominous cloud, and over the Greeks as well. Athens and other cities of Greece had intervened against Persia in the revolt of the Greek cities of Ionia, led by Miletus—thus tempting Darius to ambitious attacks upon Greece itself. Persia suffered a series of defeats—not merely at Marathon and, a little later, at Salamis, but in Asia itself. Yet for a long time its imperial prestige remained unimpaired, as a man of enormous wealth is not impoverished by money losses that would mean ruin to others.

Even when the Ionian cities at last broke away from Persian rule, the result was not a surrender of world-leadership to Greece; these cities still found themselves comfortable under Persian patronage. In Greece, in fact, there had not yet arisen any power to compete with Persia in leadership and influence. Until the reign of Philip of Macedonia, the Persians alone, in this part of the world, exercised political and financial mastery on an extensive scale. Their vigorous grace of character had during this time degenerated into a lazy assumption of superiority; but by comparison the Greeks were still a people of small stature, unequal to attempts and achievements of majestic proportions. The Persians admired, and made free use of, their talents and arts and energies—without dreaming that the Greeks could ever dislodge them from their prerogative of empire.

And indeed, though it was a fury blowing from Greece that finally scattered the cloud of Persian power, the Greeks cannot be said to have succeeded the Persians in imperial dignity. Philip and his son Alexander, and all those generals and kinglings with whom Alexander shared the death-banquet of Persia, were men of middling scope, none of them a hero, none even a monster. No great light, either terrible or glorious, illumined the destruction of Persia. It is a lurid period—that which we are now to look into—and its great men are of a sickly colour. But the women whose names are associated with them make a more full-blooded show of life. Some of them achieve the reality of seeming monsters.

Yet were these not the times in which Aristotle lived—and was his not a noble life? Does he stand out of his times, a freakish immortal—or, were not his times somewhat good, somewhat wholesome, to have borne him? If this man was so far involved in the historical drama of his period as to have been the tutor and friend of Alexander, can it have been so inglorious a one—can Alexander's have been so mean a greatness? And was not Aristotle the intellectual heir and peer of Plato, who had known Socrates, and whose mind was salted with Socratic wisdom, and whose heart was even sweeter than his master's? Did not Aristotle preside over what we now regard as the grand age of human thought?

But we must see how the age of Aristotle looks by the light of the age of Alexander. And we must also take into account the lives of the various wives whose husbands gave this period their name: for the way in which women live their lives is an eloquent commentary on the circumstances with which men fill them.

2

PHILIP THE GREAT AND HIS WIFE OLYMPIAS

ALEXANDER THE GREAT, the third Macedonian king of this name, was born in 356 B.C. His character was made of patches, and so was his life. There is no real beginning to his story, and no real end; it is a ragged bundle of episodes, without any single force of temperament or purpose to give it either charm or heroic coherence. Alexander's spectacular conquest of the East cannot be regarded as a grandiose achievement. He sped restlessly and furiously from place to place, destroying what was already destroyed, reducing to dust what needed only the impatient touch of a child to prove it corrupt and vulnerable. Alexander was never more than a stepchild of history. He lacked the gift of luck that enables a man to accumulate round him a lasting legend of greatness, though to his own misfortune—and though the living stuff of the legend be mean or spurious or somehow hateful.

For his father, King Philip, Alexander had no love. Philip was boorish, ignorant, brave, honest, surprised always by his successes; laughing against himself at a setback, grinning over a triumph like a man who claimed no credit for it. All his pride of kingly superiority lay in his conviction that other men, whatever their pretensions, were as foolish as himself.

Alexander feared his father, but hated him and felt humiliated by his clownish acting of the kingly rôle. He feared his mother Olympias also, and had no more love for her than for his father. But she was proud, and longed to be a queen with more dignity and elegance than she could enjoy as the wife of Philip. It was through his mother Olympias's efforts that Alexander gradually came to hate, and then despise, his father. Olympias used Alexander as an instrument of revenge on her husband.

Philip provided Alexander generously with tutors and gave in to all Olympias's wishes for his upbringing and education. He took little interest in his son himself, regarding him as a thing of his mother's. But from time to time Olympias would make Alexander appear before his father and display his acquirements. On these occasions Philip would behave with exaggerated boorishness, frightening Alexander's horse if it happened to be a demonstration of his skill in manly sports—or, if a moral discourse, affecting a repugnance for virtuous conduct not at all natural to him. Philip was a short-tempered, self-willed, but—when not opposed—good-humoured man. His decisions were speedily taken, his worries easily forgotten. He had the typical Macedonian traits; the Macedonians were richer in northern blood than the Greeks, less agile-minded, more stubborn, more resistant to influence or interference. Philip was slow to speak, quick to exclaim, suspicious, intolerant, careless of the effect he produced on others. He could be kind on impulse, though he generally took little notice of the feelings of others; but he was seldom cruel, never vindictively deliberate in any act.

In converting the broad peasant land of Macedonia into a formidable political and military power, he had gone about his work like a tribal chieftain rather than like a king—following no set plan of expansion, mixing the small affair with the great, turning from one affair to another at apparent random, seeing the impressive structure that was year by year building itself up as a domestic conglomeration, never as a feature of the world scene in which it stood out so harshly and provocatively. That Philip achieved so much is less remarkable than his failure to achieve more.

Philip's lack of world-wisdom infuriated Olympias as much

as his unkingliness of speech and person. She herself came of a distinguished line, being a sister of the King of Epirus, which lay far to the west; the son of Achilles had migrated to Epirus after the Trojan War, and the royal family claimed descent from him. This grandeur of blood was the ground of a frequent taunt of Olympias's: 'My son,' she would say to Philip when he mocked Alexander's attempts to acquire the graces of a prince, 'is two sons—mine, but also yours. The descendant of Achilles must ever be on his guard against the son of the barbarian fool.' To such words as these Philip would answer: 'But the son of the barbarian fool sometimes takes possession, and the descendant of Achilles will be famous for his follies.'

Olympias had not always looked upon Philip with disdain and resentment. She had first met him when he came to Epirus to visit her brother Alexander, then a young and inexperienced king grateful for Philip's support and encouragement. During this visit she had seen Philip at his best: he was gay with her brother, engagingly shy with herself, anxious to be liked by all. His presence in Epirus had entirely silenced the opposition that still had existed to her brother, who with Philip's help had seized the kingship from a cousin. A year after this visit Alexander of Epirus paid a return visit to Philip, and Olympias accompanied him. Before Philip's departure from Epirus he had spoken to Alexander of his desire to marry Olmypias, but without making a formal proposal— since it seemed doubtful to him whether a young woman of so many refinements would wish a rough and clumsy stranger for a husband. The subject was not again mentioned; and when Philip heard that Olympias as well as her brother was coming to Macedonia he did not dare regard this as a sign of her consent. But it was Olympias who had urged Alexander to undertake the journey. For a whole year she had dreamed of becoming Philip's queen; and the picture of her future as wife of this fair, brave soldier, who took on a radiant Homeric shape among her musings, had closed her mind to all other thoughts and hopes of herself.

Olympias married Philip immediately after her arrival in Macedonia—married the memory of her first impression of him. For a time it flattered and entertained him to be loved in this serious and ecstatic way; then he began to be irked by the demands of the part that Olympias expected him to play. He became increasingly inattentive to her talk, almost ashamed to look at her when she spoke fondly to him, and told her less and less about his doings. Just before the birth of her son Alexander, Olympias suddenly realized that Philip was disgusted by her love of him, as if there were something unclean in her thinking him a more noble character than he was or ever meant to be. What second love for him could she make out of her ruined first love? The second love that most women make out of their first love for husbands grows from a mutual and tacit sadness in both husband and wife that he is only at rare moments the man both would like him to be. But there were no such rare moments with Philip. He estimated himself at the lowest, was never guided in his behaviour by what others might expect of him, and expected only the simplest things of himself.

There was no second way in which Olympias could love Philip. He was the enemy of the elevated emotions he had stirred in her, and these emotions she now turned against him, in loathing. Nor was she happy in the heroic hopes that she transferred from Philip to her son Alexander. The fate to which she destined Alexander was a dark one—to become, in spite, the challenger of his father's fame. It cannot be said that Alexander carried on the tradition of Macedonian aggrandizement begun by his father; rather, he stole his father's part and played it more recklessly and violently, living a more tortured life and dying a more awful death.

Philip had already turned to other women before Olympias's love for him froze. These were light attachments, short-lasting and never alluded to either by Philip or the members of his court. But it came to Philip's ears that his wife was secretly engaging in witch-practices, and, knowing himself hated by her, he concluded that she must be working to inflict harm on him by supernatural means. She laughed contemptuously at his accusations, saying that such grand arts were not to be practised upon a man of vulgar character. He need have no fear: if she should ever be driven to a murderous design against him, she would use vulgar means. This so angered Philip that he swore he would divorce her and thus deprive her son of a father. To which Olympias replied that to do that he must kill Jupiter himself, since it was Jupiter who was Alexander's father, come to her in the shape of a huge sea-serpent. (But at other times she reviled Philip as the author of all Alexander's faults.) Philip had, in truth, an uncomfortable fear of Olympias and would not have dared to divorce her. Imagining her to be endowed with mysterious powers of revenge, he felt that he had less to fear from her if he kept her near him than if he sent her away under the humiliation of divorce.

Philip decided on a merrier form of punishment for her impertinence. He said: 'Since you have thought it proper to take both an earthly and a heavenly husband, there can be no impropriety in my taking other wives than yourself— whether earthly or heavenly is a matter of taste, and I think I incline to the former kind.' Henceforth Philip took pains to treat every relationship he entered into with a woman as a formal marriage, though in only one case was a ceremony actually performed—that of Cleopatra, the niece of his general Attalus. Of this marriage there was a daughter. Years later, Olympias dealt vengefully with both daughter and mother. Another of the women of whom Philip spoke as his wives was a dancing-mistress of Larissa, called Philinna. She was much older than he, and had led a somewhat disreputable life; but she was plain-spoken and kind, and Philip felt more at home with her than with any of the other women who afforded him refuge from Olympias. She bore him a son, Philip, whom he wished to succeed him as King of Macedonia—rather than Olympias's son Alexander. He did not dare to let his wish be publicly known, and obstinately resisted the persuasions of his advisers to appoint his successor; however, he made a secret will in which he named this Philip surnamed Arrhidaeus as his heir.

And then there was an Illyrian woman, by whom Philip had a daughter, Cynane; about her there is a violent story to tell. And Phila, a princess of Elymiotis. And a woman of Pherae. And the daughter of Cithelas, King of Thrace. And the concubine Arsinoë, by whom he had Ptolemy, who became Ptolemy of Egypt—the ancestor of Cleopatra.

Olympias could hold herself much offended against, as Philip's lawful wife; for he not only played husband to half a dozen other women, but denied her the attentions and honours she ought properly to have enjoyed as Queen of Macedonia. Yet it was not so much Philip's infidelities that inflamed her feelings against him as his mocking defiance of her early expectations of him. Olympias's scorn provoked in Philip brutalities of language and behaviour with which even he reproached himself.

Olympias took no lovers; nor was there any consoling softness in her regard for Alexander, or in his for her. She felt cheated of the exalted pleasure that Philip had seemed to promise, and could not resign herself to a quiet sadness in its place. Every woman must live by some sense of victory over disappointments, and Olympias was not the sort of woman to find compensation in her own powers of self-control and endurance. Her parents had died while she was still a child, and her brother, who doted on her, had never restrained her wild impulses and imaginings. When she reached maturity she was initiated into the Orphic and Bacchic rites, and became fanatic in both. It was at a mystic orgy that Philip had first seen her and fallen under her spell; and it was by an orgiastic light that his barbaric robustness, which she was later to despise and loathe, appeared a symbol of heroic strength. In place of her young visions of Philip's destined grandeur there could only be a bitter enjoyment of his failure to be what she had wanted him to be, and a loveless triumph in her son's superiority over his father. Everyone whom Philip in any way favoured was odious to her; she was ready to despise Alexander for any passion or vice that seemed inherited from his father rather than from herself.

Besides Alexander, Olympias had another child by Philip—a daughter, Cleopatra. (This Cleopatra must be distinguished from Cleopatra the niece of Attalus, whom Philip married.) She was born four years after Alexander. Philip had ceased consorting with Olympias. But she began to fear that the children whom Philip had by other women would later contest Alexander's right to the kingship and perhaps even succeed in assassinating him; and she therefore wished for a second son, to take Alexander's place should he be violently removed. Calling Philip and his retinue to her apartments one night, she pretended to fall in with his boisterous mood—making jokes of the sort he delighted in, drinking freely, urging him to drink. There were many witnesses to her seduction of him: she flirted with him, drew him into an inner room, and came out an hour later to ask his men, who were still carousing, to carry him off and put him to bed. When Philip learned that she was pregnant, he was annoyed at the trick that she had played on him—he did not want another son by Olympias. But when the child was born and proved to be a girl, he taunted her with having played a trick on herself; and as Cleopatra grew up he took pains to make her fonder of him than of her mother, and to be more tender with her than with Alexander.

Olympias tried to incite her brother Alexander, King of Epirus, to enmity against Philip. But Philip had treated him generously, and it was important to both, for political reasons, to remain friends. Moreover, Philip secretly promised Alexander to give him Cleopatra—Alexander's own niece—in marriage when she grew up, and sent her to Epirus on long visits; and Olympias, who could not bear the sight of the child, was only too pleased to have her out of the way. When Cleopatra was sixteen, Alexander of Epirus came to Macedonia to marry her. At the marriage-feast Olympias brought a cruel thing about, of which we shall hear. But Cleopatra went back to Epirus as her uncle's bride and lived happily with him.

It must not be thought that Philip was entirely uneducated, or lacked respect for learning and the learned. His simplicity of manner was what he thought proper to himself, and he was too honest and proud to imagine that he might owe anyone more delicacy than his impulses dictated. His history before he married Olympias, early in his reign, will reveal how his life came to be divided between the brutalities and the refinements of kingship.

His father, Amyntas, had been defeated in a war with the Illyrians, and obliged to pay a heavy tribute, and to yield Philip, his youngest son, as a hostage. The Illyrians sent Philip to Thebes, from where Amyntas would have difficulty in reclaiming him should he later inflict defeat on them. This in time Amyntas did, and the Thebans supported the Illyrians by refusing to yield up Philip to him unless he abandoned his demands for tribute from them. But Philip's mother feared his return, since another son of hers had recently been assassinated; in Thebes he would at least be safe from the intrigues which were tearing Macedonia. So Philip remained there, and was provided with tutors befitting a boy who would perhaps one day be King of Macedonia. Philip had another brother, heir now to Amyntas; but he was a hard-fighting soldier and might die in battle— as indeed happened.

Epaminondas, later to become a renowned Theban general, was a fellow-pupil of Philip's, and together they studied military arts with patriotic earnestness. Epaminondas, who was the elder of the two, taught Philip to hate the greater city-powers of Greece, which he pictured as in corruption and envious of the fresh riches of the northern places. The comparison between his sentiment as a Theban and Philip's as a Macedonian was a somewhat forced one, since Thebes had an ancient title to political dignity. But, compared with the Athenians and other Greeks, the Thebans were of a rude culture—heavy-witted, slow to change, stubborn and ineloquent in communication, always suspicious of the stranger. There was thus some ground for their both feeling themselves uncontaminated by the civilization of the South. And Epaminondas could point to the injuries that Macedonia had suffered from the Athenians—just as Thebes had been the victim of Spartan aggression.

All this had its effect on Philip. Yet his mind was also drawn to subjects of a different sort during his schooling at Thebes. He was initiated into Pythagorean ideas, and followed the usual course of philosophical studies—which included a schoolboy's acquaintance with the work of Plato, who was then coming to be a respected name. He was not stimulated or influenced by this part of his education, but it taught him his own incapacities of mind and was perhaps responsible for his rather ungracious scrupulousness in disavowing pretensions of high character and intellect.

During his military studies at Thebes Philip first came across the massed phalanx as a battle-formation. But he would not have ventured to introduce it into the Macedonian army, accustomed to fight in open order, had it not been for Olympias. When she married him he was engaged in fighting many enemies, besides those at home: the Illyrians, the neighbouring Paeonians, and both the Thracians and Athenians, who had intervened in Macedonian affairs to support rivals of Philip to the kingship. Olympias, who was well-educated in Homeric lore, reminded him with what boldness and stoutness the heroes of Troy had faced battle, drawn up in a close body, their shields locked together. This recalled what he had seen at Thebes; and so he instituted the phalanx throughout his forces. Not being bound by Greek military conventions, he changed its structure, making it more bristling and terrible.

When Amyntas died, Philip's surviving brother became king, but was killed in battle soon after his accession. It has been said that Plato used his influence with the Thebans to persuade them to allow Philip to return to Macedonia in order to act as regent to his infant nephew, whom his brother had named as his heir. However it was, the Thebans certainly released Philip at about this time; and after a short period as regent he seized the kingship for himself.

These are the military achievements of Philip, from his accession. At the age of twenty-four, in one year, he defeated the Illyrians and the Paeonians, driving them out of the towns they had captured; and made a favourable peace with the Athenians. He then formed an alliance with the powerful city of Olynthus in Chalcidice, an enemy of Athens, manipulating their conflicting interests to his own advantage. He not only put an end to the interference of the Thracians in Macedonian affairs, but drove them out of Crenides, an important settlement that they had made on the eastern borders of Macedonia—sending a large number of colonists there and changing its name to Philippi. Around Philippi were goldmines that had long been worked, but in an unsystematic and desultory way; he now organized the working of these mines so effectively that they brought in a high yearly revenue. Moreover, he had gold pieces coined, called Philips, with which he hired many mercenaries and which he used also to buy favour for himself in Greece. And all the time he was continually fighting.

At the beginning he was regarded in Greece merely as a barbarian soldier-king, whose military operations were too scattered to be politically menacing. Greek statesmen could not imagine that the king of this upstart country might change the fortunes of the southern states: Persia was still the all-preoccupying thought. In 354 the Athenian orator Demosthenes, declaiming against Persian imperialism, made no reference whatever to Philip. And Philip himself at this time certainly did not see his achievements in political perspective. His imperial powers seemed to accumulate as something apart from his battle victories—as if thrust upon him by Fate. Perhaps the most conscious motives in his perpetual campaigning were a desire to escape from Olympias, who had him watched by her spies when he was at home and whom he believed to be a witch, and a defiant will to prove to her that he could fight battles successfully without her fanatical inspiration.

It was not until 352 that Demosthenes delivered his first oration against Philip. By this time Philip's warring had brought him to interfere in the affairs of the island of Euboea; to capture Methone, which brought him close to Thessaly; and to range into Thessaly itself. In a battle during these campaigns Philip lost an eye—a misfortune that he attributed to Olympias's magic. Now he struck still farther south, as far as Thermopylae; but this drew such angry protests from the Greeks that he turned elsewhere. Also, at about this time, he was once more called upon to intervene in Epirus on behalf of Olympias's brother; it was after his return from this journey to his capital, Pella, that Olympias contrived to become pregnant again by him. Then he left Pella, to make an attack on Olynthus, his former ally, which he suspected of treacherous negotiations with the Athenians. He not only razed the town, enslaving many people, but took possession of the whole triple peninsula to the south. This war provoked from Demosthenes three hostile orations.

Demosthenes was one of the Athenian embassy that went
to Pella to discuss the peace terms. When the embassy came
again to Pella for the ratification of the treaty they found
Philip already departed for Thrace. His absence on this occasion was looked upon by the Athenians as a crafty evasion
of his part in the agreed bargain over Chalcidice, but there
was no craft in Philip: he had merely gone off to do the
next soldierly thing that came into his head.

After the conquest of the Thracians, which damaged
Athenian interests in the Thracian Chersonese, Philip conquered Phocis. Thus he gained control of the important
Delphic trade, and Phocis's place on the All-Greek tribunal
that dealt with disputes between the Greek states. However,
Philip was never able to take the ceremonial side of his new
importance seriously. At his introduction to the tribunal, he
wore common hunting-clothes. When he was given a share
in the Presidency of the Pythian Games, he accepted the honour
so coolly that Athens was unwilling to send the usual deputa-
tion to them. At the Olympic Games held after his taking
of Olynthus, he behaved with drunken joviality; and gave
presents on an over-lavish scale—disregarding distinctions of
personal rank and of civic dignity. But in thus shocking
Greek sensibilities he was innocent of any intention to offend.
From his own point of view he was being friendly and
benignant, in matters that could be of no great importance;
since they did not concern war-making or money-making.

It was at about this time that Isocrates wrote the dangerous
oration urging Philip to go against Persia. Isocrates was a
sincere Athenian patriot, and the accusations of disloyalty that
many prominent Athenians made against him, because of this
appeal to Philip, were quite unjust. It is difficult to estimate
what effect this oration had on Philip. His conflict with
Persia resulted from steps of war, rather than of policy. But
he undoubtedly read the oration, since he referred to it in a
reply to Demosthenes's attacks upon him. He had at first

mocked Demosthenes in gross soldier language, treating the Philippic orations as personal, not political, attacks. Philip heard from his spies at Athens that Demosthenes had called him a barbarian drunkard, with no beard to catch his wine-drippings; and, being also informed that Demosthenes secretly frequented low wine-shops, he addressed the distinguished orator as a drunkard who wore a soaked beard, full of hidden wine-drippings. But when Demosthenes went into the Peloponnese to persuade various Greek states to resist Macedonian influence, even though it might for a time be of use to them against Sparta, Philip grew seriously angry with him, for his hostility began to take on military significance. By the time that Demosthenes had delivered his third Philippic, active conflict had taken place between Philip and the Athenian commander in Thrace. Athens had even gone so far in its new alarm at the Macedonian advance as to make a temporary alliance with Persia.

When Philip attempted the siege of the town of Perinthus, on the island of Euboea, which had become a centre of anti-Macedonian machinations, he found the inhabitants supported by Persian and Byzantine troops. He therefore proceeded to the attack of Byzantium; but here found the fleets of several Greek states opposed to him. Realizing that Athens was the chief force behind all this opposition, he resolved to settle with it before long. Many in Athens would now have attempted to conciliate Philip, but Demosthenes urged resistance and encouraged them to form an alliance with the Thebans.

3

THE LAST YEARS OF PHILIP

DURING the minor wars that Philip prosecuted after his return
from Byzantium he had received a severe wound, from
which he was slow in recovering. The Athenians hoped
for his death, and he himself was afraid that he might never
be able to fight again. Once more he thought himself the
victim of Olympias's arts. Lying long ill at Pella, he finally
asked her to come to him: for they lived in separate houses,
and usually no communication passed between them except
upon matters relating to Alexander, whose needs and rights
Olympias had constantly to keep before his father.

'Are you about to die, then, that you send for me?'
Olympias asked, as she entered his chamber.

'It seems your wish,' Philip answered.

Olympias, knowing that Philip thought her responsible for
the festered state of his wound, determined to terrify him
into conceding still greater honours to Alexander. She said:
'I have long ceased to have wishes on your account. But I
will not deny that I have wishes for Alexander, who suffers
for your hate of me.'

'I do not hate you,' Philip protested weakly.

'It is indifferent to me whether you do or do not. But to
the injustices inflicted on Alexander I cannot be indifferent.'

'Wherein have I been unjust to Alexander?'

'You have deprived him of his natural part in your wars
and battles, though he is perfectly skilled in soldierly feats.'

Philip at first found no answer to this. It was true that
he had kept Alexander from all contact with his soldiers:
he feared the consequences to himself should Alexander, so

much under Olympias's influence, become a hero to them. Two years before, when he went to attack Byzantium, he had refused Olympias's request that her son accompany him—instead, appointing Alexander a member of the council that was to govern Macedonia during his absence. This was a meaningless honour, since all the other members of the council were men of solid years, not likely to consult or be helped by the opinions of a boy of sixteen. Alexander, now eighteen, was still unfit for responsibilities of state, but he was of soldier's age and ripe for daring exploits. Under superstitious dread of death, Philip was moved to further what he feared. After a long, sad silence he sent for his general, Attalus.

When Attalus appeared and saw that Olympias was with the King, he drew back in surprise and displeasure. Between him and Olympias there was deep and constant feud, since he more than any other of Philip's generals was opposed to Alexander's presentation to the army; and he was the uncle of Cleopatra, whom Philip had taken as wife. Moreover, he had gone out of his way to persecute one of Philip's pages, Pausanias, who belonged to a noble and influential family and was known to be a spy of Olympias's. Believing that Philip would die of his wound, Attalus was alarmed for his own fate, and the fate of his niece, at the prospect of Alexander's assumption of the kingship: for this would mean the rule of Olympias. He therefore bore himself toward her now with a show of courtesy—and Olympias enjoyed his embarrassment, aware of what was in his mind.

'It is my desire, Attalus,' Philip said sternly, expecting opposition, 'that my son Alexander share the command with me in the war we must make on Athens when I am well enough to rise.' But Attalus only bowed—ironically, in the direction of Olympias. 'Go to him,' Philip continued, 'and inform him of his new position, and let all my generals pay proper homage to him, calling the army to parade before him. And while I lie here, instruct him respectfully in the duties of a commander.'

When Attalus withdrew, Philip said to Olympias: 'Alexander's rights have now been fully accorded to him—but it remains for me to be healed.'

He dared not look at Olympias as he said this. If she refused to lift her curse or to reveal by what means he might be cured, he was not only doomed but without means of revenge—for he had solemnly appointed Alexander second in command, which amounted to declaring him his heir.

Olympias smiled contemptuously. She could not feel grateful to Philip for granting her petition, since he had done so only in selfish trembling for his life, not in justice or in love of his son. Yet she indulged his faith in her power to cure him: there was more satisfaction for her in seeing him live to witness Alexander's success as a soldier —she was confident of this—than in letting him die, of fright, while Alexander was still too inexperienced to take firm hold of the kingship. At her girdle Olympias wore a pocket of Carthaginian embroidered cloth. She put her hand deep into this and, feeling carefully among the objects it contained, drew out a small ebony box. This she held out toward Philip on her palm; but she closed it teasingly in her long fingers before giving it to him.

'I think your wound will heal if bathed frequently with water to which a little of this powder has been added. Yet there is one other point upon which I should like to be made easy before I give it to you: Pausanias. This youth is under my protection and dearly regarded by Alexander—reasons, it would seem, for his being subjected to indignities by your other pages and for your own and Attalus's abuse of him. I should like these to be reasons for treating him with especial delicacy and consideration.'

'Ask anything of me you desire, cruel woman,' Philip answered wearily, 'for you know that I have no strength at this moment to refuse it. I shall make Pausanias first page of my court, if that will appease you. Only give me the powder—and leave me. My wound throbs, I have talked beyond my strength. I think we can have no more to say to each other.'

'I think not,' Olympias said. She tossed the little box on the bed and left the chamber coolly, as if she had been ministering to a slave.

Philip was soon well. With Alexander at his side, he led his soldiers against the combined forces of Athens and Thebes: defeating them overwhelmingly at Chaeronea, in 338. Alexander distinguished himself in this campaign, but his manner with his father was strained and distant; and Philip for his part was disturbed by the enthusiasm of his soldiers for a son whom he could not love and whose presence had been forced upon him by circumstances of which he was now ashamed.

After the battle Philip indulged himself and his officers in rich banquets, at which there was much free drinking and rough entertainment. During one of these he amused the company by having all the prisoners pass before him, throwing scraps from the table to the most miserable and taunting the proudest-looking of them with their defeat. One of them retorted thus: 'Fortune, by your victory, grants you the right to assume the airs of Agamemnon—but you prefer, it seems, the unheroic part of a Thersites.' At this Philip turned pale, for the words might have been spoken by Olympias herself. He was the more mortified in that Alexander was present and undoubtedly relished the reproof. Instead of ordering the prisoner to be punished, Philip rose from the table with a violent movement and left the banquet-hall. And all wondered.

In spite of such irritations, it was a triumphant time for Philip. Yet he had no acute feelings of spite against the Athenians—except Demosthenes, whose utterances against himself, composed in iambic meter, he chanted derisively as drinking-songs. On the whole he was generous to Athens, even adding to its territory; but more severe with the Thebans, perhaps because he regarded them as better soldiers. By this time Epaminondas, with whom he had studied at Thebes, had been killed in a campaign against Sparta. Perhaps, too, Philip was moved to punish Thebes for having held him hostage during his boyhood.

A great congress was held, at Corinth, of all the Greek states—with the exception of Sparta. Here the leadership of Philip was acknowledged, the various delegates consoling one another with the assurance that without Macedonia's help Persia could not be resisted. But Isocrates, the Athenian orator who had first addressed Philip on the subject of Persia, killed himself after Chaeronea, to prove that he had never meant his country's dishonour. Demosthenes, however, survived the defeat—not feeling the need of death until, over fifteen years later, Macedonia had inflicted a second defeat on Athens.

Sparta was angered by Philip's latest success, and particularly that it should have been at the expense of Thebes: regarding itself as deprived of its own rightful field of conquest. And Philip was angered by Sparta's refusal to participate in the anti-Persian congress at Corinth. This was no mere question of ceremony, but contained the threat that Sparta might become troublesome while Philip went against Persia. He therefore led his army into the Peloponnese, forcing Sparta to surrender several towns and adding some of the territory thus gained to the dominion of Argos.

Alexander did not accompany his father on the Lacedaemonian campaign, but returned to his mother at Pella. Now, just before he left for the campaign against Athens and Thebes, Philip had unwisely sent for his son Philip Arrhidaeus, whom the dancing-woman Philinna had borne him. He was at this time about fifteen years old, and Philip

intended to establish him at Pella in magnificent style, still
hoping secretly that Philip, and not Alexander, might be his
successor. The boy was amiable and intelligent, unlikely
to become involved in plots, as Alexander was through
Olympias. Nor had Philip feared, in granting Olympias her
wish that Alexander be given a responsible military command,
that she would want to take any revenge on young Philip
during his absence. That he left his other son at Olympias's
mercy shows how unreal to Philip were her grounds of
resentment against him. He saw her as a wild-mannered,
wild-minded woman, dangerous when her whims were not
satisfied; but he had little comprehension of what the
grandiose dreams of her girlhood had meant to her, and
what furious energies his disappointment of them had released
in her. It was only after young Philip became her victim
that he began to feel the full weight of her terribleness pressing
upon him, like a doom he could neither avoid nor understand.
Alexander himself was shocked by what Olympias had done,
though accustomed to accept all her acts as necessitated by
his father's stupidity and brutishness.

She had feigned a desire to deal kindly with Philip
Arrhidaeus and caused the page Pausanias, who was handsome and lively and winning, to become his constant companion at Pella. Young Philip soon adored Pausanias, and
would not be without him. It cannot be known whether
it was Pausanias himself who administered the debilitating
poison, or some slave of Olympias's, introduced by Pausanias
into Philip's household. Pausanias was almost certainly aware,
however, that frequent doses were being administered to
Philip, for he better than anyone else could observe the gradual
disordering of Philip's mind and health. Finally Philip fell
into a fever, of which he did not die; but recovered to be
feeble-witted—foolishly amiable, soft and tottering in body.

By the time Alexander returned to Pella, his half-brother
Philip Arrhidaeus had already been reduced to helplessness.

But this was not the full extent of Olympias's work against him. King Philip, before leaving Pella, had sent agents to Asia Minor to arrange a marriage between young Philip and a Carian princess reputed to be of great beauty. Olympias now urged Alexander to send agents of his own, to persuade the Carian satrap to reject Philip Arrhidaeus, because of his ruined body and mind, and accept Philip's legitimate son in his place. If this could be arranged the whole world would be witness to the setting aside of the one son in the other's favour; and Philip could not renounce Alexander without involving himself in a war with the Carian satrap and his allies. But Philip, having finished the war against the Spartans, had already determined on campaigns in the East: considerations of prudence did not cool his anger at Olympias's tampering with young Philip and Alexander's impudent meddling in the Carian affair. When he heard what had happened he ordered Alexander's agents to be imprisoned, and returned to Pella with the intention of punishing both Alexander and Olympias.

At Pella, Philip found that Alexander had fled to Illyria, and Olympias to Epirus, to her brother Alexander's protection. Philip passed certain decrees against them, depriving Alexander of his command and banishing Olympias permanently from Macedonia. Olympias's brother was bound by fraternal obligations to protest against Philip's severity; he declared that his marriage with his niece Cleopatra could not be fittingly celebrated that year, as had been arranged, while her mother was in exile. Philip relented, for he had set his heart on the marriage, and lifted the decrees. Alexander was recalled from Illyria, and Olympias returned to Macedonia with her brother Alexander. Philip trusted to her brother's presence and to the happy atmosphere of the marriage festivities to soften Olympias's fresh resentment against him; he now preferred to believe her innocent of Philip Arrhidaeus's ruin and to forget her and Alexander's part in the Carian affair. He planned gorgeous entertainments for the guests whom he had invited to the nuptials at Aegae. Representatives from all the Greek states were to come, and from many far countries, and wonderful gifts were arriving in advance of them. Philip was anxious that Olympias should be impressed by these evidences of his power; and even hoped for a lasting reconciliation with her.

Almost a happy time for Philip. He was marrying a daughter for whom he had tender feelings to a king who was his friend and the brother of Olympias: a proud woman, commanding in stature, surely a more queenly queen than any country in the world could boast. And he could also present his son Alexander to the assembled guests without shame—a worthy soldier, though too sullen and mysterious in character to be dear to him. And his generals Attalus and Parmenion were moving at the head of an expedition of ten thousand to free the Greek cities in the Troad and favour them with the protection of Macedonia. So far they had only occupied Abydos and Rhoetion; and opposition from various quarters, and difficulties of various kinds, seemed to prevent further progress. But that was as it should be: the swift and large successes must wait on his arrival there, after Aegae. He now looked forward delightedly to all the banqueting and drinking and parading with which the two nuptial days would be crowded.

On the first day the marriage itself was celebrated; and at the banquet that followed it Philip made a speech which he had carefully prepared to flatter the feelings of Olympias.

He began by a recital of the battles he had won, and described how after each victory he had banqueted and drunk with his officers and soldiers, dwelling on the particular merriment of each occasion. By the time he had finished this part of his speech he was already very drunk, and the point that he had intended to make—that no occasion was so pleasant as that celebrating family joys and the noble graces of peaceful friendships—was lost in his hoarse chuckling over battle orgies of the past. Long before this banquet was over, Philip had to be carried out, senseless from drink. Olympias exerted herself to be friendly to her husband's guests, especially the foreign ones, and to dispense the host-courtesies in which he had failed. She thus won for herself the only kind of homage acceptable to her as Philip's queen—insinuations of sympathy of the kind commonly offered to wives who are ashamed of their husbands. But she was far from being content with such a minor triumph at a moment when she felt Philip's very existence to be an obstacle to the great events that she wanted to happen around her, and through her. She was not altogether sure of Alexander as an instrument, but it was too late to hope for other turns of life than those that might come to her by his becoming King.

That night she slept little; and during part of it Pausanias was with her. But Alexander did not know what was being plotted.

The next day Philip could hardly restrain his excitement: a surprise was in store for the wedding-guests at Aegae. He called Pausanias to him to help him dress. When the royal party left for the theatre, Philip walked between the bride and bridegroom in a white robe of many folds, his demeanour unsmiling and his step slow and solemn. At the theatre a different ceremony began. Images of the twelve gods appeared, wearing white robes and decked with golden cloths. Pausanias now threw a golden cloth over Philip's shoulders, and Philip joined the procession of images as a thirteenth god. His life-guards, who attended him on all occasions, clustered round closely; but Philip, in a gesture of good-natured confidence that included the whole assembly, motioned them to follow at a distance and ordered only Pausanias to keep close. Pausanias carried, these days, a Celtic sword that Olympias had given him; she had brought it with her from Epirus and valued it for the mystic signs

engraved upon it, and for the legend associated with it—
that it would turn blunt and harmless if the enemy on whom
it was used were truly loved by a single person, but would
instantly kill if he were not.

When the procession came before the seats where Olympias
and the rest of the royal party were, Philip paused. All rose
to hail him, and pages stationed here threw flowers at his
feet. Philip bent to pick up a flower; the gold cloth slipped
to the ground. Pausanias ran to pick it up, then draped it
deftly over Philip's shoulders. As if taken suddenly ill,
Philip fell backwards.

The life-guards hastened up and carried Philip out of the
theatre. He lay still and unconscious on the litter on which
they brought him home; but no one thought of death until
they laid him on his bed and saw that the litter was stained
with blood. Then, searching for the wound, they found
Pausanias's sword plunged into Philip's back, under the
golden cloth.

Meanwhile, in the theatre, the guests and the crowd waited
silently, almost resentfully. Many assumed that Philip had
fallen from drunkenness and would return when the guards
had revived him. Olympias had withdrawn, making
Alexander accompany her; and Pausanias had disappeared.
But their absence was not thought significant until news of
Philip's death reached the theatre.

Horses waited at the gates of Aegae, for Pausanias's escape.
No one would have troubled to pursue him had not Alexander
of Epirus insisted on his capture, from a sense of duty to his
new wife, Philip's daughter, and in loyalty to Philip himself.
Olympias's probable part in the murder did not at first occur
to him; if it had, he would perhaps have tried sadly to
shield her.

But Olympias made no attempt to shield herself. When
Pausanias was caught, the horses by which he had escaped
were recognized to be hers. And when his crucified body

was displayed in the market-place near the theatre she came to the spot attended by her suite and had a golden crown put upon his head. The crowd assembled there may have taken this to mean that she thought Pausanias innocent of her husband's murder; they were not, at any rate, sufficiently devoted to Philip to raise an outcry. There could be no doubt in the minds of those close to Philip and Olympias as to who had committed, and who inspired, the deed. But with Philip's death Olympias became, for the time being at least, the most important person in Macedonia. It was clear to everyone that accusations of complicity in the murder did not offend her; and, if they had been distasteful to her, all would have been silent on the matter.

At Philip's funeral the body of Pausanias was burned over Philip's by the order of Olympias; and soon afterwards a monument to Pausanias was erected on the spot. What was Pausanias to Olympias that she should have taken him so dangerously into her confidence, that he should have done her bidding so faithfully? It could not be that she valued him for her son's sake; she knew that Alexander was secretly jealous of his beauty and of her attentions to him. Nor was there any real warmth in Pausanias's feelings for Alexander: his subservience to Olympias could not be so accounted for. There is no mystery, however, in Pausanias's short life. His family was a noble one, but impoverished, and Olympias could be sure of his devotion by keeping him well supplied with money and fine clothes. He was lazy, sprightly and without great ambition for himself—the perfect accomplice. If he had become a difficulty, Olympias would undoubtedly not have hesitated to destroy him. Her tenderness toward his memory made many think that he had been her lover. But it signified no more than her satisfaction with herself for having chosen so convenient an accomplice, one who had no care for his own interests beyond a love of the baubles of good living. Olympias intrigued and plotted persistently

during her life, but of her other agents and accomplices none
had so little reason for serving her as Pausanias.

After Philip's death, Alexander did much that Olympias
could not have hoped of his father; yet his achievements
did not brighten her old age. Her life grew darker than it
had ever been in Philip's time—not only because her part
in great events could now be only a mother's, but because
they were still far from being those she had dreamed of.

All women would like things to happen swiftly and
largely—but, the things they would have happen being so
different from the things likely to happen, most of them
prefer slow, small lives to naked contact with the insufficiencies
that their times and their husbands represent. A few are too
proud to accept for natural what is the nature of the world
in their years of existence; and their hatreds and revulsions,
while not humanly forgivable, must be regarded as hard
weights in the scales of truth against the soft hearts and light
judgements that other women lay there. Perhaps the angry
and tortured ones would have been less intractable in an
earlier age than their own, or better pleased with the world
in a later. But they are not to be extricated from the black
pages in which they invariably occur, as they could not
extricate themselves. The frighteningly ungentle women of
history are eloquent memorials of the desolation of the
times through which they lived—more so than any stories of
men descended to us from the horrors or poverties of the past.

The figure of Olympias is not easy to conjure up; in her
blackness she seems to have been almost invisible in the
scene in which she moved, though so ominously there. Philip
was at first fascinated by the sight of her, and then ceased to
look. Her son Alexander was intensely and fearfully aware
of her all his life, but as if by a spell cast upon him rather than
through any lucid picturing of her power and terribleness.
When he learned at Aegae that she was concerned in his
father's murder, he hurriedly left the city without seeing her,

and had departed from Pella to present himself to Philip's soldiers before she returned there; for a long time he could not bring himself to meet her.

Cleopatra begged her new husband to take her away as soon as possible to Epirus. She had lost her childish reverence for Philip, and was shocked rather than grieved by his death. Her one thought was to be out of Macedonia: Macedonia and Olympias were to her the same nightmare. Alexander parted with his sister Olympias in pain and dumbness; he was too puzzled by her character to reproach her for Philip's death. He had loved her when she was a girl: it had been exciting to have her as an elder sister. But the experience of seeing her in her maturity had shaken him. It was not as if she had changed into something horrible, but as if, rather, he had been deluded in his early view of her. He began trying to see her then as she was now, and this soured many other memories of his youth.

Olympias knew very well the feelings she inspired, but in her ecstatic and disdainful misery could not treat them as having anything to do with herself. No one ever dared to speak to her of her relations with other people; and, since she avoided the company and friendship of women, she had few questions of any kind asked of her. During the day-time she was much alone. At night she interviewed her agents and spies, and men of importance who sought her influence or feared her enmity—and always it was someone different: no constant ally or returning friend or long-trusted servant. She had abandoned her interest in mystic cults and magical rites. Nothing burned in her mind now but a will working toward she did not care what end—a heat that she could not make burst into flame. Indeed, she was as dark within herself as she seemed to others; and had that mistrust of dark which prevents hot-tempered people from giving themselves up innocently to sleep. In Olympias's bedchamber the lamps were not extinguished until dawn.

4

MODERNITY AT ATHENS

ALEXANDER's first tutor of importance was old Leonidas, a native of Epirus and a relative of his mother, who attempted to inculcate in him the ancient virtues of that land—silence, indifference to hardship, and the love of friends. Then for a time he was much under the influence of the young courtier Lysimachus, who accomplished feats of strength and military skill with a smiling ease that made them seem fashionable vanities; and who taught Alexander to value most in himself those endowments and talents that won most praise. The youth whose education Aristotle was called upon to complete had a mind full of ill-mixed notions, and a character of changeable shape.

Olympias showered luxuries upon her son—which Leonidas, stealing into his apartments, would remove; so that Alexander grew up to be both covetous and careless of fine things and to disprize what he had struggled to possess. He learned from Leonidas to long for dear friends, but from his mother to be readier with contempt than love; and from Lysimachus to console himself with flattery. The habit of silence that he acquired under Leonidas's tutelage strengthened his natural tendency to put the burden of speech on others except when he was angry or exalted. He fell easily into moods of sullen dissatisfaction with himself, but the effect of Olympias's bitterness on him was to make him regard others always as the source of unhappy feelings and crossed desires. In his early experiences and contacts, he learned no lesson to help him to subdue the enemy that haunted him all through his life—the horror of being alone with himself.

Aristotle added to these confused elements a dressing of equanimity; and, as Alexander was never in truth at peace within himself, it may be said that philosophy made a hypocrite of him.

Was Aristotle, then, a false guide and unvirtuous philosopher? His name has come down to us as a high and honourable one, and his works are still a resort of wisdom to many serious seekers after fixed truths. But let us look into his life and consider what kind of man he was in his own time—whether his firmness in the midst of its turbulent uncertainties was by grace of an immortal calm of mind, or whether it was the achievement of a prudent and obstinate intelligence. What was Aristotle in Athens, and what Athens when Aristotle taught there?

First of all, we know that Aristotle assumed the rôle of philosophic educator with such energy that Plato's name fell into dimness, as if he had lived centuries before Aristotle rather than been his master. The difference between them was not a difference of view, so that it might be said that Plato was of one age and Aristotle of another, but a difference in the quality of their ambitions. Plato set himself the end of exploring the difficult realms of thought with patience and serenity; the greatest sin a philosopher could commit, he taught his pupils, was to be hasty for solutions and over-successful in argument. 'It is our part to study what problems are contained in existence,' he would say, 'but time alone can solve them. And to seek to frame modestly the questions to which we cannot find answers—rather than to offer our poor conjectures to the vulgar for truths.' But Aristotle was all otherwise. He learned quickly, and even while at school felt that he had mastered all the subjects on which Plato lectured: because he understood the nature of the problems defined by Plato, he thought he must certainly have it in him to solve them. To Plato's perfect ideal of the true answer he opposed the more comfortable notion of the reasonable answer; and as his self-confidence grew and his method swelled into a semblance of philosophic achievement, he became more and more content with commentary in place of thought.

Before Aristotle, the popular way with a perplexing subject was the way of superstition. For superstition Aristotle substituted common sense, and appealed to the vanity of dull or vulgar thinkers to support him in his presentation of common sense as the opposite of superstition. He was himself more sanguine and untroubled by the hideous disunion of the world in which he lived than any contemporary of public note. The fashionable mood at Athens, among people aware of the destructive significance of every event of their time, was one of gloomy curiosity and knowledgeable despair. If Aristotle in his smoothness of temper could have bestowed some strength or ease of spirit on his time, it would be no accusation to call him an optimist. But his optimism was of that inglorious kind which is a mere resolve of invulnerability: the noble optimists do not refuse pain. And to this failure in the responsibilities of wisdom is to be added the poor use he made of the opportunity for wise influence that his close association with Philip and Alexander gave him. If these seem severe judgements, since it may be argued that a man who has devised a philosophical system has already done service enough to the happiness of his world and his fellows, we must let the matter be decided by more intimate tests.

Aristotle arrived at Athens in his eighteenth year, a wealthy orphan with an indulgent foster-father. His father had been physician to Amyntas of Macedonia, the father of Philip, and he had occasionally accompanied him to Pella; Aristotle was three years older than Philip, who had looked on him with wonder for his grown-up ways and knowing talkativeness. Years later, when Aristotle had become a celebrity, Philip was very curious to see into what sort of man he had grown. The sight of Aristotle grown up amused him greatly, for he found him still comically like the big-headed, precocious boy he remembered—the same pompous lisp and important little black eyes, and his legs spread out colossus-like when standing as if to compensate for their extreme thinness.

We must not, therefore, think of him as an inexperienced youth making his way shyly into the mysteries of Athenian sophistication. He came armed with introductions to the most respectable personages of the city, and the conviction of a distinguished future, and ample means of living meanwhile in accordance with his expectations. The elegance with which Aristotle always dressed—his expensive clothes, handsome rings and modishly arranged hair—gained him easy entrance into the best Athenian circles when he was a new-comer to the city; and, later, added an air of prosperity to the career of philosopher which made him as eminent a figure in the popular eye as if he had been an orator.

Aristotle took care to avoid the mistakes of Plato in addressing the public. For one thing, Plato's frequent references to Socrates, and his repeated professions of gratitude to his master, detracted from his own impressiveness. When Plato came to deliver in the Peiraeus the address that should have been the high point of his career—his lecture on The Good—the crowd gradually dwindled away to his few constant followers: because he allowed his audience to feel that the person addressing them was far less important than the problems he was discussing. Further, Plato made it difficult for people to estimate the value of his wisdom, by teaching gratuitously. And he pursued his profession with a gentle informality that led people to think of him as someone apart from the conventional courses of life. He not only lectured his pupils in the regular way at the Academy, but would talk to anyone who came to him in his garden at Colonus. He interrupted the programme of his school for visits to other cities, to talk with other philosophers and give lectures where he found interest in his ideas; he had travelled even as far as Egypt. When Aristotle arrived at Athens he was on a journey to

Sicily and southern Italy, from which he did not return for three years.

Aristotle prepared himself for attendance at Plato's school during his absence. But even before he became Plato's pupil he had already begun to disapprove of his prospective master's disregard of professional formalities—and formed a resolve to become, in good time, a different sort of philosopher himself. And it can be said that he fulfilled this resolve faithfully. We find no such unprofessional tenderness toward his master, in the works of Aristotle, as we find in those of Plato toward Socrates. Nor did Aristotle ever make his audience feel that the philosopher was less important than the matter of philosophy. He was not so disregardful of the human weaknesses of his public as Plato—who throughout his addresses and writings referred only twice to himself, and on both occasions in humble relation to Socrates.

Aristotle's most persistent criticism of Plato was that he had 'failed to come to an understanding with the public'. In appealing to everyone, Aristotle said, Plato succeeded in appealing to no one: his pure-minded impartiality was excessive in that he did not make it clear to which class or party he was friendly—and so was without public credit or importance. The Athenians were never moved to use Plato as an ambassador, as they used Aristotle. Plato condemned the crowd as capricious. Aristotle was careful to distinguish between different elements of the crowd and thus to endear to himself that section of it which was most desirable as an audience. He condemned those who worked at crafts or trades as necessarily unvirtuous—all manual workers, in fact; yet he was at pains to except those who worked in forests and mines. This mysterious exception becomes comprehensible if we consider that much of the wealth of Macedonia came from its forests and mines, and that Philip made forestry and mining dignified and lucrative occupations in order to attract workers to them.

Aristotle's Athenianism was never so extreme that it allowed him to forget his Macedonian affiliations. He was nevertheless sufficiently attentive to the prejudices current at Athens to win the good opinion of its most sensitive class—that which suffered most from the general decrease in wealth, and the consequent rise of large numbers in the class scale, by being constantly forced to demonstrate its superiority over classes equally poor. The laws at Athens restricting the activities of resident aliens were rigorously enforced. That Aristotle was allowed to keep a school shows how assiduously he practised his belief that a philosopher must come to an understanding with the public.

Aristotle, of course, loved his school—we must not make it seem that he was altogether without feeling in his designs and courses. He loved his school; and he also loved his wives. The Lyceum was dear to him as a comfortable centre of intelligent activity in a distressed world; and he was even extravagantly affectionate to his wives, in his conviction that a philosopher must ensure his peace of mind by every possible means. When his connexion with Macedonia made it dangerous for him to remain any longer at Athens, he went to Euboea and built up around him there another school, in loving memory of the Lyceum. So upon the death of his first wife, after due celebration of her contributions to his happiness, he speedily took her closest companion to fill her place and formed his second household in loving imitation of his first.

But Aristotle did not officially found his school at Athens until he was in full middle age—after a long period of absence. His first period at Athens had lasted twenty years; he spent much of this time in learning all he could from Plato, in order to become an able adversary. And likewise he did not take a wife until he had passed the age of forty, when he felt he had acquired sufficient control over his emotions to rule his household with an easy but firm benevolence.

Aristotle, as has been said, was in his eighteenth year when he first came to Athens. Plato was then in Sicily, and Aristotle had already been three years at Athens when Plato returned. During this time he worked hard to prepare himself for his studies with Plato, reading books with which Plato would be surprised to find a new and young pupil familiar, learning much from Plato's associates about his ideas, methods and habits, courting the good opinion of the people of whom Plato would be likely to inquire about him. Plato's favourite—if not most brilliant—pupil was one of his companions on the Sicilian journey. This was Xenocrates, who was twelve years older than Aristotle. He was a hesitant and inelegant thinker, but so earnest and loving in character that Plato spoke of him as 'an example of the results of philosophy rather than an example of its practice.' Plato also had with him his nephew Speusippus; it was Speusippus who was to succeed Plato as president of the Academy, by Plato's wish. He was more quick-minded and energetic than Xenocrates, but, like him, a man of simple qualities. In his devotion to his uncle he was more loyal than loving —greatly concerned with the spread of Plato's teachings, yet not deeply reverent toward Plato himself.

Soon after Plato's return from his travels, Aristotle presented himself at the Academy and was received into the fortunate number of the philosopher's daily intimates. By now Aristotle was thoroughly at home in Athens. He had rented a comfortable house in a street less dirty and with fewer shops than most; he was well provided with money by his guardian, and could afford Athens's best. The finest houses were shabby enough, compared with what was considered respectable in Stageira, his native town, and there was nothing in Athens besides the public buildings to match the magnificent private mansions he had seen in Pella. It would be good for Athens to come under Philip's dominion, Aristotle felt—to be ruled by a warrior king might have an invigorating effect on it.

Aristotle's father and mother were both dead by the time he came to Athens. His mother belonged to a noble family of Chalcis, and had left him some property there; and he had inherited the whole of his father's fortune, apart from small sums set aside for his younger brother and sister. His parents had expected great things of him, and had instructed Proxenus, whom they chose to be his guardian after their death, to deny him nothing reasonable for a youth of his powers; Proxenus came from Atarneus in Mysia, but had long been settled in Stageira. Aristotle lived so extravagantly during his early years in Athens that he used up nearly the whole of his inheritance. But Proxenus did not have the heart to deny him and supplied him from his own purse: thus Aristotle's relations with his guardian were of the tenderest. By the time that Proxenus died, Aristotle had become prosperous in his own right. When Aristotle discovered how severely Proxenus's fortune had been depleted by his early demands on him, he generously adopted Proxenus's son Nicanor.

In justice to Aristotle it must be said that, in insisting on so much material dignity of life, he had ever in mind his needs as a philosopher. That he had chosen a house unmarred by having a shop in its front was not due to mere foppish vanity: he had the justification of requiring quiet surroundings for his thought and reading. And he was an enormous reader. Indeed, only just enough was spent in dressing in the style he considered becoming to his chosen profession. He had clothes in almost every colour—and would, his friends said of him, have dressed himself in yellow if this had been permitted to men; with borders and fringes and tassels in the newest taste. But he spent almost as much on books as on clothes—in not many years he had accumulated the finest private library in Athens.

Aristotle was never quite sure of Plato's attitude to him. Plato said nothing of him that could not be favourably interpreted—and yet how often were Plato's phrases used by others to mock him! Once Plato came to call on Aristotle, who had been absent from the Academy for a few days because of a slight indisposition. Aristotle responded delightedly to his master's desire to see the whole house. Plato was tall and broad, but he never stood to his full height: as he walked by Aristotle's side, stooping to speak with him, it seemed that the master was showing deference to the pupil. On this occasion Theophrastus was present, a fellow-pupil and devoted admirer of Aristotle: it was he who made a report at the Academy next day, to the other pupils, of Plato's remarks during this visit. Plato had lingered in Aristotle's wardrobe-room and shown interest in every petty detail of the dressing-table. Aristotle had an exception-ally large hand-mirror, of polished bronze, which Plato picked up and looked into with a kindly smile: 'Surely, Aristotle, you had this made to hold the image of your head!' Certainly Aristotle's head was of an impressive size, and for the moment he was pleased. But he could not help doubting Plato's good-will toward him when he heard the phrase given a sly turn by Isocrates, not long afterwards.

Aristotle was making a laboriously amiable criticism of Plato's estimate of women: 'Our master's philosophy is so reasonable,' he had said, 'that he avoids systematizing such beings as women, that would prove weak in reason if fitted into a system. Now, if I were bold enough to prescribe a philosophy, I should make it as small as man's reason, not as large as man's reasonableness: and what did not fit into my system from vagueness of nature I should reduce to the proportions imposed by man's reason. But our master in his loving spirit prefers not to look upon reality in a clear mirror—the mirror he studies is as flattering to all contained in it as the sky.'

'True,' answered Isocrates, 'whereas your mirror was made to hold the image of your head, neither more nor less. You must let me see it when I next call upon you: our master was much taken with it.'

Two other phrases used by Plato on that visit to Aristotle clung to him for many years. When Plato left he had said: 'Be not too long away from us, Aristotle, for during your absence the school has felt itself deprived of its intelligence.' Probably Theophrastus, in the ingenuousness of his devotion, had reported to the others that Plato had called his friend 'the intelligence of the school.' They repeated the words, however, with an intonation that stung Aristotle; and he could not forget who had first spoken them. Then, after Plato had left the house, in Theophrastus's company, he had met someone in the street and said: 'We come from the House of the Reader!' Had this been another's phrase, Aristotle might have been pleased with it. But Plato had said so many other complimentary things of perhaps double import.

He had one day come upon a group of his pupils listening admiringly to a discourse of Aristotle upon a discourse of his own. Plato had been censuring poets for not matching beauty of language with clarity of thought. 'A poet,' Plato had said, 'is a lover of truth. But custom has taught him to be more concerned to express his love than to know well what it is that he loves. Therefore it falls upon philosophers to attempt to know what poets ought to know, and to stutter the truth while poets tell eloquently of appearances.'

'It is well to withhold the highest honours from poets,' Aristotle argued, 'but let us not at the same time withhold them from ourselves. The prize of truth is to him who can seize it. As for ascribing to poets exclusively the gift of beauty of language: if they have separated beauty of language from clarity of thought, does not beauty of language then become unbeautiful? And if we, having clarity of thought, have also clarity of language, is not clarity of language more beautiful than beauty of language? And who now would win the prize of beauty? When the Athenians climb eagerly to the Pnyx and the orator of the hour steps upon the platform to harangue them, soon they bestow upon him the prize of beauty: what he by poetic eloquence makes seem virtuous they applaud for virtuous, and whom he eloquently vilifies they condemn. Who would not confuse virtue and vice like an orator must forswear the beauties of eloquence: which is the philosopher's noble part. Let us not look upon ourselves as unfortunate in not being gifted with poetic graces.'

Plato had approached the group not long after Aristotle had begun to speak. But Aristotle continued nevertheless: for had not the master encouraged them always to make their own opinion of his ideas—to be, as he put it, learned as well as taught men? When Aristotle finished, Plato lingered pleasantly with the group. 'Is it not a fine thing,' he said, 'that the youngest of us should guide us away from the errors of the eldest? Thus, it is the colt that first dares to run into new fields of pasture. We must all be thankful, Aristotle, that you are not a born Athenian, for then by the law we should have been compelled to part with you for two years while you bent your great mind to the problems of soldiering—and without your vigilance what a tangle we should have made of philosophy! But there, don't grow red, don't sulk at me, Aristotle: I do sincerely mean to praise you. You are more vigorous in your studies than any other of my pupils, and would I not be an ungrateful teacher to upbraid you for that?'

Aristotle could not help feeling pleased with the interest with which Plato undoubtedly watched his progress; and, as the traits that Plato singled out for comment were those that he most valued in himself, he gradually developed a confident indifference to whatever disapproval might be implied in Plato's observations.

Once, when Plato was walking with a number of his

pupils in the park of the Academy, along the bank of the Cephisus, they met a policeman come to inform Plato that a man had been caught prowling in his garden at Colonus during the night. 'And what did he find?' Plato asked. The policeman, a Scythian armed with a bow, said: 'He seemed to have found nothing, but his look was miserable and guilty.' To which Plato said: 'Alas, poor man. But, had he found something, I should have offered it to him, and then he would have had to choose whether to be innocent and miserable or fortunate and guilty.'

'Is this not to put philosophy in place of the laws,' asked Aristotle, 'and make philosophic justice a rival to legal justice? Should we not use philosophy to strengthen the laws rather than to compete with them?'

Theophrastus said: 'Aristotle is ever jealous of the dignities of philosophy, is he not, Master?'

And Isocrates said: 'Our master needs no lessons from Aristotle in loyalty to Athens. Does Aristotle claim to be a better Athenian than Plato?'

Aristotle hated Isocrates. He replied: 'You would not call me so good an Athenian as yourself, I suppose, since I do not go daily after my bath to play with the women of the town, or bring dancing-girls into my house.'

'No,' answered Isocrates, 'you sit bent over a game-board, solemnly studying the draughts, to keep your wits sharp for future engagements of argument.'

All this time the Scythian policeman stood nervously fingering his bow, understanding nothing of what was being said, not sure what Plato's wishes were with regard to the arrested man and hesitating to press the matter for fear of seeming stupid.

Plato turned to his nephew Speusippus. 'And what is your opinion of the matter?' Speusippus answered: 'I would not publicly express a difference from you, Uncle, nor in private do anything so foolish as to waste time in disagreeing with you. For clearly you have thought longer and more earnestly on all subjects than any other man.'

'And you?' Plato appealed to the gentle Xenocrates. Xenocrates blushed. 'It seems to me, Master,' he said, 'that the words you used of the prisoner were generous and wise, and the proper retort of a philosopher to a policeman.'

At this the policeman became still more embarrassed.

'But have you nothing to say,' Plato persisted, 'to Aristotle's dissatisfaction with them?'

'I would first attain the art of understanding you, Master, before attempting that of differing from Aristotle.'

Plato sighed and turned to the policeman. 'My young friend Xenocrates requires the spur, you see, where Aristotle requires the curb. I am sure that must be plain to you?'

'Yes, Master,' answered the Scythian.

'You hear what he says, Xenocrates—and Aristotle?' Xenocrates smiled; Aristotle walked stiffly away.

'But the prisoner, Master Plato?' pleaded the Scythian.

'Why, I suppose we must do as Aristotle says and make philosophy the support of the laws. Therefore, do as you please with him.'

'If you make no complaint against him he will probably be freed.'

'There is nothing in philosophy to move me to prevent such legal justice.'

When the policeman escaped to make his report Plato sent Theophrastus after Aristotle. 'Tell him that, acting upon his very pertinent objection, I have resigned to the police authorities the happy privilege of declaring the man innocent.'

And now we have learned enough about the behaviour of Plato to Aristotle, and Aristotle to Plato, during the years when the younger philosopher was under the tutelage of the elder.

5

THE RISE OF ARISTOTLE

GRADUALLY Aristotle gathered round him a group of scholars who looked upon the Academy as representing the old school of philosophic thought, themselves the new. These met at the Lyceum, a gymnasium built near the banks of the River Ilissus on the south-eastern edge of the city. Here Aristotle established himself in a rival position to Plato without breaking his connection with the Academy. And here came, of course, Theophrastus; and among others, toward the end of Aristotle's first period in Athens, Callisthenes, a cousin of his mother's.

The most important member of this group, for the future course of Aristotle's life, was Hermias of Atarneus. Hermias, a eunuch, had proved so astute in affairs of state that his master Eubulus, a resolute enemy of the Persians in Asia Minor, had made him his successor as dynast of the prosperous cities of Atarneus and Assos in Mysia. During a period of peaceful relations with the Persians, Hermias had come to Athens to observe the military strength of the Athenians, form a clear notion of their policy toward Persia and, if possible, get a promise of support from them in any conflict in which he might be involved with the Persians. Atarneus was the birthplace of Proxenus, Aristotle's guardian, and thus it came about that Hermias was Aristotle's guest while he was in Athens. Having failed to extract any definite promises from the Athenians, Hermias attempted to enlist the interest of Philip of Macedonia. It was Aristotle who suggested this, for he frequently wrote letters to Philip on the state of affairs in Athens, in token of his gratitude for Philip's generosity to his father—and also because he was resolved to make the career of philosopher comprise dignity of a worldly degree. Philip was at that time not ready to think of adventures in Asia, but he thanked Aristotle for bringing the matter to his attention.

The Athenians were aware that Aristotle wrote frequently to Philip and occasionally received letters from Macedonia: for he made no secret of it. Indeed, it added considerably to his prestige. Very few people in Athens felt serious concern at Macedonian expansion. Athens itself did not seem directly threatened, and it was the mood of the time to make a leisurely best of a bad situation instead of straining to replace it by a good one. For many years there was far more complaisance toward Macedonian activities than hostility; even the professional patriots varied their attitude according to the changing look of events. So well-intentioned a man as Isocrates did not become irreconcilably anti-Macedonian until after the battle of Chaeronea; he was moved to suicide as much by shame in his fellow-citizens as shame in the defeat itself.

Athens was, in fact, a comfortable place to live in at this period, for a person who wished to be in the midst of events without feeling their impact sharply. In all that passed nothing seemed threatened but the good name of Athens; and there was a wide margin of opinion as to the extent to which its good name was affected by the changes it did not resist, and also a wide margin of philosophic indifference to the importance of a good name when other things remained tolerable.

'Tolerable' was a favourite word of Aristotle's. When Hermias of Atarneus complimented him on the position he had built up for himself at Athens, on the number of his friends and followers and the handsomeness of his house and its amenities, his answer was, 'Yes, I find existence tolerable at Athens.' His home was particularly tolerable to him during Hermias's stay. Hermias had his sister Pythias with him, and the presence of these two guests made Aristotle exert himself pleasantly for their entertainment. At all times there was a glow of ease about his house; there was now a radiance that embraced him warmly in his own hospitality.

Hermias was fond of luxury, as an Easterner and a eunuch; but also, somewhat in Aristotle's way, as a philosopher— because luxury contributed to evenness of humour. Between Aristotle and Hermias there was a deep understanding on the wisdom of good living, if not on the reasons of philosophy that supported it. And Pythias was intimately included in this sentimental bond. She had been brought up by her brother to be greedy, covetous and lying, but also very loving and flattering with others; and so her vices seemed no more than an excess of unselfishness toward those whose interests she made her own. As soon as she was settled in Aristotle's house she constituted herself the champion of his self-indulgence, and incited him to displays of vanity for which he might otherwise not have had the courage. She was plump, tidy-looking, shrewd and always in a happy temper— always confident that things would go well with her, since she had easy appetites, and no difficult scruples to stand in the way of her satisfying them. Aristotle liked her enormously, and she herself made it clear that he would be most acceptable to her as a husband. He would have married her at once, if he had not already made up his mind that his wife should play no part in forming his greatness, but rather be one of its adornments.

They were both moderately sure that they would one day marry, and Hermias smiled upon the prospect. The association of the three at this period had therefore all the charm of a family alliance, with none of its responsibilities. Hermias repaid Aristotle's hospitality by adding many new beauties and comforts to his house. Pythias appointed herself his domestic manager and made such a bustle of good food and merriment that Aristotle's house acquired a new popularity among his friends. The gentle Xenocrates came more frequently than any other: he had, alas, fallen in love with Pythias, and did not suspect any engagement between her and Aristotle, since they behaved in such a simple, comradely way to each other.

Xenocrates had confided his feelings for Pythias to Aristotle. 'Her goodness of heart has inspired in me a lasting devotion,' he said. 'But I think her brother might not want her to marry a barefoot philosopher, with untrimmed beard and meagre mantle. She has been brought up to love elegance— though I think her virtue would resign her to a humbler way of life.'

'I am sure she would adapt herself comfortably to any sort of life,' Aristotle replied, 'where she esteemed the man.'

'Ah, that is it,' Xenocrates sighed, 'I am afraid my qualities are advertisements for philosophy rather than for myself, as Plato always says of me. Now, you would have no such difficulty with a lady. You wear a neat beard, and your nails are prettily manicured. No one seeing you in the street on your way to a party, with your brightly dyed shoes and gold-knobbed stick, would think "There goes a philosopher."'

'I trust I am no less the philosopher for that,' answered Aristotle haughtily—on his guard whenever Plato was mentioned.

'I am not criticizing you, but myself,' said Xenocrates. 'I am sure I should do the thing clumsily, if I attempted it, and so it is just as well that I have pledged myself to the traditional philosophic dress. I suppose it is presumptuous of me to aspire to Pythias. But the thought that she will soon be leaving Athens saddens me.'

'You must not forget that Hermias has invited us to come to Atarneus whenever we find it convenient.' And this was all that was said between them on the subject of Pythias, Aristotle giving no hint of his own feelings for her.

But, when they were alone together, Hermias and Aristotle and Pythias referred freely to the proposed relationship, about which there were many tender jokes. For instance, Aristotle was afraid of mice. 'When we are married,' Pythias said, 'we must have a snake to keep the house clean of them, for I don't think it becomes a philosopher to be forced to draw his legs up under him as you do when a mouse runs near your chair.' And Aristotle, on leaving the house to go to the market to do Pythias's shopping, would say with all the suave correctness of a newly-made husband: 'I'll try not to be too long, my dear.'

Aristotle enjoyed these visits to the Agora. Here were the public offices, and the banking establishments, and the offices of many business-men of the Peiraeus—the port of Athens, connected with the city by two long walls. Aristotle cultivated the friendship of people of every influential class, and was particularly attracted to those engaged in practical affairs, such as would naturally be conducted in the Agora. Usually he had little excuse for visiting it, and his presence there would have provoked comment, especially in the afternoon, when he was expected at the Lyceum. Now he could say, 'I am just doing a little shopping for my guests,' and everyone would think that perfectly reasonable. At least, so he assumed. There was, as a matter of fact, a good deal of talk about his relations with Hermias and Pythias, it being generally said that he was preparing a comfortable home for himself in Asia, should he by some chance lose popularity at Athens; philosophers stood upon slippery social footing, particularly those who mixed in politics—and Aristotle was a resident alien besides. It was even insinuated that improprieties took place between Aristotle and his eunuch friend. All this gossip reached the ears of Theophrastus, who, not daring to speak to Aristotle about it, spoke to Xenocrates instead.

'A horrid witticism is going round Athens,' he said. 'That, in the eyes of Aristotle, Hermias and Pythias are sisters.'

Xenocrates was indignant. 'If Aristotle were merely a philosopher, his friendship with the dynast Hermias might indeed justifiably arouse suspicion. But he is also a man of worldly affairs. And as for Pythias, I have spoken of her to him myself, and I know that there is nothing of the lover in his feelings for her.'

And the placidity in Aristotle's manner, as he went the round of the stalls and shops of the market, buying the very best fish and table-dainties, certainly did not bespeak the lover. Even when he bought personal articles for Pythias, the way in which he bargained over the prices, felt the stuff and joked with the merchant, was more eloquent of the cool-tempered master of the household than of the doting lover. The responsibility of choosing for her a new pair of white slippers seemed a domestic triviality, which he was pleased to control along with larger responsibilities—not a lover's delightful privilege. Once he brought home to her a handsome peacock-fan that had taken his fancy: it would be a pretty sight to see the estimable young lady residing in his house fanned by such a fan. Another time, a parasol of the newest fashion: it was proper that his guests should advertise their satisfaction with their stay in Athens by patronizing Athenian modes and cultivating Athenian tastes.

He was managing his life and his career very well, and needed no assistance from anyone. The gossips of the market-place said of him: 'He has shown that he can get along without Plato. And now he is showing that he can get along without a professional match-maker. If all men were as Aristotle, the match-making women would soon have to go out of business.' At the Lyceum his affairs were proceeding nicely. In the morning he would meet the members of his circle there and deliver a long formal lecture, leaving time for a little discussion afterwards, but not enough time for organized disagreement. In the afternoon, after the meal, there would be a leisurely talk with Hermias on world-politics. Sometimes this would last for hours; sometimes it would be cut short by a marketing expedition to the Agora.

If he lingered in the market-place, to chat with a banker or a business-man of the Peiraeus, or to watch a parade, he would send his purchases home with a slave. Then from here to the Lyceum. Arriving thus late at the Lyceum, he did not have to interest himself in the physical activities of the gymnasium, which bored him. By this time the men would have finished with their athletics; they would be sitting, fresh from their baths, on the benches in the porticoes, or walking at their ease among the colonnades and strolling out upon the terraces.

When he paused to talk to a group, he would make no challenges—no 'And what is your opinion of our discussion this morning, did I not see you there?' or 'Demosthenes spoke rather incoherently yesterday, don't you think?' or 'Isocrates's speech was as crabbed and whining as usual, was it not?' Rather: 'A delightful day—I heard at the Agora that a very fine load of Paphlagonian chestnuts has arrived—but the wood-shipments from Macedonia have not yet come in.' Or: 'What do you think a slave of mine did yesterday? Got into a brawl with one of my neighbour's slaves who said that working for a philosopher was no better than having a woman for a master—and stabbed him with a meat-knife. My neighbour did not dare to be very angry, though the slave won't be able to work for a day or two—he had obviously said something against me which the slave had overheard. But I paid him handsomely for the inconvenience—and for the pleasure of demonstrating that philosophers are at least able to meet their liabilities.' Then, after a few cheerful words of greeting to everyone in sight, he would walk off by himself, his face set for contemplation, attended perhaps by Theophrastus, Xenocrates when he did not happen to be at the Academy, his young cousin Callisthenes, and a few other intimates who found it useful to know the probable subject of his evening talk. In the evening, when members of his circle, and a number of casual friends as well, assembled at his house, ordinary political and moral subjects were discussed, rather than purely philosophical ones; and Aristotle encouraged a certain amount of disagreement—as evidence of his tolerance and his liberality as a host.

When Hermias and Pythias left Athens, no definite date was arranged for Aristotle's visit to Atarneus; but it was agreed that, if Aristotle found it difficult to leave Athens, between his responsibilities at the Lyceum and his obligation of service to King Philip of Macedonia, Hermias would bring Pythias to Athens to be married to him. Nothing of this was told to Xenocrates, who was greatly saddened by Pythias's departure—and who took Aristotle's tearlessness as proof of the falsity of the rumours current about him and Pythias. Hermias and Aristotle exchanged vases bearing complimentary inscriptions. Aristotle presented Hermias with a dozen casks of the finest wine for export that he could buy in the Peiraeus. While he was making this purchase and arranging for the casks to be put aboard the ship in which Hermias and Pythias were to sail, he noticed some very elegant blocks of marble on the quays, ready for loading. Instantly a pretty resolve took shape: he returned to the exporting-offices and bought a block of similar marble for Hermias to take back to Atarneus with him. And this is why it was a pretty resolve: Hermias was to have it carved into a statue of Pythias, which was to be sent to Aristotle on its completion.

The visit of Hermias and Pythias had been of much benefit to Aristotle. It had made his house more popular, generally increased his prestige in Athens—and endeared him to Xenocrates. Xenocrates's affection was no small gain, for it meant that he attended the Lyceum more frequently; and, since his devotion to Plato was unquestionable, this established a precedent that other loyal disciples of Plato could honourably follow. Even Plato's nephew Speusippus came; and he was now the active head of the Platonic school, Plato having gradually renounced all the formal burdens of mastership.

Plato was old and ill, but the chief reason for his retirement was grief over the spirit that had come to prevail in Athens. Large changes were going on in the world. The crowd was aware of these only at moments when an orator moved them to pleasure or displeasure—and then their emotions were fixed upon the personalities of the day, not upon the year-long events. And those who saw the way of events either did not care, or cared with such astute self-interest that it would have been better had they understood nothing. There were the wicked, and the ignorant; and, where one might have looked for goodness, only calm. The few who were good, like Xenocrates, were too humble for passion. Plato knew that, if he continued to control his school, his un-happiness with the state of things at Athens would urge him to attempt to arouse passion in the minds under his influence. Feeling it a philosopher's duty to let men be what they were fated to be in their time, he withdrew to make some order in his disappointments before he died.

At the Lyceum, Aristotle treated Plato's withdrawal as a sign of the victory of his own system over his former master's. Every philosophic argument was made to seem a rebuttal of a parallel argument of Plato's, although his system was but a narrow frame into which the substance of Plato's thought was squeezed. When Xenocrates and Speusippus attended his lectures he softened his attacks on Plato; but Speusippus, a little sharper than Xenocrates, grew irritated by Aristotle's harping on the theme of Plato's vagaries, and toward the end of Aristotle's first period at Athens ceased visiting the Lyceum altogether.

Aristotle had meanwhile kept up his correspondence with Philip, and many people felt that Philip's condescension to Athens was in part due to Aristotle's influence with him. When a delicate situation arose over a tax levied by Philip upon the Thracians, that involved the property of certain Athenians, Aristotle was asked to go to Philip and get as favourable terms as he could. He did in fact succeed in getting such terms as earned him the esteem of the few rich men whom his visit benefited and inspired the crowd to regard him as the friend of Athens. But, more important even than this achievement, was his success in ingratiating himself with Queen Olympias. For it was she who later persuaded Philip to summon Aristotle to be tutor to Alexander. Philip did not like Aristotle, though he found him useful. 'He is too clever,' Philip said of him. 'A true philosopher is always something of a fool.' Olympias thought Aristotle capable of supplying an element of reserve that was missing from Alexander's character and of which he would have great need if he was to be a more dignified monarch than his father—natural dignity he did not possess.

When Aristotle returned to Athens from this visit to Macedonia, he was accompanied by Antipater, a brilliant officer of Philip's who was charged with making final arrangements with the Athenians over the Thracian affair—since Aristotle as a resident alien had no power to pledge the word of Athens to anything. Antipater was Aristotle's guest during his brief stay in Athens; and from him Aristotle learned much about Macedonian intrigue that he had not known before. Antipater had the confidence of both Olympias and Philip, each of whom thought him an ally against the other. But he had little affection for either, and his position was a dangerous one. However, he explained, Philip might be killed in battle, since he always went where the fighting was bloodiest, or be assassinated by one of Olympias's agents. Then Alexander would be King, and Olympias would undoubtedly rely on him to assist her against her many enemies. He did not have a high opinion of Alexander; once he was in power, he would know how to rid himself of both of them. Aristotle did not fail to realize the value of friendship with such a man. From now on he corresponded not only with Philip, but with Antipater as well. And occasionally he took the liberty of addressing himself separately to Olympias, giving her such good advice on the development of kingly vigour in her son that she made up her mind to put Alexander, when he was old enough, under the tutelage of this cool-headed man.

Plato died while Aristotle was on his way home from Macedonia : he arrived just in time for the funeral. But he did not attend it, being occupied with conferences on his Macedonian mission and with the entertainment of Antipater. He did, however, send the finest wreath that the most expensive florist in Athens could provide. To appear at the funeral, he told himself, would possibly have been interpreted as an act of hypocrisy : he had had no direct contact with Plato for several years. Moreover, the contents of Plato's will were already known. In it he expressed a wish that his old pupils would continue to frequent his house and garden at Colonus ; there was mention of all whom he imagined as coming there to honour his shade, but none of Aristotle.

Aristotle soon had far more serious public incidents to ponder than the little matter of the Thracian tax. Philip was waging a ruthless war in Chalcidice. The city of Olynthus was utterly destroyed; and Stageira also, Aristotle's birthplace and the home of his father, who had for so many years been court-physician at Pella. The news was mortifying enough to have made Aristotle break off relations with Philip and join the anti-Macedonian party at Athens—had he not felt that he had other friends besides Philip in Macedonia, who might be more regardful of his feelings when the rule passed into their hands. Therefore, when he next wrote to Philip, he allowed no reproachful reference to Stageira to mar the tone of decorous familiarity that he customarily adopted with him. Aristotle had, after all, no property in Stageira except his father's house. His dear guardian Proxenus was dead. Proxenus's son Nicanor was safe, though beggared. In inviting him to come to Athens, Aristotle offered him

adoption, hospitality and training in philosophy in return for
secretarial services. Aristotle's brother had been killed in the
taking of Stageira. His sister had fled to relatives at Chalcis,
in the island of Euboea, their mother's birthplace.

Thus Aristotle recovered quickly enough from the personal
injury sustained in the outrage committed upon Stageira by
Philip. Also, the slight resentment he felt gave him reason
for added friendliness toward Antipater, and toward Olympias;
so that the event led to his being more intimately involved
in Macedonian affairs, which did not displease him. But his
position at Athens was a somewhat awkward one at this
period. There was now great fear of Macedonia in the air,
and Aristotle was suspect, as a self-declared friend of Philip.
Demosthenes had delivered an angry oration against the
Macedonian king; sharp phrases were in everyone's mouth.
Aristotle did not dare to speak on the subject, and hostile
interpretations were put upon his silence. It occurred to no
one to regard him as a victim of Philip's destruction of
Stageira, since there were no evidences of his having suffered
from it except Nicanor's arrival at Athens; and Nicanor was
obviously being very useful as a secretary. Besides embarrassment of a political nature, Aristotle also had academic
difficulties—which, although not serious in themselves, added
to his general uneasiness. Speusippus, now in full control at
the Academy, was having remarkable success with the school.
Plato's death had stimulated new interest in his ideas; and,
Aristotle told himself, Speusippus had taken advantage of the
anti-Macedonian feeling of the moment to make it seem
traitorous to attend his lectures at the Lyceum.

6

THE MARRIAGE OF ARISTOTLE

For the first time Aristotle felt himself not thoroughly at home in Athens. He wrote to Hermias, and Hermias sent him the kind of letter that he could show at Athens, to account for his departure—asking Aristotle to come to Atarneus as soon as possible, to advise him in the dangerous conflicts he was having with the Persians. The letter contained an invitation to Xenocrates as well, and in such affectionate terms that he was tempted to regard it as a sign of Pythias's favour. Xenocrates consented to accompany Aristotle, who could now leave Athens without any appearance of flight. A rich and powerful dynast of Asia sought his counsel; and with him went one of the strongest and most honourable supporters of the Platonic school. Theophrastus also sailed with Aristotle. He was a native of Lesbos, which lay near Atarneus, and was desirous of paying a visit to his family. Should Aristotle be condemned during this absence, such a devoted disciple as Theophrastus would not escape animosity—so it was just as well that he could not endure to be parted from his master.

Aristotle spent over three years in Atarneus. Throughout this time he felt in no hurry to return to Athens. The letters he received from his adopted son Nicanor convinced him that he was not strongly missed. A long absence would at least have the effect of making his return an important event. They would say, not 'Aristotle is back again' but rather 'Have you heard? Aristotle has arrived in Athens!' Meanwhile there was much that he could do: get his lectures written out in order, elaborate and perfect his system, make himself known abroad—since Atarneus and Assos were busy centres of commerce, visited by traders and travellers from many far places. He could also familiarize himself with the political situation in Asia and thus increase his usefulness to the Macedonians. His relations with Philip, however, grew cool. He had tried to persuade Philip to come to the support of the independent cities of those parts against the Persians; but Philip became annoyed at his attempts to force a complex imperial policy upon him. Aristotle wrote more and more to Antipater, who found Aristotle's views in harmony with his own ambitions. Sometimes, too, Aristotle exchanged letters with Olympias.

Aristotle had persuaded himself, moreover, that a long rest at this period of his life, when he was approaching his prime, was a necessary preparation for the burdens of fame that he felt certain would be his. It had been maliciously said of him at Athens that he worked too hard, that he had a thinking-engine rather than a mind. He would show the world that he could follow nature's course as heartily as another man. He allowed Hermias to initiate him into luxurious practices that in Athens would have been considered oriental depravities. He rose late, and trained himself to depend on slaves for everything that it was possible not to do for himself. Between Pythias and himself there were delightful intimacies—a whole morning might be spent, for instance, in choosing perfumes from the stock of an Egyptian trader who presented himself at the Palace. Xenocrates, being also a guest at the Palace, exerted himself to fall in with this idle way of things; but his awkwardness made him miserable. Unlike Aristotle, he had no reasons other than his love for Pythias to induce him to linger in Atarneus.

For a long time Xenocrates continued to believe that Aristotle's feelings for Pythias were of a mild brotherly kind, and to trust Hermias's good-natured and apparently sincere encouragement of his suit. Pythias herself showed no con-

tempt for his love. When he pressed her to marry him and
return with him to Greece, she would answer that she was
still too young to leave her home and settle in a foreign place;
and, further, that if she married a stranger he must first become
familiar with her own kind of life. However, Pythias was
not altogether hypocritical in allowing Xenocrates to hope for
her. Aristotle was her first preference, and he had privately
pledged himself to marry her when his position at Athens
was secure. But with a man who meddled in politics, and
in such changing times as those, the chances of prosperity
had to be measured against large chances of misfortune.
Xenocrates, even because of his simplicity and unambitious-
ness, might well be the better bargain. She had decided,
at any rate, that it would be either one or the other. Her
brother Hermias, because of his defiance of the Persians, was
in a dangerous situation. She would be safe with none but
a Greek husband, and Aristotle and Xenocrates were the only
Greek suitors she had.

But something happened which made Xenocrates withdraw
his suit abruptly and utterly. He received a letter from
Speusippus asking him to return to Athens. Speusippus was
planning to go to Italy to revive interest there in Platonic
studies, and wanted Xenocrates to be in charge of the Academy
school during his absence. When Xenocrates told Pythias that
he must leave Atarneus immediately, Aristotle was present.
Xenocrates would have preferred to talk with her and Hermias
together; but Hermias was just then in Assos, and Aristotle as
the friend of all three might be the best person to bring about
a happy arrangement. If Pythias would only say that she
would give him a definite answer if he came to Atarneus
again when Speusippus returned from Italy, in about a year
from then—Xenocrates felt that without such an assurance
he must give up all thought of her. Although he loved her
dearly, he could not make a division in love between her
and philosophy. Already he felt ashamed, before the ever-

close shade of Plato, for these many idle months to which his desire to be near Pythias had reconciled him.

'Will you, Aristotle,' he said, on the occasion of his leave-taking, 'use your brotherly influence with Pythias to persuade her to say now whether or not she will become my wife—or, should she still wish more time for reflection, to promise that if I come again, after a year, she will then give me a frank and decisive answer. But should you be unready to do one or the other, Pythias, I must order my mind to a life without you, and without any woman. I have taken as much thought for my happiness of the heart as I dare: if I took more, I should become unworthy of that happiness of the mind which Plato bequeathed to me. Speak, Pythias! Speak, Aristotle!'

Pythias did not speak. She looked expectantly toward Aristotle, feeling that he knew her thoughts and could argue Xenocrates into letting things be as they were. But a sudden recklessness of pride took hold of Aristotle at this moment. He resented Xenocrates's assumption that he had not sufficient manliness to be in love with Pythias himself, and resented also Pythias's demand that he intrigue with her like a eunuch. So he said with a sly emphasis that Xenocrates could not possibly misunderstand: 'I am naturally impartial in this matter, Xenocrates, as the honour of friendship requires. But there is an honour that I owe Pythias, of another kind.'

Xenocrates gasped, seeing in an instant what he had been blind to for months, and years. Pythias was annoyed with Aristotle. She had not meant him to hint at so much, and disliked being made to seem a deceiver. She had not really practised deceit on Xenocrates: she had seriously considered him as a possible husband—more seriously than Aristotle realized.

'Aristotle should know me better,' she said defiantly, 'than to think that I choose easily between two men whom I esteem so highly.'

Xenocrates, however, was not to be flattered into his old innocence. He was horrified—less with them than with himself.

'I have been more stupid,' he answered sorrowfully, 'than a man of my kind has a right to be. The humiliation I suffer is merited, and I blame myself more than either of you.'

When Xenocrates had left them, Aristotle and Pythias were sullen and silent, each dissatisfied with the other for reasons they preferred not to discuss. Aristotle was not ready to marry Pythias, Pythias was not at all sure of Aristotle in spite of what he had said to Xenocrates. Neither had expected Xenocrates to behave with such firmness. But they were a well-matched pair, and soon found a way of being at peace with each other—that of blaming Xenocrates for having behaved dishonourably. Aristotle told himself that the incident would teach Pythias that the sister of an Asiatic dynast, in those uncertain times, could not afford to be captious in choosing a husband. Pythias told herself that for the future she must be as much on the alert with Aristotle as with any other.

Hermias was indeed being more unlucky in his conflict with the Persians than either he or Aristotle had anticipated; he had intrigued with every anti-Persian dynast of Asia Minor, bribed every satrap who seemed disposed to treachery, and contributed heavily to the maintenance of a number of small armies that the cities of his neighbourhood held ready against Persian interference. But the Persians continued to be dominant everywhere—not because they were strong or skilful, but because there was no large single opposing force. In 344, the fourth year of Aristotle's stay in Atarneus, Hermias was confronted with a painful choice. The Persians, irritated by his persistent defiance, threatened to invade his province; and, at the same time, offered to come to an understanding with him by negotiation. In spite of all that he had done to organize resistance to the Persians, he could not, he knew, rely on his allies to give him the support he needed if he decided to meet the Persians in battle. He therefore decided to yield a little to them this time. Aristotle continued to give him hope of future help from Macedonia. Philip seemed little interested in Asiatic adventures; but at any moment Philip might fall a victim to one of the many conspiracies against him in Macedonia, and then either Antipater or Olympias would dictate the policy of the new government. Aristotle felt himself of sufficient influence with them to be able to engage the interest of either in anti-Persian operations.

Hermias went under sworn safe-conduct to make an amicable arrangement with the Persians through their general Memnon, a Greek. But Memnon, as if anxious to prove his zeal in the Persian cause by treachery to its enemies, violated the safe-conduct and carried Hermias off to the court of Arta-xerxes III, the Persian Emperor. Pythias was frantic when Hermias did not return, Aristotle gravely concerned. He decided that he must leave Atarneus immediately. The Persians had too much fear of Hermias to let him escape, once they had him in their power. If they killed him, a ruler friendly to Persia would govern in Atarneus, and all who had been connected with Hermias would be in danger. Aristotle was all the more uneasy in that, Hermias's capture being unforeseen, he was caught without any definite plan for the immediate future. He would probably return to Athens; but he would be at a disadvantage if it seemed that he came back merely because he could no longer stay comfortably in the East.

During these years Aristotle's follower Theophrastus had been in Lesbos. He had frequently visited Aristotle, sailing from Mytilene, a port on the eastern coast of the island just across from Atarneus. He was ready to accompany Aristotle wherever he should decide to go next; meanwhile he was assisting his aged father in his fullery at Eresus, on the western coast of Lesbos. Aristotle now wrote Theophrastus to meet him as soon as possible at Mytilene, prepared to depart with him. Aristotle sent off three other letters. One was to his adopted son Nicanor at Athens, telling him to write to Mytilene whether he thought this a propitious moment for a return. He asked Nicanor to sound Xenocrates; if Xenocrates bore him no ill-will because of Pythias, he would be very useful in helping him to re-establish himself. The second letter was to Antipater, and the third to Olympias. In these Aristotle said that he had decided to return to Athens, in response to the insistent pleas of members of his school at the Lyceum; but that, since there had been occasional references to a possible demand on him to instruct Prince Alexander, he would delay at Mytilene until he heard from them again—regarding Macedonia as having first claim upon his energies.

While Aristotle was thus concerned with his plans he saw little of Pythias, and told her nothing of them. But she did not press him to console her or inquire what he meant to do. Her spies had brought her his letters; she had read them and sent them on their way, after sealing them again with his own seal. She allowed him to see that she despaired of Hermias's return. Her intention to follow him wherever he went she did not, however, reveal. She had made everything ready for a hasty departure, and sat weeping many hours every day, thinking of her dear, kind brother and easing her anger at Aristotle's avoidance of her. She knew that she would have her way in the end, but she disliked having to outwit a person in whose fortune she took so warm an interest. She was sure that she could be happy with him and make him happy to be her husband. Why should he be so foolish? It was proof of her tenderness for him that she did not regard him as having behaved with guile; she told herself only that he was behaving 'just like a man'. That she could view him in this homely way as a man made him more attractive to her than Xenocrates, who never stopped for a moment being a philosopher.

Meanwhile this is what was happening with Hermias. Artaxerxes held him prisoner in his palace, but with so much courtesy that Hermias was confident of being able to win his freedom and the advantage, besides, of a personal friendship with the monarch, above the spiteful reach of his ministers and generals. Artaxerxes was weak, and his court was a web of plots and disloyalties in which he scarcely dared move: he needed friends. But he was also cruel—of a line that had exhausted its ancient energies and had no power of revival except in cruelty. Artaxerxes himself had killed his brothers; his vicious grandmother had killed his vicious mother. Hermias counted on his weakness. And it was of Artaxerxes's weakness that he became the victim. For it had three degrees: dependence, then suspicion, then the revulsion of cruelty. So it was that, after confiding his suspicions of everyone else to Hermias, he turned suspicious of him. And one day on waking up he cried: 'Have the eunuch strangled!'

During Hermias's imprisonment at Artaxerxes's palace he made two real friends. One was the old king's youngest daughter, Parysatis, who was frail and shrinking and in fear of everyone about her. Hermias told her: 'When I am released, little Parysatis, I shall persuade your father to let me take you to Atarneus, to visit my sister Pythias, whom you will love. She will make you strong and happy.' The other was Barsinë, the daughter of Artaxerxes's nephew Darius. She was a sturdy and bold child, who tumbled hilariously over Hermias's knees. This Darius became Emperor of the Persians six years later, murdering the heir of Artaxerxes, who was then reigning. Both Parysatis and Barsinë were to be married by Alexander the Great on the same day.

Let us now move quickly to Athens. Aristotle is back, and married to Pythias. There is no general enmity against

him, and Xenocrates has remained friendly—as Nicanor fore-
told in the letter he wrote to Mytilene. Aristotle is again
at the Lyceum, his house is much frequented. But he does
not feel at his ease as he used to feel. His welcome was not
a warm one, news of the manner of his departure from
Mytilene having somehow preceded him. People unkindly
seized upon the fact that he left Mytilene while Hermias was
still a prisoner, not yet murdered. Soon after his arrival he
wrote a beautiful poem in memory of Hermias, full of the
most affectionate and reverent protestations, but this was used
mockingly against him; the old witticisms about his relations
with Hermias were revived and are still to be heard. Further,
there is the nonsensical talk caused by the statue of Pythias.
Pythias has insisted on keeping it in the house, for the luck
she says it has brought her. He has had it placed in a little
closet off their bedroom; but this makes people say that he
worships there, as at an altar. Besides a vague, continuous
sense of instability, there is a particularly biting irritation:
Xenocrates, and not himself, has been used by the Athenians
on occasions when it was necessary to send an embassy to
Philip.

Aristotle knows that this was largely because of an antipathy
that Philip has developed toward him: Philip probably
indicated that he would prefer Aristotle not to come. Philip
must have learned by now of his correspondence with Antipater and Olympias. When Aristotle heard from them at
Mytilene that there was no immediate chance of his being
called upon to instruct Alexander, but that they had hopes
of being able to invite him later, he understood very well
where the difficulty lay. He regards his transference of
loyalty as judicious, but it is unpleasant, nevertheless, to be
temporarily at a disadvantage.

Here is Aristotle, then, keeping his own counsel and cauti-
ously enduring something less than success, with Pythias's
help. Two years of life together have proved her right in

making him marry her. They have not been prosperous years, but they have passed quickly because of her cheerful contempt of them as unworthy of Aristotle. This is a phrase frequently on her lips—it may be about a fish for dinner or about the small number of pupils in attendance at his school : 'unworthy of Aristotle'. Such is her devotion to him that what is unworthy of him is also unworthy of her. Nothing crosses their intimate life. She gets on well with Nicanor, Aristotle's adopted son. He is of her own age, and teaches her how to write nicely; and she gives him courage to be less nervous of Aristotle, toward whom he has always borne himself with timorous gratitude. Scandalous tongues impute more than a friendship of household convenience to them. But Pythias is too fond of Aristotle ever to deceive him without his knowledge . . .

Aristotle had behaved good-humouredly about the marriage. He had sailed one night from Atarneus without having informed her of his intention, leaving a note of farewell in which he explained that he loved her too dearly to be able to endure the pain of a farewell interview. His continued presence in Atarneus, he said, would only embarrass her, and Hermias also on his return, since circumstances would now force him to adopt a pro-Persian policy for a time; the Persians would presumably blame Hermias's previous policy on himself. When circumstances were healthy again he would, of course, renew connexion with his beloved friends. Meanwhile he must bend himself to the re-establishing of his own career, which was greatly set back by these events.

Pythias, however, knew of his intention. She would have liked to hide herself away in the boat in which he was sailing and then surprise him when they were out at sea. But she had much to arrange, even though she was ready to depart— for one thing, the seizing of the city's jewelled regalia, which could only be done at the last minute. Instead, she sent on board that famous statue of herself.

With the statue went this message to Aristotle: 'By my fond interest in your movements I have learned that you leave Atarneus this night. I know that you would have asked me to come with you to share the uncertainties of your fortune, had you not felt that this was too great a sacrifice to ask of me. But I shall sail for Mytilene in the morning, not long afterwards, and join you there, and in love give my word that I shall never reproach you for any hardships I may suffer from having joined my fate to yours. You have taken pains not to let it seem that you had entirely lost faith in our Hermias's safe return—this is most delicate. But I am sure that my brother will never see Atarneus again, and have resigned myself mournfully to regarding him as lost. Since I cannot join you this night myself, I send after you the statue of me that you desired dear Hermias to have made. Thus you do not go forth from Atarneus alone. And soon I shall be with you doubly, in the loved appearance and in loving flesh also. The captain, who hands you my message, has my authority for delivering the statue to you, and will lend men from the crew to bear it where you wish. He has been well paid, therefore do not feel ashamed if you are unable to offer him a reward for his service. However, I should not mind your making him a present of the little golden bedside-lamp which the slave who helped you to pack apparently mistook for yours. But if you are fond of it, keep it, with my love. Pythias.'

Although Aristotle was dismayed by being encumbered with Pythias at this difficult moment, he could not help feeling a flattering glow of excitement. He had put off the responsibilities of marriage as long as he could, having intended to wait until his fortune permitted of his fulfilling them creditably. There was no escape now, but he made up his mind to look upon the marriage as a favourable omen for the future. Perhaps he had been too careful, too modest; his achievements in philosophy and his reputation in Athens and the world were surely solid enough to justify a little risk. The thought that he was taking a risk warmed him strangely. And Pythias had brought a handsome dowry with her in gold and jewels. It was suitable, after all, that it should be she rather than he who insisted upon the marriage; the kindliness with which he yielded would earn him her everlasting gratitude.

Theophrastus was waiting for him at Mytilene at the house of a relative, ready to depart with him wherever he went. Of the statue of Pythias, which the captain of the boat sent after him, Aristotle said to Theophrastus: 'You must not wonder at my bringing it. I had designed this charming girl for my wife. She was unable to leave with me and may be unable to join me here. If she cannot, I shall have need of something to hold my memories of her. A philosopher does not forget.'

Then Pythias came, and the proprieties required that they be immediately married. It was necessary to linger in Lesbos until he should hear from Macedonia whether he was wanted there; if he was called upon, he would prefer not to go by way of Athens. He wrote a second letter to Antipater, to account for his sudden marriage: it would damage his dignity to arrive in Macedonia with a wife whom he seemed to have picked up on the way. But he was not wanted in Macedonia, and so finally set sail for Athens—with Theophrastus and Pythias, and the statue.

When, two years later, Antipater again suggested to Philip that it would be wise to call upon Aristotle to tutor Alexander, Philip yielded. Antipater argued that it was better that Alexander should receive training in the political arts from Aristotle than from Olympias. To which Philip answered: 'You may be right. His mother teaches him only how to outwit me. This Aristotle will perhaps teach him how to outwit his mother. I care very little—except that I do not wish to see the man about at Pella. I liked his father, but the son has turned out to be a pushing and vain fellow. I do not disrespect philosophy, but I like openness and some clumsiness in a man. Aristotle is too cunning and smooth for my taste. I'll tell you what we'll do. We'll set him up in his birthplace, Stageira, and give him the sort of thing they have abroad—a gymnasium with shady groves and columns, and benches to sit about on when they ponder their problems.'

Antipater then said: 'What if he is offended at our having taken so long to send for him, and stands upon his pride?' Philip answered: 'Have you not learned, Antipater, that no city is impregnable through the gate of which a mule with a load of gold can pass?'

Pythias remained in Athens during the eight years of Aristotle's tutelage of Alexander. She was greatly liked there for her gaiety and her fine dinners, and with Nicanor's help kept up the social repute that Aristotle's house enjoyed; the invitation to be tutor to Alexander had done much to revive the esteem in which he had formerly been held. Pythias's good sense and her affection for Aristotle prompted her to write to him that Nicanor helped her to endure his absence, that she was sure that he would commend, in a philosophic spirit, her not making a gloomy widowhood of these years of separation. And Aristotle's good sense and affection for her caused him to reply that he could not but think it well that in keeping up his house for him at Athens she should take what little rewards of happiness seemed just.

Thus each made it easy for the other to be as reasonable as possible. Aristotle would not have asked Pythias to waste her best years in lonely fidelity; and to have taken her with him might have given the impression both at Athens and Pella that he was attempting to attach himself permanently to the Macedonian court. And Pythias had too high a respect for Aristotle to treat him like an ordinary husband. It was plain to everyone who frequented the house what her relations with Nicanor were. But the times were lenient, Aristotle was always spoken of by both with the frankest affection, and undoubtedly when he returned an arrangement would be made in accordance with the proprieties. A girl child was born to Pythias during the first year of Aristotle's absence; and, when it was learned that Aristotle was pleased to regard it as his own, everyone felt comfortable and behaved with the friendliest magnanimity toward the young couple.

7

ARISTOTLE'S ROYAL PUPIL

THEOPHRASTUS accompanied Aristotle to Macedonia, and so did his cousin Callisthenes. Aristotle went first to Pella, and remained there nearly a year, until the gymnasium which was being prepared at Stageira was ready. During his stay in Pella his relations with Antipater knit into a close friendship; and, although he regarded Olympias as mad, he showed so much agreement with her views about Alexander's education that she was persuaded that she had made Aristotle one of her creatures. Callisthenes, a young man with complete confidence in himself and a natural directness of speech, won Alexander's affection immediately. The two people who had been nearest to Alexander up to this time, besides Olympias, were old Leonidas and the elegant Lysimachas. Leonidas was severe with him, but always formal: never forgetting that his charge was a prince destined to reign. And Lysimachas flattered and indulged him as if he were king already. Callisthenes was the first who treated him as an equal and whom he could both love and respect.

Aristotle was not altogether easy about Callisthenes's manner with Alexander. 'For the present he enjoys the liberties you take, but watch his mood carefully, lest one day they feed a spite.' Theophrastus, on the other hand, he was always urging to be less timid. 'Alexander is not a brave boy, though rash-hearted. He will perhaps be made into a brave man, but he will never trust himself. Therefore he will seek others in whom to trust. He will be a monarch of many friends—and it will be no small distinction to be one of them, if I

144

judge the times rightly.' But Theophrastus preferred to share humbly in Aristotle's fortune rather than reach after glories of his own.

Aristotle never succeeded in endearing himself to Alexander. However, he convinced Alexander that there was to be learned from him something that he could not learn so well elsewhere: the art of making plans. Of the making of plots Alexander already knew all too much; but the confusion of his boyhood, lived in an atmosphere of uncertainty and hatefulness, and his own confusion of character, were not favourable to the building up of a steady will. By nature Alexander was wilful, but without a will. To have a will, one must have some degree of admiration for oneself and for one's ideas, and this Alexander never had except in flashes—when, remembering Aristotle's precepts, he forced himself to believe that he was a great man.

'Greatness is absolute in no man,' Aristotle told him, 'as truth is absolute in no mind. Power and wisdom lie in being somewhat stronger and somewhat shrewder than others. God is that which is somewhat above what men commonly are. And those men who stand a little above their fellow-men have the secret of divinity.' Thus Aristotle encouraged Alexander in that contempt for humans which he inherited from his father, Philip—save that Philip included himself in humanity. The most stalwart exponent of modern philosophy was conniving at the making of a proud oriental despot out of an unhappy and unfortunate northern prince. This work was done not only while Alexander was under Aristotle's tutelage. For, even after Alexander had begun his Asiatic conquest, he communicated frequently with Aristotle; and until a few years before his death he relied on Aristotle to stimulate his appetite for empire and justify its excesses.

At the charming gymnasium in Stageira, Alexander spent altogether four years with Aristotle. Olympias did not wish her son to be entirely cut off from her influence, and she had come to mistrust Aristotle because of his friendship with Antipater, in which she played little part. Further, Alexander was obliged to break off his studies when he was called to be regent of Macedonia during his father's expedition against Byzantium. A small part of the education that Aristotle gave him was concerned with the ordinary subjects of formal schooling—the study of Homer, and of the history of philosophy. But the larger part was a course of study in political reasoning, especially prepared for Alexander's benefit: maxims for the alert execution of kingly duties, studies in theories of conquest and colonization, and in principles of policy in dealing with the Greeks. 'Treat all conquered barbarians as mere instruments,' Aristotle counselled, 'but treat the Greeks as friends, if you would conquer them.'

As Alexander never returned from his Asiatic expedition, he had no direct dealings with the Greeks after the first two years of his reign. All his diplomacy, therefore, was exerted upon his own supporters, starting mischief where there was none, goading it to action where there was. He made the mistake of treating his generals and officers as beloved friends, attempting to subdue them by extravagant affection—and they in turn treated him as a heartless schemer, crediting him with far more insincerity than he actually had. Toward those whom he conquered he behaved without weak scruple or sentiment, but also without prudence or dignity. Everywhere reckless and uncertain, Alexander had not even the satisfaction of feeling himself a worthy pupil of his preceptor. Only when he made some new resolve of glory did fortune, and Aristotle, seem to smile on him. But then, once in the train of events, wildness and a bitter sense of isolation came upon him: and his only comfort was in hate, and in acts of boorish folly that his father would have regarded as fitting revenge on Olympias, who had believed the blood of Achilles a safeguard against his grosser inheritance.

It was an uneducable boy whom Aristotle was given to

educate, as he soon realized. A less resourceful man would have abandoned the task. But he could make Alexander more dangerous, if not more wise. The world would not be the worse off in the end, he felt. Alexander would probably add fresh confusions; but these would make the times richer in event, and philosophic equanimity a still more golden possession. Besides, a primed Alexander could enliven the conflict for dominance which was bound sooner or later to break out between Olympias and Antipater. And meanwhile, in the disordered condition of the world, what could be more pleasant than to reside aloof in Stageira, yet holding a position of undeniable honour and importance? Xenocrates sometimes visited him when he came to Macedonia on an errand of state, Stageira being not difficult to reach from Pella; thus they would know at Athens in what circumstances he lived, and how strong his influence was with Philip's heir. And not only Alexander was his pupil, but other youths certainly destined to prominence. Among these were Ptolemy, an illegitimate son of Philip's, and Nearchus the Cretan, both of whom Philip banished during the later years of Aristotle's stay for participating in the intrigues in which Olympias and Antipater involved Alexander.

Apart from the beautiful park and fine buildings of the school prepared for Aristotle and Alexander and his young friends, Stageira was still in the ruinous state to which Philip had reduced it. Naturally, this caused Aristotle some sadness, but not enough to make living in the town intolerable to him. Indeed, the comparison between his own little domain and the wreckage marking the site where his parents' house had stood, and that of his guardian Proxenus and many other familiar places of his boyhood, provoked consoling thoughts of satisfaction with his own fortune. So much had had to make way before the Macedonian advance—his native city, Athens itself. The old Stageira was no more, yet he stood secure upon the crumbled remains. He belonged culturally

to Athens, and Athens was in the main content to let the
barbarians be masters of the day—in his heart he knew the
Macedonians for barbarians; yet he went about the world,
and even among the Macedonians, a free man.

Nor was he at all uneasy about the reception that he
would have from Pythias when he returned, nor about
the talk that there would be about his evident indulgence
of Pythias's relations with Nicanor, when he was again the
master of his household. Xenocrates had tried to hint at
something during his visits, but the subject was too sad a
one for him to be able to play the friend's part smoothly.
Whenever he referred to it, Aristotle's cheerful manner,
which might be due either to innocence or indifference,
made the task seem not worth the pain it would cause him
to speak out.

It was only after eight years at Pella and Stageira that
Aristotle returned to Athens. During the last years of his stay
Alexander became King—Philip having been at last assassinated. It now remained to be seen who would gain the as-
cendancy—Olympias or Antipater. Aristotle wished to avoid
being torn between them, and would have returned at once
to Athens upon Philip's death. But it was not a propitious
moment for Aristotle to reappear in Athens. Athens became
suddenly patriotic, thinking that, with the new king scarcely
established, it would be easy to throw off Macedonian rule;
Thebes was always ready to bear the brunt of any military
attack, and it seemed that Alexander could do little against
the two cities, with rebellious northern tribes to pacify.
Aristotle advised Alexander to go against Thebes first. When
Thebes was reduced, Athens would be indifferent again:
the northern tribes could meanwhile do nothing very serious.
And so it happened. Alexander sacked Thebes; and not long
afterwards the assembled Greeks (except the Lacedaemonians)
flatteringly elected Alexander to the military command of a
league against the Persians. Then the young king went

against the northern tribes, penetrating as far as the Danube. Rumours of his death reached Thebes, which was secretly pressed by Athens to take up arms again. Alexander made a lightning descent on Thebes, this time punishing it cruelly; Athens now became enthusiastically pro-Macedonian.

Aristotle lingered in Macedonia a little longer, nevertheless, at Alexander's request. Antipater was against the proposed expedition into Asia, fearing that, if Alexander succeeded too well, he and Olympias would become inconveniently popular. Alexander hoped that Aristotle would be able to persuade Antipater to co-operate in preparations for the expedition. This Aristotle did, by arguing that Alexander's absence from Macedonia would weaken Olympias's party: Alexander would be gone a long time if, as Aristotle expected, he followed the ambitious scheme of conquest that they had worked out together at Stageira. The generals Parmenion and Attalus were still in the Troad, with the ten thousand that Philip had sent there in the year of his death: Parmenion was ordered to bring the men back. But Attalus, the uncle of the Cleopatra whom Philip had married, was secretly killed. He had been exchanging traitorous letters with Demosthenes, and these fell into the hands of Antipater's spies. In one of Demosthenes's letters Aristotle was accused of conspiring with Antipater against Alexander and Olympias; for this reason little was said of the matter to Alexander—the order for Attalus's death came from Antipater.

Before Aristotle left, the expeditionary army was nearly ready to depart, and he had the pleasure of seeing the first review of the forces—thirty-seven thousand men altogether. They had already received their new campaign equipment—new helmets and greaves and leather cuirasses. This was an extravagance, but it pleased the crowds, and would impress the Persians. Above all, it pleased and excited Olympias. The soldiers carried, besides their swords and small shields, long, heavy pikes, some standing taller than three men—

which gave them the look of an army going out to fight not men, but gods. Aristotle thought to himself: 'In a sense, this is true. It is the destiny of the Macedonians to destroy the old days and all their obsolete gods and philosophies.' The cavalry, leading the parade, rode with a brisk careless-ness and ease—the horsemen sat upon a blanket and used no stirrups. At the end of the parade came the engineers and the instruments of the siege-train: rams, towers, catapults. And then, having reviewed the troops, Alexander himself stepped out before the populace, attended by pages and body-guards, his battle-council of ten, and his picked guardsmen.

'This,' said Aristotle to himself, 'is the future.' And his heart swelled with the feeling that he had contributed to its making.

Callisthenes did not return to Athens with Aristotle, having been urged by Alexander to accompany him on the expedition to Asia. Two other young comrades were also pledged to go: Philotas, son of the general Parmenion, and Hephaestion, a new and much-adored friend. For a secretary Alexander chose Eumenes, a Greek of advanced age but still vigorous, who had been secretary to his father. Aristotle knew him well, and arranged with him before departing for Athens that he should keep him informed of the situation in the East: thus Aristotle would have another source of private information besides Antipater—he could not count on Callis-thenes, who was stiffly honourable in such matters. Nearchus the Cretan and Ptolemy were of course recalled from exile. With Alexander surrounded by so many people whom Aristotle could regard as friendly to himself, including several old pupils, he left for Athens in highest satisfaction: it could not but be soon manifest there what standing he had in the world of affairs as well as in the world of thought.

This was toward the end of the year 335. In 334 Alexander

crossed the Hellespont. By 330 he had driven the armies of Darius far eastward. Sardis, Ephesus, Miletus and Halicarnassus were his; Tyre and Gaza had been captured. Thirty thousand Tyrians were sold into slavery, and the lovely island-city, so long a prosperous centre of civilized commerce, deprived of all its trading advantages: in the year after its capture Alexander founded Alexandria, which he intended to become the first port of the world. At Jerusalem the High Priest had received him in so flattering a way that he forgave the city for having failed to help him. Then he had gone into Egypt, which offered little resistance, since it hated the Persians. After the founding of Alexandria he went south into the desert, to the Oasis of Siwa, to worship at the temple of Jupiter Ammon, and was saluted by the priests as the son of the God. In the spring of 331 he crossed the Euphrates and Tigris, and this time Darius was defeated beyond all chance of recovery.

It was now that Alexander assumed the airs and habits of an oriental despot. He wore the Medic dress—the robe, turban and cloak, though not the tiara or trousers; he took to himself all powers, including those of a divinity, requiring anyone who appeared before him to prostrate himself. Babylon, Susa and Persepolis surrendered pacifically; and at Persepolis he paused to celebrate these four brilliant years of conquest. The generals on whom Alexander most relied at this time were Parmenion and Hecataeus and the one-eyed Antigonus, and Nearchus and Ptolemy, and Seleucus and Perdiccas; and in his secretary Eumenes's judgement he trusted particularly. Between the friends, officers and generals surrounding Alexander there was ardent jealousy and distrust. Hephaestion, Alexander's favourite, loathed the sober Eumenes, Perdiccas felt a deep enmity for the ambitious Antigonus; and there were few whom Callisthenes did not a little despise.

With Eumenes, Aristotle corresponded frequently; and, as it was Eumenes whom Alexander heeded more than any other, Aristotle was perhaps justified in feeling himself the brains of the expedition. Naturally there were scandalous incidents which would not have occurred had Alexander been a more civilized person. But, being turbulent and child-like, and the king of a people without a well-matured history, he would be more successful in tearing off the old crust of the world than a man of suaver temper and traditions. 'The half of his achievement,' Aristotle said to himself, 'is that he does not know what he does. For it is not a pretty tale—and it will be centuries before it has been sufficiently forgotten to seem a glorious one.' It was to himself always that Aristotle confided such frank judgements; all his honesty, indeed, was with himself. The times were not safe for open comment on world-events. If Alexander succeeded, his supporters would be first lords of the earth. But meanwhile, anxious as the Athenians were for the defeat of the Persians, he was the disturber who might make more changes in the world than the world was ready for. 'In the distinction between sympathy and advocacy,' Aristotle said to himself, 'lies the whole art of self-preservation.'

He even refrained from discussing these matters with Pythias. She rejoiced heartily in every victory of Alexander's over the Persians, and Aristotle was obliged to excuse her somewhat indiscreet enthusiasm as natural to a woman whose brother had suffered a cruel death at their hands. Pythias and Aristotle understood each other as perfectly as ever, but her association with Nicanor had of course caused certain differences; and one was a seeming separation of views and interests, which public decency required and Aristotle's delicate political position recommended. Where a wife is the ardent ally of her husband in argument, dangerous opinions may be suspected. Playful variance between husband and wife is always taken to be proof of law-abiding innocence.

When news reached Athens, in 330, of the excesses that

had attended the capture of Persepolis, there was more amusement than horror in the general disapproval of Alexander's conduct. A well-known Greek courtesan, Thaïs, had attached herself to Alexander—a woman of beauty, intelligence and worldly experience. Alexander did not love her; but, in his ignorance of the ways of the world, he had looked to her for instruction in the behaviour becoming to a conqueror. It was she who encouraged him to adopt oriental trappings of dignity, and she was right in the judgement on which this advice was based: that for Alexander the grandeur of person necessary to impress the world could only be achieved by a lavish display of power, never by a display of qualities. His greatness would last only so long as he could dazzle the world with the effects of greatness, seized from the corpse of Persia.

Thus, upon his entry into Persepolis, which marked the end of the first stage of his triumphs, at the instigation of Thaïs he celebrated the event with a royal wildness that could not fail to send blazing rumours across the sea to Greece. Although the inhabitants had offered no opposition to his entry, at the height of the banquet that he gave at the royal palace on his last night in Persepolis—before leaving for Media in pursuit of Darius—he ordered a massacre of the people assembled outside, killing them even in the midst of their acclamations. And then, when dawn began to show the colour of blood upon hands and swords and the palace esplanade and gardens, he set fire to the palace: his armies marched out of Persepolis by the light of the flames, and the day seemed ominous of glories to come.

But now Alexander began to resort less and less to Thaïs, who attached herself to his general Ptolemy. Ptolemy had long coveted her, and they were married soon after Persepolis: Ptolemy wishing so clever a woman to be bound permanently to him, secure from the temptations of fortune that usually beset courtesans who went to the wars. This marriage was never publicly acknowledged, and he made others. But he never repudiated it, keeping Thaïs always near and drawing always on her advice. When he ruled in Egypt, she lived in honour in a palace of her own, and their children, two sons and a daughter, were brought up in royal style.

8

THE PHILOSOPHER AT HOME

'A MAN of Alexander's genius,' said Pythias, 'cannot be expected to conduct a war in the dull, orderly way in which any common general would.' She was speaking of the scandal of Persepolis and of Thaïs's part in it: the occasion was one of those evening parties at Aristotle's house that had earned it the name of 'the second Acropolis of Athens'.

'It is a mistake, my dear,' commented Aristotle, 'to make orderliness identical with dullness. What is philosophy but orderly calculation—and surely you would not call philosophers dull? Alexander has admittedly a certain genius, yet there is so much wildness in it that one may wonder which is master, he or it. I tried to give his character a seemly shape, but I fear the mould has not held firmly.'

Having said this, he sighed and smiled gently, trusting that his part in the making of Alexander would be neither forgotten nor recalled to his disadvantage. The mood of Athens was now lazily pro-Macedonian, and his own standing and fortune were all that he could desire. The school at the Lyceum was at last officially recognized, in spite of his being a resident alien and by law forbidden to preside over a public institution. The relations between his own school at the Lyceum and that at the Academy, to the Presidency of which Xenocrates had now succeeded, were as amicable as possible, Aristotle by common agreement taking those pupils who wished to follow a learned career, Xenocrates taking those who wished merely to study.

Nicanor continued to serve Aristotle in a secretarial capacity, assisted by Theophrastus—Aristotle was still at work upon the full and revised collection of his writings. Frequent presents of money were sent to him from Macedonia at Alexander's bidding; and, as Athens now used Macedonian coinage, the source of his added wealth could not be the subject of unsavoury rumours. By Alexander's generosity and Eumenes's interest he also received rare botanical specimens from Asia, which the vice-regents of the conquered provinces had been ordered to seek out for him. His botanical studies were an especial satisfaction to him, since they enabled him to demonstrate the busy many-sidedness of the ideal philosopher. The basis of his attainments in this and other physical branches of knowledge was some manuscripts that his father had bequeathed to him, which he was carefully amplifying and correcting for inclusion among his own works.

Pythias's relations with Nicanor were so decently managed, and all three were motivated by such a pleasant spirit of co-operation, that theirs seemed even more respectable than other households. When intelligent people add formality to socially irregular behaviour, fashionableness and decorum are happily joined; and so it was in Aristotle's domestic life. On his return from the North he had had to be very careful in the way in which he took up his position in the household again. There could be no pretence that he was unaware of Pythias's adultery with Nicanor, since she herself had been delicately frank—thus disarming public opinion. Aristotle had a husband's right to kill Nicanor if he caught him in adultery with Pythias; and he therefore treated him with condescension, as if he had indeed considered exercising this right and decided to forgo it. Convention and law forbade a renewal of marital relations with Pythias—the penalty would have been loss of all civic rights. To protect himself from the accusation of having sexual commerce with an adulterous wife, he took to himself Pythias's charming slave Herpyllis, of whom both were fond. She was very like Pythias in feature, and had all her mistress's gentler graces; so that Aristotle had a second Pythias, and a more pliant and untroubling one.

Pythias's own position might have been painful if the times had been less cynical. There was only one disability from which she suffered for her sin, and this was no inconvenience to her: she could not worship in any temple, and if she attempted to do so anyone might do anything they pleased with her, short of mutilating or killing her. It was a subject of humour within the family, and between Pythias and her friends—Pythias having always been lax in her temple-going. 'It is as if they punished criminals by forbidding them for ever after to obey the laws.' On the whole, then, Pythias had more dignity in her new status in Aristotle's household than in her former simple wifeliness. She was still the mistress of the house, but she was also an interesting personage on her own account. Latterly she had resumed the title of princess, which was hers before her marriage to Aristotle: it was natural that an Eastern princess should live differently from other women. Yet she was more zealous than ever in making Aristotle's hours at home as agreeable as possible and in advancing the fame of his house as a meeting-place for the best society of Athens.

In Nicanor's devotion to Aristotle there was now a new warmth. Aristotle was not merely a patron fulfilling a duty to one to whose father's kindness he was indebted for his own easy youth: he was the husband of the woman Nicanor loved. And it seemed to Nicanor that Aristotle was not displeased to be no longer called upon to minister to the affections of so exactingly passionate a woman as Pythias. Aristotle was as fond of the little girl that Pythias had borne to Nicanor as he was of the daughter he had had by Herpyllis. The children played together as sisters, and Aristotle was already thinking of desirable marriages for them when they were grown up. It was no secret in the family that Aristotle hoped that Nicanor would one day marry Herpyllis's child: he had set aside for her a generous dowry, and if Nicanor became her husband Aristotle would have satisfied both his daughter's and his protégé's claims upon him.

What was Nicanor like? It was to the credit of Pythias's discretion that he was neither taller nor handsomer than Aristotle, and altogether of a slighter build; and he had the pinched, uneasy look of a man who has no cause for complaint but is always aware that the life he lives is not of his own making. Pythias was more than kind to him, but he knew that he was not respected. Aristotle's manner with him was hearty but carelessly rude, and it was no consolation that Aristotle was somewhat rude and sarcastic these days to everyone. There was a difference: with others Aristotle's manner seemed a flattering familiarity, with him it seemed a challenging, though not threatening, reminder of his many obligations. Yet Nicanor was not unhappy, and to the end of his life remained loyal to Aristotle's memory. He had cause to feel obliged to him.

By this time Aristotle's philosophical theories were so well organized that he was more sprightly in talk, feeling no need to prove their correctness in persistent argument. If anyone disagreed with him he would say, 'To-morrow I will show you what I have written upon that head.' In two matters Aristotle was orderly to the point of fidgetiness: in his clothes and in his writings. Yet the rooms he occupied were always in disorder; and he was more nice in the use of perfumes and pomades than in the taking of baths. He gave the impression of being a prim, tidy person, and Pythias of being radiantly sluttish; Pythias, however, was very exact in the care of her person, though her clothes were generally in disorder. There is a popular prejudice that untidy people are unselfish, and that tidy people tend to be selfish. But in truth the unselfishness of very untidy people is often merely a sign of the low value they place on everything; and there is no one who can be so genuinely generous as a person who knows where each of his possessions lies and what its worth is. Pythias, indeed, valued very little but the comfort of her physical person, and Aristotle in so far as he and she shared the material securities of life, and Nicanor in so far as he contributed amiably to her enjoyments. Yet she was noted for the lavishness with which she dispensed hospitality and bestowed gifts and affection on her friends : for she did not care what happened to the good things that overflowed from her own sufficiencies.

Aristotle was cautious with money, except in the buying of clothes and books and in expenditure that seemed necessary to the dignity of his position ; and he was equally cautious in pledging himself in friendship. Yet at the evening parties at his house a continuous glow of good humour came from him, while Pythias, for all the enthusiasm of her welcome, seemed ready upon the instant for malice. One might have thought her heart the narrower—but there was really little difference between them in this respect. Both were well regarded, and neither greatly loved.

Of the people who visited Aristotle's house, many were not of his intimate circle of scholars, and yet, he could boast, his ideas were perfectly clear to them. 'I have brought philosophy down from the elusive heavens in which up till now it has lingered. Before our time the science of first principles resembled a lisping child.' And as he said this, in his lisping voice, none would smile, for it was perfectly true that he had made philosophy commonplace; up till then philosophers had been, if not quite lisping children, at least as curious-minded as poets. 'Plato should have been a poet,' Aristotle said. And he was right.

'The universe attains reality only in the individual,' said Aristotle. 'In man the thought of the divine reason becomes complete.' And no man could hear this without feeling flattered in his humanity. Even the women—for the tone of Aristotle's evening parties was so fashionable that a few women always came—shared in this gratifying sensation: watching their husbands from their chairs, they could feel that these homely reclining figures were the best the world had to give in the way of creatures. Some of these women were wives of wealthy business-men of the Peiraeus, among whom philosophy was a favourite pursuit. A successful merchant or banker naturally inclines to the belief that the works of man have the essence of divinity in them; Plato's view that the works of man were an incomplete example of that of which the divine was the perfection would not have sat well upon people who felt that all the pleasures of existence proceeded from their ingenuity. 'From lower to higher, not from higher to lower, is the flow of being' was a favourite dictum of Aristotle's: and this seemed to them a just account of the laws of material prosperity as well as of the laws of the whole universe. Oxen were beasts of burden, slaves were born to subservience—and the farther away one got from degrading employments the nearer one came to divinity. Or, one might say, it was no more marvellous than the difference between barley and wheat.

If Xenocrates happened to be present, there was less talk of a philosophic kind, since Aristotle knew that he would have been a little shocked by the ease with which his guests ventured into these abstruse subjects. Xenocrates was bound to Plato's view of divinity as an absolute condition, not merely the result of the flow of being from lower to higher levels of happiness and virtue. Just once, when Xenocrates was present, a guest indulged himself in a philosophic pleasantry of the Aristotelian style, and Xenocrates could not resist opposing what he regarded as rankly anti-Platonic sentiment. Pythias had been talking about the vileness of slaves, and saying that a high price paid for a slave was no guarantee against vicious qualities: of the nine that she and Aristotle had, the gentlest was the one which had cost them least.

Eupompus the painter was there that evening, and from his many consultations with Aristotle upon theories of art he had acquired the Aristotelian habit of applying philosophy promptly to any topic whatsoever. 'Yet a high price,' he said, 'is nevertheless a token of high value. If prices were put upon the good qualities of character, they would be very high ones. But it is not so much lack of wealth that prevents our purchasing them, since there are those in the world with money enough to purchase anything, as an uncertainty as to the prices which they would be worth in comparison with other things. The price put upon slaves is an estimate of their usefulness, not of their moral character. They may prove useless from some defect of character, but equally from stupidity or physical imperfection. That your best slave cost you least means only that we have not reached a point in the knowledge of value where the financial worth of good character can be accurately measured. In future times, when these matters are less mysterious and better regulated, the purchasers of slaves will be neither so lucky with low-priced slaves nor so unlucky with high-priced ones.'

At first Xenocrates tried to smile with the others; but, as he realized that they, and even Aristotle, did not regard Eupompus's argument as entirely frivolous, he felt moved to make a serious comment upon it. 'Do you not confuse several things, Eupompus? Surely it should not be very difficult for an honest man to estimate the goodness of a slave he wishes to sell, and to put a price upon him above the ordinary in accordance with the added usefulness he will have for his new master in being more than merely strong and skilful. To do so would be to put a price upon goodness of character in a slave. But is that not very different from putting a price upon goodness in people in general? And suppose that were possible: it still would not mean that one could acquire good qualities for oneself by purchase. If one pays for good-ness in a slave, the qualities remain with the slave; they do not become one's own, although one has the benefit of them.'

Aristotle was reluctant to answer Xenocrates, not wishing to engage in controversy with him, and anxious that none of his guests should defend Eupompus or Eupompus himself speak—lest Xenocrates be discouraged from coming again. And yet courtesy demanded that someone take notice of what he had said. Fortunately, Pythias understood Aristotle's feelings and came to the rescue.

'You make goodness such a sacred property, Xenocrates, that I do believe you would hesitate to imitate a virtue in another that you admired for fear that this might be stealing. Certainly you are the only person I know who has no adornments that have been either borrowed or bought.'

And everyone laughed, including Xenocrates himself, who was not offended by her reference to the meanness of his dress. It was quite true that he could not remember ever having bought himself new clothes; and, if he had indeed borrowed those which he was wearing, he had forgotten from whom. Aristotle was delighted by the double sense of Pythias's witticism—which was also directed, all were aware, at the bareness of his virtues and the simplicity of his talents.

Lysippus the sculptor carried the conversation forward another step away from danger. 'There's no craft in which the prices are so uncertain as in sculpture, I think. In earlier times the sculptor worked to dictation and was paid according as he did or did not please his patron. Nowadays there is more talk of freedom in workmanship, which is of course necessary and proper. But the sculptor who sets out to satisfy his own view of beauty must not forget that his work must be sold. The more faithfully he observes his own ideas, the lower the price he is likely to be offered for his handicraft—for most people love to use their money in a masterly way and feel cheated where they can't. When one adheres to the principles of art, one would like to put a very high price on the work, yet dares not. And when one indulges untutored tastes, one thinks too little of the work to dare name the price that could probably be got for it.'

Lysippus sighed, and the looks sent toward him were sympathetic, but no one made any comment. The rich men present were probably thinking that, however true Lysippus's words were, they for their part would not buy anything that did not please them; and the others were perhaps of the opinion that a clever craftsman ought to be able to please himself while seeming to work for the pleasure of his client. There was, at any rate, some suspicion of Lysippus, even in Aristotle, because he frequented so many different circles of acquaintance; he was interested in nothing except success in his art, and used this company as he used others—to help him talk himself into fame. Yet Aristotle tolerated the man as one of those whom he called 'new people'; and also because, in the discussions of art in which they sometimes engaged, Lysippus helped him to broaden the application of his theories. Lysippus, moreover, was very insistent that contemporary sculptors of the first class must throw over the rules of Pheidias. Having himself thrown over the rules of Plato, as old-fashioned encumbrances, Aristotle could not but feel a partiality for this ambitious innovator in another field.

Whenever the conversation got out of her control, or Aristotle's, as it did on this occasion after Lysippus's complaint of the difficulty of fixing prices for works of sculpture, Pythias called for music. Music was not a customary feature of these parties: it was Aristotle's desire to provide comfortable rather than merry entertainment. He did not wish to seem to be competing with other distinguished hosts of Athens—not only because he preferred his guests to remember that his was the home of a philosopher, but also because too much popularity would arouse envy. In another house the husband would say to the wife: 'I think we might have the music now!' At Aristotle's, the preliminaries were a little more intricate.

On the evening of which we have been speaking, when the conversation took an awkward turn, Aristotle felt that music would be at that moment suitable. But he said nothing, only tapping his fingers together thoughtfully. Pythias, understanding the sign, at first pretended that she had noticed no lapse of genial ease in the company.

'It is a pity for modern sculptors,' she said, talking upon the subject that Lysippus had brought up, 'that all the traditional statues have been made already. If you could invent new gods, your problem would be solved until all the possible sorts of statues of them stood in all the possible places—and you would not mind their priests having some say in what they were to look like. Every imaginable kind of representation of the old gods has certainly been devised—and I should not be in the least surprised to learn that sculptors had as great a part in the forming of religions as priests. The huge Athene-the-Champion, of Pheidias—of course he didn't invent the idea, but he invented the size. When there's nothing more to invent about gods but statues of larger size than before, then it's time for new gods—dear me, the dreadful things one can say when one starts talking—do you think, Aristotle, we might have a *little* music, or I don't know where my tongue will lead me next.'

Aristotle smiled and nodded indulgently, and a *little* music was had. The music currently played in Athens at this time was oriental in flavour; the musicians that Pythias employed were themselves from the East—they had, in fact, been attached to her brother Hermias's court and through her influence had found their way into the best houses of Athens. Aristotle really delighted in listening to music, especially of the modern sort. 'It loosens the mind from its strict boundaries, and feeling leads thought into strange lands of desire where, however, one cannot come to grief, since they are unreal.' Of what nature the desire, he did not say. Perhaps in such moments his mind followed after Alexander, and his fancies were not unlike those that whirled in the head of his former pupil.

Alexander's movements in Asia were more interesting to the intelligent part of the population than anything else going on at the time. Indeed, gratitude for the excitements that his activity caused seemed to have suppressed all fear of what would happen if he should turn his appetites loose upon Greece. True, the masses were hostile to him—being of simpler imagination, they regarded a conqueror as one who might conquer them also. A small faction of politicians, headed by Demosthenes, urged a policy of impartiality—which the pro-Macedonians found tiresome: world-politics, they said, could not be conducted like a lawsuit. Demosthenes lacked the natural graces of eloquence and persuaded no one but those who were already persuaded. His harangues were long and over-laboured and his temper not winning, and those who were not against him were tired of saying that he was an honest man. He had for years bored Athens with the suit about his inheritance—until it was felt that the side upon which Demosthenes stood in any matter was probably the right one, but the other side the more agreeable. He had studied with Plato, but had ceased going to the Academy before Aristotle came to Athens. Isocrates, whom Aristotle had never liked, had trained him in oratory; and, although Demosthenes had long since repudiated his teacher, Aristotle counted them both as of those narrow patriots who would have made Attica an isolated second-class state like Sparta. In the intransigence of Demosthenes there was more ill-temper than idealism—but Aristotle regarded all brands of civic patriotism with equal disdain.

It seemed unlikely, however, that there would be an obstructive stiffening of spirit in Athens. Aristotle had no exact picture of how Greece would be ultimately affected by Alexander's conquests in the East, but he felt confident that the world would undergo an enlivening change of colour because of them. In spite of his staid behaviour and style of reasoning, Aristotle had a rebellious disrespect for the past. In one who is not himself a man of action, this can inspire a sympathy for the most violent of his contemporaries. If Aristotle had not been as shrewd as he was rebellious, he would certainly have been tempted to bring himself closer to the scene of the great events of his time. Athens was not really part of the scene. It was, as he put it to himself, the audience; and he chose to be of the audience until it was clear how the drama went. He had once nearly wrecked himself by experimenting with fortune—when he allied himself with Hermias. Of that adventure he had Pythias for a reward; she had not proved an inconvenience, but he would have hesitated to say that he felt altogether lucky in her.

They had got on well, and she had added many interests to his life, as an ordinary woman of Athens could not have done. Nor did he mind her relations with Nicanor—they were both considerate and attentive, and public opinion did not require him to feel outraged; moreover, there was Herpyllis, who cosseted him sweetly and asked nothing in return. Yet he could not help regarding his domestic arrangements as impermanent. When, in 330, Pythias died, he was naturally much affected—but not surprised. He had reconciled himself as gracefully as he could to their alliance, which had been more of her making than his own. As he did not spurn the honours that he had won at Athens, yet privately held himself worthy of higher ones, so he had always looked on Pythias as a sign of Fate's partiality for him rather than as his full due of personal bliss. He took a similar view of his part in the affairs of the world. In spite of his having intimate connexions with the chief personalities in Macedonia, the first power of his day, his influence was indirect, almost intangible; yet he was resolved not to lose by impatient pride what he might get by proud patience. Soon after Pythias's death he went through a homely form of marriage with Herpyllis, such as was permitted with a slave; and he felt that his dignity was the greater for his condescension. Had not Pythias herself been a slave by birth—though raised to the rank of a princess by her eunuch brother's talents? (Needless to say, he had never reproached her with this.)

Nicanor remained with him, and all the members of the household were on excellent terms with one another. The statue of Pythias was now moved from the sleeping-quarters into the courtyard. She seemed to smile approval on the composite family she had left behind, and which was, indeed, the product of her lively affection for Aristotle. Besides the girl that she had had by Nicanor and the girl Herpyllis had borne to Aristotle, there was Nicomachus, Herpyllis's second child. (This boy grew up to be an earnest but undistinguished scholar, devoting himself entirely to the editing of his father's works.)

9

ALEXANDER'S FRIENDS AND WIVES

In 331, the year before Pythias's death, Antipater suppressed a rebellion in Thrace and made a successful expedition against Sparta. This news, and the complaints against Antipater with which Olympias's letters were filled, caused Alexander great uneasiness; but he knew no way of checking Antipater's growing power except by proceeding feverishly forward in the path of conquest upon which he had entered. It was a long, tortuous path and he could not see the end of it. Wherever he paused, that became for the moment the capital of his chaotic empire. There was no place that he could think of as home—certainly not Pella; and no place in these new regions the capture of which could mean to him the possession of a natural seat of royalty.

As he had no friends in Macedonia whom he could trust to defend his interests against Antipater's ambitions, he made as little as possible of his mother's outbursts in answering her letters. Olympias herself he did not trust—not because he doubted her loyalty to him, but because he had acquired enough political sense to understand that the violence of her feelings against her enemies made her a dangerous ally. He was so afraid of the consequences of her meddling that he dealt with her letters himself when he could. In one that passed through his secretary Eumenes's hands she wrote: 'It is right to benefit your friends and to show your esteem for them; but you are making them all as great as kings, so that they get many friends and leave you alone without any.' These words Eumenes repeated to Aristotle in a letter, and Aristotle conveyed them to Antipater. Of them Antipater wrote to Aristotle: 'Poor Olympias, she understands her son well. She sees the worst in people, and she is generally right. Upon this matter of Alexander's friends she speaks wisely. In his extravagant favours to those around him he is contriving his own ruin. For which let us be grateful, since his successes would otherwise not mean ours.' Aristotle doubted whether Antipater had enough talent in him for world-leadership—there was no madness in him, as there was in Alexander, to make up for deficiencies in wisdom or will. Nevertheless he was flattered to be included in this conspiratorial 'ours'.

Suspicious as he was of Antipater, Alexander was obliged to remain on friendly terms with him. Antipater could at least be relied on to keep order in Macedonia and to prevent Olympias from indulging her passions in open acts of vengeance. She had already, in the year after Alexander's departure, committed one violence that but for Antipater might well have provoked a rebellion. She had induced Cleopatra, Attalus's niece whom Philip had married after herself, to come to Pella with her daughter; and caused them both to be murdered. Such an act, at a time when Alexander's enemies were eager to make the most of any ground of accusation against him or his mother, would have had unfortunate consequences if it had not been for Antipater's skill in covering it up. His own interests required that Macedonia should be in a tranquil state at this time, since any disorder might overthrow him as well. The best that Alexander could do was to urge his mother to be patient with Antipater until his return from the East, and to send her wonderful presents from his spoils: there was nothing that pleased her so much, he knew, as evidence of her son's grandeur. In his correspondence with Antipater, he excused his mother of the things complained of by dwelling on his great affection for her.

One of those whom Olympias bitterly attacked in her

letters to her son was Cassander, Antipater's son—who was in fact so sly and vicious that Antipater himself mistrusted him, keeping him in Pella instead of asking Alexander to appoint him to a command in the East. A constant object of her hate was Alexander's beloved Hephaestion ; she accused Alexander of loving him in an unclean way, that shamed his dignity. Aristotle, too, she had come to dislike, aware now that he corresponded frequently with Antipater. That Cassander sometimes visited Aristotle at Athens made her think that he acted as his father's messenger in a plot in which Aristotle's advice was being used ; yet it was not remarkable that a young Macedonian noble should occasionally take in the sights and pleasures of Athens and call upon the famous men of the city.

To have heeded all her insinuations and charges would have been impossible for Alexander, even had he taken them seriously. During these many years in the East he had never paused to measure his friendships or his deeds. A huge tangle of circumstances had knit itself round him, in which he could not distinguish between what was good and bad, lucky and unlucky ; and so he clung helplessly to the whole. Yet everything that his mother wrote lingered in his blood, if not in his memory, and in time sprung up as a rage of his own. There were very few of those whom she attacked whom he did not later turn against himself.

The first to suffer was Philotas, commander of the cavalry and son of the general Parmenion. This was after the murder of Darius in the Parthian desert by the satrap of Bactria, who intended to resist Alexander after he had routed the remnants of the Persian army. Alexander honoured the body of Darius and rescued his baggage and harem ; wishing to impress upon the restive satraps of this region that he alone had the supreme right of victory over the Persians. The women he sent to Susa ; among them were Parysatis, the daughter of Artaxerxes III, and Barsinë, the daughter of Darius. Then he pursued the fleeing Greek soldiers who had served in Darius's army and incorporated them in his own. It was while he was engaged in subduing the Parthians and Bactrians that Alexander became inflamed against Philotas, because of a rumour that he was concerned in a treacherous plot, and his father as well. Under torture Philotas said things that were construed as a confession; he was stoned to death. Then an order was sent for the death of Parmenion, who was at Ecbatana. Other executions followed, alike based upon rumours. Parmenion had been the loyalest of Alexander's generals; Philotas had always fallen in with Alexander's whims cheerfully and uncomplainingly. This was in 330.

But there remained many other companions with whom Alexander could share his hours of rest. One of these was Cleitus. In the winter of 329, after the Bactrian satrap had at last been caught and killed, Alexander murdered Cleitus with his own hands, in a drunken fit at a banquet. His remorse was great the next day, when he was sober, and all his intimates exerted themselves to console him—except Callisthenes, Aristotle's young cousin. Callisthenes was still a favoured friend, although Alexander's old admiration for his proud, frank ways had weakened, since he had come to expect only softness and pliancy from those who surrounded him.

During the next two years Alexander continued the work of subduing the great outlying provinces. A few Bactrian princes still resisted him; chief of these was Oxyartes. Oxyartes had placed his family, for security, in a strong hill-fort called 'The Rock'. Instead of pursuing the prince, Alexander stormed the fort. He had heard that Oxyartes's beautiful elder daughter was so dear to her father that through indulging her caprices he had made everyone his enemy. She had, it was said, refused every suitor who had asked her in marriage; and, as her father would not make her marry against her will, many quarrels had resulted. Alexander thought that, if he captured the daughter, the father would certainly be driven to submit. This would save him the trouble of further fighting in Bactria: he was anxious to proceed to the conquest of India.

Alexander captured 'The Rock', and Oxyartes submitted without fighting. His elder daughter was called Roxana. She was indeed very handsome, very straight and tall and commanding. Seeing in her a resemblance to Olympias, Alexander married her—as if to escape from his mother, and yet to someone the same. But she was not the same. She was a brutal, rather than cruel, woman. Olympias, feeling pain, inflicted pain, but Roxana's hates were simple and gave her more pleasure. Alexander sent her to Susa, to await there his return from India.

Alexander was by now discontented with Callisthenes and had almost decided to leave him in Bactria. He had tried to be indulgent to Callisthenes's honesty and outspokenness, telling himself that he had, after all, encouraged these presumptuous habits; he felt that, when he had conquered India and was lord of the world, his old companions would no longer dare to be so free with him. Moreover, he was rather weary of punishing misbehaving officers and friends, having just witnessed the execution of a number of men, in whose loyalty he had trusted, for having meddled in a plot to assassinate him. Of all the plots that had been brought to his attention he had very little proof, but he agreed with his generals that severity was a wiser policy than justice at this stage of his career: when his power was everywhere established and recognized, it would be time enough to be just.

Callisthenes's name had been mentioned in connexion with this last plot, but Alexander had preferred not to know whether he had taken any part in it or not. Alexander was still fond of Callisthenes; and then there was his relationship with Aristotle. Aristotle and Antipater were friends: if harm came to Callisthenes, Aristotle would certainly complain to

Antipater, who as Governor of Macedonia had it in his power to hamper the expedition of conquest in many ways. But at a banquet celebrated in Bactria just before the departure for India, Callisthenes so conducted himself that Alexander forgot all prudence. Callisthenes had delivered a speech praising the achievements of the Macedonians, which, coming from one who was not a Macedonian, Alexander naturally found pleasing. Then Alexander challenged him to try his rhetoric in an attack upon the Macedonians, thinking that this would afford great amusement, Callisthenes being very sharp and witty. Callisthenes, however, took the challenge seriously, and not only described the faults of the Macedonians, but touched upon some of Alexander's own weaknesses.

In his rage Alexander remembered the accusation of conspiracy against Callisthenes, and ordered that he be immediately seized. As if he wished to prove, on the eve of his departure, how oriental he had become in his whims, he used a form of punishment that was favoured by tyrants of the East when they wished to make an example of someone who had offended them. Callisthenes was closely chained and put into a cage. Alexander commanded that he be sent from one place to another, and displayed as a warning against insolence. All means of cleansing himself were denied to him; his body was soon covered with vermin, and he grew so fat for want of movement that after a time no one could tell that this inactive mass of filth and flesh had once been a young and bright-minded man.

To Antipater, Alexander wrote: 'Knowing your friendship for Aristotle, I have as yet not harmed Callisthenes, who is his cousin. For myself, I have come to doubt whether I owe Aristotle any debt of consideration. It may even be that he is concerned in the plot. But I shall not press this, and for your sake will continue to send him presents and order my governors to supply him with botanical specimens for his collection. I do not know why he should be interested in such matters, being a philosopher and not a gardener, but perhaps it is best to humour him. It is at least a safer subject than some others that I think he meddles in.'

Antipater, in replying, was careful to avoid the appearance of defending Callisthenes; nor did he protest against Alexander's suspicion of Aristotle. Aristotle might well have had correspondence with enemies of Alexander in the East, thought Antipater, of which he knew nothing. If Alexander died or were assassinated, it would be useful to Aristotle to be on friendly terms with those who afterwards ruled the East—for Antipater's ambitions were centred in Macedonia itself. Why Aristotle ventured outside the field of learning, however circumspectly, Antipater did not quite understand—unless he meant to acquire political power in Athens one day, with Macedonian help, and, through this, an active part in the affairs of the world. Whatever his reasons were, Antipater valued his friendship, which included the giving of much shrewd advice.

'Would it not be best,' Antipater wrote, 'to try Callisthenes in the presence of Aristotle? Then you could tell from the philosopher's behaviour and words to what degree he is implicated, if at all. And if he is innocent you will have the benefit of his wisdom in judging Callisthenes fairly.' By suggesting such a trial Antipater disclaimed responsibility for Aristotle's activities and at the same time showed the warm interest on his behalf that Alexander would expect. To Aristotle, Antipater wrote: 'I have urged Alexander to give you the opportunity of refuting these absurd charges.' When Alexander received Antipater's letter, Hephaestion was with him, whom he loved so dearly. Hephaestion was like an immature girl, both in appearance and character. He was sulky, always under some cloud of self-dissatisfaction, and imagined that no one loved him. It pleased Alexander to coax him constantly into a good humour, for this is how he would have liked to be treated himself. As Hephaestion looked over Alexander's shoulder to read Antipater's letter, Alexander reproved him; he burst into tears.

'But you know that I could never be angry with you, sweet Hephaestion,' Alexander said. It was on this occasion that Alexander appointed Hephaestion chief of his body-guard, to win a smile from him—though up to then he had held no important office, being without any talents except those of sentiment.

Alexander then dictated a letter to Aristotle, in which he invited him to come to the East for Callisthenes's trial. 'If you make this journey,' he said, 'go to Susa and wait for me there should I not yet be back from India. If you do not come, I shall be obliged to keep Callisthenes in confinement until I return to Macedonia, which you can more easily reach. For I am resolved, because of all I owe you in knowledge and calm judgement, not to punish him without your consent.'

Aristotle did not go to the East. That Callisthenes had disgraced himself was his own fault, Aristotle argued. He had frequently warned him that his bold ways put him too much in Alexander's power. 'It is for my honesty that Alexander values me,' Callisthenes had said. 'If I cease to be honest, he will find nothing pleasing in me, for I am not gifted in flattery.' To this Aristotle had answered: 'You are a philosopher, Callisthenes, and should know how to go only half-way in everything. I do not mean that you must be false: but the wisdom of a wise man is not so much in what he does as in what he does not do.' Callisthenes had made this retort: 'Then I had rather not be a philosopher in friendship.'

Seven months later Aristotle heard that his cousin had died from the effects of his cruel imprisonment. 'I hope that in his sufferings,' Aristotle said to himself, 'Callisthenes returned to the precepts of philosophy and knew how to taste but the half of his pain.' If he felt any guilt for not having gone to

plead for Callisthenes, he did not show it in the letter which
he wrote to Antipater on the subject. 'Since this is Alexander's
temper,' he said, 'it is fortunate that I was not tricked into
going myself.' He hoped that Antipater would guess from
these words that he knew from where the suggestion came
that he should be present at his cousin's trial. The incident
increased rather than diminished the regard of Antipater
and Aristotle for one another; the less trust there is among
conspirators, the more elegance in their intercourse.

It was just as well that Aristotle had not gone to Susa,
for Alexander did not arrive there from India until 324.
He had conquered everywhere—that is, he had marched on
swiftly, without resting long enough to allow resistance to
show itself, fighting battles occasionally, ordering a town
to be founded here and there where a site pleased him, and
thoroughly exhausting his army. The most substantial result
of the Indian expedition was the fleet that Nearchus the Cretan
built there for the transport of soldiers; in it he brought
the greater part of the army safely across the perilous Indian
Ocean to the Persian Gulf. Alexander travelled overland,
meeting Nearchus and the disembarked army in Carmania,
east of the Gulf. Being very weary from the journey, he
proceeded himself in leisurely stages to Pasargadae with a
small body of soldiers, ordering the rest of the army to march
along the shore of the Gulf to Susa, and await him there.

Let it be understood that Alexander returned from his
Indian conquests in no elated mood. He was not only worn
out physically from the exertions of the campaign, but
frightened and depressed by the responsibilities that faced him,
now that he had won an empire. He had no one to help
him, no one to lean upon: Hephaestion, whom alone he
loved, leaned upon him. His generals were already dividing
the empire among themselves in anticipation of his death.
His mother was loyal to his interests, but too full of reckless
hates to be trusted as an adviser. He had been obliged to

take his witless half-brother Philip out of her reach and carry him about with the army—and this imbecile was his heir. If only Aristotle had been possessed of a heart, he was the one he would have chosen to help him govern his empire. Plato had dreamed of establishing in Sicily a government that would be an example to the world of wise rule. What happiness he and Aristotle could have together bestowed upon the world—by such an alliance of wisdom with power as the world had never before seen! Aristotle thought him vile, he knew, and had imparted to him only the means of covering up the vileness.

'I shall at least be what I am before the world,' he swore. 'If I am in truth vile—then to be honestly vile.' He had come so far toward an understanding with himself by the time he reached Pasargadae.

Here was the tomb of Cyrus, and Alexander looked forward to seeing it. But he found that it had been looted by the soldiers who had preceded him. The disrespect shown to the royal tomb seemed like an affront to himself. 'However little dignity and sweetness there be in empire over others,' he cried, 'where is there more?' Those who had committed the outrage were executed.

It was while he was at Pasargadae that he heard of the flight of Harpalus from Babylon, where he was governor. Harpalus was Alexander's treasurer, and if he fled it must mean that he took much money with him. But he had been a friend of Alexander's from his youth, and his vices were rather those of self-indulgence than of treachery. So much Alexander could not say of any general. Therefore he sent messengers after Harpalus, urging him to return to Babylon and to regard himself as pardoned for whatever offences he might have committed. Harpalus, relieved of the necessity of giving an account of his abuses, returned, and was even more lustful and extravagant than before. He lived as a king and had for his amusement the most expensive courtesans of Athens.

His attendants and subordinates and all who visited him on whatever errand were obliged to salute these women as if they were queens; and they conducted themselves as if they were. It was this man who of all Alexander's governors was most attentive to Aristotle, in the sending of botanical specimens; and Aristotle repaid the compliment by sending him Greek plants for his garden in Babylon.

At last Alexander came to Susa. Now he adopted, as if in despair, all the follies of the Persian monarchy that he had extinguished. He ordered that he should be everywhere worshipped as a god, even at Athens. So irresistible seemed the power of Alexander, so overwhelming the sense of his magnificence, that Demosthenes thought it expedient to defend the motion recommending his deification: in spite of the increasing violence of anti-Macedonian feeling in the populace, Alexander was added to the gods of the city. Aristotle wrote to Olympias describing the occasion, knowing that it would please her. To Antipater he wrote: 'I have done my best to discourage this, for I fear it will make the Athenians less tolerant of Macedonian interference in their affairs.'

At Susa took place that orgy of marriages which became the scandal of the world, so soon as news of it spread. First, Alexander remarried Roxana according to the Persian forms: that is, he himself performed the ceremony and declared her Queen of the East and West. She knew that he meant to take other wives besides herself, and threatened to kill them unless he came to her bed first, before marrying them—for though he had married her according to the Macedonian forms when he captured her, he had not yet lain with her, being without passion for women. After satisfying Roxana's wish, Alexander married himself the next day to Parysatis, the daughter of that Artaxerxes who had killed Pythias's brother Hermias. This was so sad and frightened a woman that Roxana scorned to be jealous of her. 'She will die,' Roxana thought, 'before I have time to put her out of the way.' Parysatis did not survive the journey to Babylon; and was probably not poisoned by Roxana.

On the same day on which he married Parysatis, Alexander also took as wife Barsinë, the daughter of Darius—whom Hermias had fondled at the court of Artaxerxes; and her younger sister Drypetis. These had been sent to Susa before the conquest of India, together with their mother, who had since died. Alexander had also sent here the women of Darius's harem, whom he now bestowed as wives upon his generals. There being not enough women to go round, all the palaces and mansions of Susa were broken into and the marriageable women seized. Eighty of Alexander's generals were married in this way, and to every soldier who took a Persian wife a dowry was promised: ten thousand soldiers married Persian women—laying hold upon them in the streets and raiding the villages in the neighbourhood. And all this took place in one week. 'We shall be more Persian than the Persians,' Alexander cried, 'since there are no new ways of greatness left in the world.' While at Susa he added thousands of Persians to his troops.

Roxana, whom Alexander feared as he feared his mother, offered no opposition to his taking Barsinë and Drypetis for wives, since she felt these marriages to be necessary to his imperial dignity. But, when the marriages had taken place, she would not permit him to lie with the women; and after a few weeks she insisted that he cast off Barsinë and marry her to Nearchus, and give Drypetis to Hephaestion. Barsinë rejoiced in this change of husbands, not only because Nearchus was a more sane and amiable man than Alexander, but because she now felt herself out of reach of Roxana's jealousy. Hephaestion was disconsolate to be forced to marry Drypetis. He was even more passionless toward women than Alexander; and he knew, moreover, that Roxana meant to separate him from Alexander by the marriage.

At Ecbatana, Hephaestion fell ill and died. 'It is you who

179

killed him,' Alexander said in his grief to Roxana, 'by denying him my love. Our hearts were close, because we were both unhappy—you have made a dead man of me as well.' Roxana did not attempt to console him. She herself felt that Alexander had not long to live, and schemed rather as his prospective widow than as his wife. After this, Alexander was nearly always drunk, and when sober went about in such black, dangerous gloom that it became the object of those around him to fill him with wine whenever possible.

10

THE DEATHS OF ALEXANDER AND ARISTOTLE

IT was at about this time that Olympias's brother Alexander, King of Epirus, was killed in battle. Her daughter Cleopatra —at whose marriage to Alexander Philip had been assassi-nated—regretfully returned to Macedonia. Cleopatra had been happy in Epirus, and looked upon her mother with horror; but as Olympias had become ambitious of seizing Epirus for herself, Cleopatra could not safely remain there. She was timid, soft-tempered and now utterly hopeless. Her mother hated her for the love that Philip had borne her, and would have ruined her had she not felt that in Cleopatra she had a prize to hold out to Alexander's generals.

But, before attempting to dispose of Cleopatra, Olympias went daringly to Epirus herself to press her claims. 'While I am gone,' she said to Cleopatra, 'you must be as friendly as possible with Antipater, and keep a sharp watch upon him, and let me know of anything you learn that looks like treachery. My spies will report to you, but their eyes will be on you also, so have care.'

Cleopatra became friendly with Antipater, but not in the way Olympias had ordered. He was the only one in whom she dared to confide her fear of her mother; another might prove to be a spy, but in his hatred of Olympias she could trust. Antipater wrote to Alexander of his half-sister's pre-dicament. Alexander in reply asked Antipater to send Cleo-patra to the East: he would find a husband for her himself. When Olympias returned from Epirus, Cleopatra was already in Sardis. Alexander would not have her nearer to him than this, since he already felt unjustly burdened by the presence of his half-brother Philip and feared that she might become a centre of intrigue. Indeed, he scarcely knew her. Perhaps she would have been a comfort to him, for she was loving and gentle-hearted; but she was not strong enough to have saved him. She stayed in Sardis year after year, forbidden to go elsewhere yet treated with honour at Alexander's command. Several of his generals visited her there, wishing to marry her and thus increase their prestige, but she refused them, one after the other; she was too unhappy to be able to forget her first husband.

When Alexander died, she was still unmarried. Then she became so weary of her friendless life at Sardis that she consented to marry Ptolemy, now King of Egypt. Ptolemy, at least, was known to be kind, and in Egypt she could feel at a safe distance from Macedonia and Macedonians. But Antigonus, the great enemy of Ptolemy, had Cleopatra assassinated before she escaped from Sardis.

Olympias's journey to Epirus was partly successful. She had not been able to collect enough friends to help her seize the rule from her cousin, who was now king; but, trying another plan, she had endeavoured to gain her cousin's friendship and inflame him against the Macedonians. On her departure he promised to support her in war against the Macedonians when the time seemed suitable. Antipater suspected that she had formed a plot of some kind with the Epirot King, but could learn nothing of it.

Soon after the arrival of Olympias at Pella, one of his spies, a slave in her service, brought him a cup of a poisonous metal that had been made to resemble perfectly the cups she used at banquets of state. It bore a mark to distinguish it from the others, and the slave knew its nature, for Olympias had cautioned him never to pour wine into it for anyone unless she told him to do so. This curious metal was found in Epirus. Antipater could only conclude that she meant to try the cup on himself, at a banquet in celebration of her return to which he had been invited. He therefore ordered the slave to steal it, promising to send him to some place out of reach of Olympias's vengeance. Antipater did not like to keep the cup about him or to entrust it to anyone in Macedonia, and decided to send it to Aristotle by the slave. He would make Aristotle a present of the slave, to repay his guardianship of the cup.

Infuriated by the loss of the cup and the disappearance of her daughter, Olympias attacked Antipater in her letters to Alexander more bitterly than ever before. By this time Alexander was already established in Babylon. He lived in a feverish confusion of moods—now planning new conquests and new works in the already conquered lands, now torturing himself with self-pity and raging against those around him for not loving him well enough. His mother's letters threw him into fits of torpid despair, for he could not be angry with her. Roxana, he knew, thought him mad and was already scheming with his general Perdiccas for his ruin. She had not yet had a child, and hated him on this account— her position would be insecure if he died and left her childless. Most of the time she treated him with scorn, as depraved and unmanly; but there were occasions when she tried him with soft ways, hoping to stir in him some natural feeling for her as a woman. Never certain of anyone, he took refuge in mysteries of his own. Sometimes he drove all Macedonians from his presence and would speak only with Orientals. Or he would shower reproaches on those who called themselves his friends, and then fall into sobs, pleading with them not to desert him. There were long spells of gloomy inactivity; then periods of excitement and over-exertion, followed by protracted banquets and unrestrained drinking.

Before Alexander arrived at Babylon, his treasurer Harpalus had fled a second time, taking with him not only a great deal of money but a body of soldiers who were weary of their long stay in the East. He approached Athens and sent into

the city as a present several ship-loads of corn, of which there
was then a great lack; and he also gave presents of money to
many important personages. He was not allowed to bring
his troops into the city, but was invited to enter it himself
as an honorary citizen. His arrival was looked upon as a
good omen by the anti-Macedonian party, and numbers of
people of pro-Macedonian sympathies were moved by
Harpalus's generous attentions to undergo a change of feeling.
Conspicuous among those who received Harpalus with
enthusiasm was Demosthenes. Aristotle avoided Harpalus in
public—not only because he would not join in anything in
which Demosthenes was associated, but also because Harpalus
was intriguing against Antipater as well as Alexander. Yet
he had a few private interviews with him, for they had in
common an interest in botany; as has been told, Aristotle
was indebted to him for many interesting specimens, and he
likewise to Aristotle. Moreover, Aristotle was curious to
learn of the exact condition of affairs in the East. He communicated to Antipater much that Harpalus told him; and thus
Antipater could not say that Aristotle treated with an enemy
without his knowledge, should news of their interviews
somehow reach him from another source.

In the matter of Harpalus's presence at Athens Olympias
and Antipater were, for once, in agreement. The Athenians
defended their hospitality to him on the ground that he was
a nephew of Philip, as indeed he was; but this excuse made
Olympias all the angrier with the Athenians. Antipater
threatened to march against them if they did not yield up
Harpalus. They then put Harpalus in prison, hoping to gain
something by negotiating for his surrender; but he escaped
and fled to Crete, where one of his own men killed him.

Now the leaders of Athens were all zeal to demonstrate
their loyalty to Antipater, and those who had befriended
Harpalus hastened to disavow or excuse their interest in him.
Demosthenes was one of many who were tried for accepting

bribes from Harpalus. He was found guilty and imprisoned, but succeeded in escaping. Aristotle had not compromised himself; his position was the more secure, even, because of the strengthened pro-Macedonian policy of the city government. But he knew that the majority of the Athenians were at heart now disgusted with Macedonian domination, and that the leaders themselves would have shown defiance had they dared. He therefore wrote to Chalcis in Euboea and ordered that his property, inherited from his mother, be put in order to receive him; and sent Herpyllis ahead to make all ready and comfortable. Although he did not anticipate a sudden anti-Macedonian rising, he felt that changes were bound to come in Macedonian affairs, which must cause changes at Athens. If, for instance, Alexander died, there would certainly be acts of retaliation against those who had been in any way associated with him.

Aristotle spoke freely of his proposed retirement to Euboea, saying that he kept postponing the painful moment of departure to have a last look at his beloved Athens, and then another and another. He would set up a school in Chalcis, but it would be a small school. 'To teach all to the few, rather than much to the many' was how he put it. Long before he was ready to leave for Euboea many had arranged to follow him—yet he still went on talking of teaching the few rather than the many. Nicanor and Theophrastus would of course accompany him, and Nicomachus and the two girls. Herpyllis travelled frequently between Athens and Chalcis, each time taking away some of the furnishings of Aristotle's house, but not so much at any time as to make his departure seem imminent. The discretion of Herpyllis in all these transactions was perfect; she behaved with the mute deftness of a slave, and where necessary with the dignity of a great man's wife.

In the spring of 323, Antipater's son Cassander visited Aristotle at Athens. He was on his way to Babylon, to protest to Alexander against accusations that had been made of Antipater's disloyalty. Had Antipater been seriously worried by these, he would have chosen an envoy in whose wisdom he had more confidence. But he had another object in sending Cassander to Alexander, one that he was better equipped to fulfil than the first. Cassander did not confide the second object of his journey to Aristotle. He merely said that his father had told him of a certain curious cup in Aristotle's keeping which he now wished conveyed to Babylon. And Aristotle gave the cup to Cassander without inquiring what he meant to do with it.

Alexander seemed to accept the defence that Cassander made of his father, and invited him to stay in Babylon for a time so that he could take back to Macedonia the full story of what was being done and projected in the East.

'The Chaldean priests prophesied that evil would befall,' Alexander said, 'if ever I set foot in Babylon. As it is now long since I first entered Babylon, let it be presumed that evil has fallen. You will tell your father whether you think the evil to our advantage or not.'

Cassander witnessed how ambassadors from proud cities prostrated themselves before Alexander and saluted him on bended knee, with upturned palm extended toward him. And he went in a boat with Alexander on the Euphrates, and was shown the works that would be done for the better distribution of the waters after the conquest of Arabia should have been effected. He was told of other conquests that had been planned, besides that of Arabia: Italy, Carthage—and then westward. An expedition had been sent to explore the Caspian; it had not yet returned, but, when it did, plans would be made for drawing on the riches of that region.

Not all of Cassander's time in Babylon, however, was spent in listening to Alexander's dreams of an even greater empire than he yet possessed. There were banquets night after night, of a splendour to make fine telling at home; at which

Cassander was so loving that Alexander called him a second Hephaestion and wept over him frequently, and begged him to remain with him always.

One night, when Alexander had again begged him not to return to Macedonia, Cassander said: 'My father would think that I was engaged in some mischief if I did not return, and write letter after letter full of complaints and suspicions. You have had enough complaining letters from him yourself —and you are his Emperor, not his son. But let me, for the time that is still left, have the honour of being your cup-bearer, and bear the title so long as I live : the cup-bearer of Alexander. It will bind me to you everlastingly if, while I am with you, you drink from no other hands than mine.' Alexander, always delighted by extravagant professions of attachment, granted Cassander this wish.

With Roxana also Cassander made a bond of friendship; and with the general Perdiccas, who had Roxana's confidence. Roxana was now in a triumphant mood; for she had at last succeeded in getting herself with child by Alexander. As the mother of his heir, should the child be a boy, she would have to be reckoned with in any important plot; and she was sure that she would bear a boy-child. Of all the generals of Alexander, Perdiccas was then the most active. Although as hostile to Alexander as the others, he had worked sincerely to consolidate Macedonian power in the East in an orderly way, being self-possessed and far-sighted. It would be better to take over a well-organized empire from Alexander, he reasoned, than an ill-mixed mass of provinces. Alexander respected Perdiccas's intelligence, and took many of his most constructive ideas from him—such as the plan for an efficient control of the waters of the Euphrates.

Finally, at the beginning of the summer, Cassander said that he could no longer delay his return to Macedonia. Alexander himself felt that to detain him any longer would anger Antipater. For the last week of Cassander's stay he ordered a continuous banquet. 'It seems to me,' he said, 'that with your departure I am losing my last friend. Therefore I wish to have you constantly before my eyes during the time that remains, and drown the future in the pleasure of beholding you again and again. Perhaps you are false, like the rest, but it is my fancy to pour out upon you all the human love that is left in me.' As the banquet went on from day to day, Alexander's talk grew wilder and wilder. He refused to stir from the banquet-hall, and grew furious when anyone else attempted to leave. Roxana looked on coldly, glances passing between her and Perdiccas and Cassander which said: 'This is the end.'

At dawn, after the last night of the banquet, Cassander sat down on the edge of the couch on which Alexander lay and raised him up. The banquet-hall was deserted now, except for these two and Roxana and Perdiccas; the dawn light deadened every feature of elegance, showed only the seven-days' dirt and wreckage.

'Alexander!' Cassander said, shaking him gently. 'It is time for me to go now. No need to waken. Smile a little and drink this for good-bye.' Alexander did not wake, but smiled in his sleep like a bewitched man and drank obediently from the cup that Cassander held to his lips. Then Cassander let him fall back again; and now all were smiling. Roxana, bending over the couch, took a ring from Alexander's hand. Without a word she placed it on Perdiccas's finger.

The death of Alexander had the effect that Aristotle had anticipated: it brought the anti-Macedonians into power and made his position at Athens not merely difficult but dangerous. He had behaved discreetly, and there would be no immediate feeling against him. It was known that he had been Alexander's friend and was highly regarded by Antipater, but a philosopher is not like another man: his thoughts rather than his conduct are the cause of any suspicion of him that may be felt, and the hostility he arouses is a slow irritation rather than a swift rush of antagonism. However, when such hostility breaks loose, it is usually more fierce than a simple attack on a simple man. Being aware that the security he enjoyed at Athens was largely due to this difficulty of making precise accusations against a person of his kind, Aristotle was gratified that Alexander's death found him with all the preparations for the move to Chalcis already finished. He was anxious to leave in a way that would give no one a chance to say that he had fled from Athens, and he showed so much ease in his farewells that it was not until early in the next year that people began to wonder why a man so prosperously established in his profession, and not yet weakened by age, should have thought it proper to retire from the world.

Only in his final interview with Xenocrates did he allow himself to speak frankly—and this was because Xenocrates alone of all his friends expressed regret that he should be forced to depart.

'As a friend who has remained loyal to you through many many difficulties, it is my privilege to tell you that I think you do well to go now, before the harsh blow falls.'

'You have information, then?' Aristotle asked.

'None,' replied Xenocrates. 'But you have walked too softly—they know that by nature you are not soft in heart or mind. We are an unhappy city, Aristotle. In our pride we do not often own to it, but sometimes we behave like other men and look where to lay the blame. And, knowing that the fault is probably all our own, we are more capricious in our accusations than would be a city in which there was less wisdom. You must forgive me if I seem to count myself an Athenian, and you a stranger. I only mean that, when the time came, I might be a worthless friend. For, although I would defend you to the last, there would be foolish and vulgar doubts of you in my mind. It would not be because you are not a born Athenian—I am not that either—but because in our despairs we feel every man a stranger and an enemy who is not also miserably uncertain of himself. This is not easy to explain, Aristotle. Perhaps the reason is that you refuse to be made unhappy by anything: it is natural to suspect the everlastingly good-humoured man. Yet there's Demosthenes, who is everlastingly ill-humoured—and would any intelligent person in Athens confess to a liking for him? We are hard to please.'

'There are all kinds of envy,' Aristotle said lightly, ignoring Xenocrates's painful efforts to get his thoughts in honest order. 'That which a successful hypocrite arouses is different from that aroused by a successful philosopher. But public opinion is a convenient shield from behind which to throw the darts. Do not take all this trouble to excuse yourself, Xenocrates. I know that you are glad to see me go. There need be no pretence between us. You have never really forgiven me for the Pythias affair.'

Now, Aristotle expected Xenocrates to deny this insinuation hotly; then he would say that of course he had not meant it, and they would shed a few tears in memory of that delightful woman and part in a mutually flattering inability to say any more to each other.

But Xenocrates, stiffening, answered: 'No, I have never really forgiven you for that.' Aristotle was so surprised that he stood speechless and vexed until after Xenocrates had left—silently, with bent head. Then, chuckling, he said aloud to himself: 'Poor old Xenocrates! Yes, we were a little cruel to him, I suppose.'

He sauntered into the court and smiled reflectively at the statue of his clever Pythias—which would sail with him, in his own care. He had already written to Herpyllis, to announce his coming; the rest of the family were there, and would be looking forward eagerly to his arrival. He would not allow those who were planning to study with him to accompany him on the journey. Better that they should leave Athens gradually, one by one, until 'to go to Chalcis' meant 'to go to Aristotle.' There were many different ways of keeping fresh the honours acquired during a lifetime of continuous achievement; not the least certain way was to withdraw a little from the scene of activity and let them be bestowed again—the second time as if unsought.

The final honour was not bestowed until the next year: Aristotle was summoned to Athens to answer accusations of impiety. The news had an exalting effect on him—he had become the Socrates of his time. Refusing to go to Athens to be tried, he wrote: 'I have long owed a debt of gratitude to Athens, which I may now at last fully pay, by preventing it from dealing with me as it dealt with Socrates and thus from sinning a second time against philosophy.' Then he waited: what would happen next? The real ground of the accusation against him was, of course, suspicion of his relations with the Macedonians. But he had been so careful that there was no mention of treason at his trial. He speculated as to what arguments would be brought forth to prove his impiety, and decided with the loyal Theophrastus and Eudemus, an old pupil for whom he had a fair regard, what should be said if they were called to speak in his defence. It would be a very good thing for Athens, he thought, to see philosophy again treated as a matter of life and death. Would Xenocrates be called upon to testify? An interesting predicament: for he would not want to say anything that could be used to condemn a fellow-philosopher, and yet he would not be able to conceal his pious disagreement with Aristotelian principles. How Aristotle wished that he could have dared to be present himself!

But when the report of the trial reached him, suavity deserted him for the first time in his life. True, he had been formally condemned to death, and there was a taste of glory in that. But there had been no impressive philosophical debate, no mention of philosophy at all. The specific charges against him were that he had worshipped the statue of a human woman and that he had written a eulogy of the eunuch Hermias in language proper to use of a god alone!

As Aristotle had trained those around him never to attempt to console him in anything, he had now nowhere to look for comfort in his shame. He lay on his couch as if he were ill, but Herpyllis knew that he was not ill—yet did not dare to show that she knew that he was only unhappy. His followers, all of whom had gone to Athens to attend the trial, had not yet returned. How could he face them? What dignity for them, to have a master against whom no more weighty charge could be brought than that of having been a doting husband and friend? He reproached himself for not having advertised his true relations with the Macedonians. But who would believe him now if he hinted that Cassander had obtained the instrument of Alexander's death from his hands—who would care?

Suddenly Herpyllis, who sat watching him, saw his expression change.

'Ah!' she cried, 'you are better!'

'Not yet, but soon—make me a brew of aconite!'

'You think you have a fever? But your head is quite cool.'

'Do as I say, Herpyllis! Yes, I have a fever. Do not contradict me. Make a strong brew of aconite—strong enough to kill. If you disobey me, I will never speak to you again. They have ruined me—and this is the only way to redeem my name. My mind is made up. Do not try to thwart me with sobs or supplications—and don't tell the children. Think how Pythias would have behaved. When my followers return they must find me dead—nobly dead: that is my answer to Athens. They would have made a Socrates of me—well, let them! Go now. Remember, you are my wife, not a slave: I have a right to expect some strength of character from you, instead of a slave's softness, having raised you from a slave's condition.'

A sharp look came into Herpyllis's eyes. 'I will do as you

ask,' she said, in a quiet, proud voice. 'Have you any wishes or orders before I bring you the drink?'

'It is all clearly set out in my will,' Aristotle answered brusquely, as if afraid that further talk would weaken his resolution. 'You need have no fear—I have provided justly for all.'

Aristotle's will was, indeed, clear upon every possible point. The two chief trustees were Theophrastus and Antipater, and these with Nicanor were also joint guardians of Aristotle's son Nicomachus. Nicanor was described in the will as 'the future husband of my daughter Pythias, who should be doubly dear to him for the dear name she bears.' Theophrastus was named as his successor at the Lyceum; to him, also, Aristotle left all his books; and he expressed the hope that Theophrastus would take for a wife Pythias's daughter, as Nicanor took his daughter by Herpyllis: 'thus becoming all one philosophic family, imbued with that spirit of divine humanity to which I have given my name.'

Finally, there were benevolent stipulations regarding Herpyllis. 'Let her remain in Chalcis if she so wishes. Or, if she would so prefer, let her go to live in my father's house in Stageira. Nicomachus will be at his studies, and the girls married—and, moreover, having been a slave, she would not receive the treatment at Athens that would befit my widow. It is best that she should not go to Athens unless a husband is found for her. Let him be a simple man, who would not boast of being married to Aristotle's widow. I am willing that he should be given enough money to make them both comfortable. If he be in a trade, and I think a respectable tradesman would be a suitable husband for her, let some money be invested in the business in Nicomachus's name; in order that he shall have the right to see that his mother is well provided for and to enjoy a just share in the man's gains after her death.'

Here we come to the end of Aristotle's affairs, and of those who lived in his shadow. Their lives faded after his death. Whatever substance was in him he had fed upon himself, leaving nothing behind but an obstinate skeleton—his work and his name. Even the manner of his death was forgotten; no Socratic aura framed the memory of him. He was a dead man, and in her loneliness Herpyllis felt this more sharply than any of his other intimates. Looking back over her years with him, she saw how her devotion had little by little brought death into her own feelings. He had not been an evil or foolish man, but good and wise always for reasons of his own. The man and his reasons were gone; but she had merged her will so entirely in his that she now seemed to herself ghostly, without shape or sense. She would marry whomever they wished her to marry, or live wherever they decided should they not find a husband of whom Aristotle would have approved.

The same year, too, Demosthenes died, after having returned in honour from exile and played an energetic part in bringing the Athenians to attack Antipater at last. But they suffered a bitter defeat, and in the ugly period of recriminations that followed Demosthenes was sentenced to death. He again succeeded in escaping from Athens; but a despairing hatred of all his contemporaries brought on a fatal attack of indigestion.

II

AFTER ALEXANDER

MANY judgements do not fall at once, but the way women live is a judgement that falls on men in their own day.

These are the ends to which some of the women came whose lives were tangled with the story of Alexander. There is Cynane, the half-sister of Alexander, daughter of Eurydice, the Illyrian woman with whom Philip made an irregular marriage. Cynane was skilled in matters of war, and she brought up her daughter, named Eurydice after her grandmother, to be as soldierly as herself. The year that Philip died, Cynane became a widow; Cynane and Eurydice lived in watchful retirement until Alexander's death, when Cynane's ambitions for her daughter led her to make a daring expedition to Asia. In this she was abetted by Olympias: it was Olympias's as well as Cynane's wish that Eurydice should marry poor Philip Arrhidaeus, who might be used as an instrument against Antipater. The small army with which Cynane and Eurydice left Macedonia was raised with Olympias's help and at her expense.

This Philip, the son of King Philip, whom Olympias had long ago reduced to feebleness by a poison, was in Babylon when Alexander died. Because he was one who could be easily controlled, he was made partner in the empire with Roxana's newly-born boy, Alexander, under the regency of the general Perdiccas—both Philip and Alexander receiving the title of King. Therefore, if Eurydice succeeded in becoming Philip's wife, Olympias would have in her a powerful ally against Antipater in the East. She would also be useful to Olympias in watching over Roxana, who was doing violent things at Babylon—so like the things that Olympias herself would have done that she felt Roxana to be even more dangerous to her than Antipater. Roxana had adroitly enticed Barsinë and Drypetis to Babylon by a friendly letter. These were the daughters of Darius whom Alexander had married at Susa at the same time as her own marriage with him. Drypetis had later been given to Hephaestion, and after his death had avoided all contact with the Macedonians; and Barsinë had been given to Nearchus, from whom Roxana had little to fear. But she suspected them because they had once been singled out by Alexander, and was certain that they must feel resentment against her for making him cast them off. On their appearance at Babylon, in response to her letter, she had them murdered.

When Cynane and Eurydice arrived in Asia, Perdiccas sent an army against them, and both women were captured. Cynane was put to death. This so aroused the troops that, to quiet them, he gave Eurydice in marriage to the witless Philip: Alexander's niece to his half-brother. There were now many quarrels over the division of power in the East, and much jealousy of Perdiccas, whom his enemies were accusing to Antipater. Perdiccas had divorced his true wife and married the daughter of Antipater. He was now intriguing with Olympias to marry her daughter Cleopatra (who was in Sardis, as has been told): of this much Antipater was aware. Antipater resolved to go to the East to put Perdiccas out of the way; and Ptolemy, who ruled in Egypt, was also persuaded to declare war against him. Perdiccas marched against Egypt, accompanied by Roxana and her child and by Eurydice and Philip. Here his army revolted against him. He was killed by his own officers; and when Roxana was shown his body, the royal ring that she had placed on his finger was gone. She had meant to marry Perdiccas and to go with him to Macedonia to outwit both Antipater and Olympias; but now she would have to fight her way alone. For the present she was in Antipater's power.

Eurydice had no fear of Antipater, but there was so much quarrelling between the various factions in the East that she could not organize a sufficient force in time to oppose him on his arrival. All yielded to him; he was made sole regent and guardian of the young Alexander, and Philip's claims to a share in the spoils of power were no longer recognized. Antipater had decided to bring all of them back to Macedonia with him: Roxana and her son, and Eurydice and Philip. Roxana was herself anxious now to take her son away from the rivalries of the East, and had written secretly to Olympias expressing a willingness to be guided by her; together—the mother, son and wife of Alexander—they could perhaps move the Macedonians to revolt against Antipater. Meanwhile, since she was at his mercy, she pretended to regard him as a friend, saying she had been deceived in Perdiccas. And his protection at this time was valuable.

Eurydice, with a soldier's spirit, disdained to hide her hostility to Antipater and her hatred of Roxana. She was the grandchild of Philip the Great, and the wife of his son: surely the Macedonians would not reject a king of pure blood in favour of a foreigner. She knew that she could not expect Olympias's support in her ambition to succeed her as queen, but she was confident of being able to win a large number of native soldiers to her side and to lead them in battle against both Olympias and Antipater. Roxana's arrival with her son would precipitate war between Antipater and Olympias, she calculated: she would defeat them in turn while they were fighting each other.

But Antipater's power had been increased by his successful management of affairs in the East. Olympias was in Epirus, undecided whether to join with Roxana, who for her part did not wish to quit with Antipater until she had won popularity as the mother of Alexander's heir. In these circumstances

Eurydice could attempt nothing; she was impatient to act, but there was as yet no propitious battle-ground.

A year after his return from Asia, Antipater died. He had appointed to succeed him not his son Cassander, but his friend Polysperchon. Antipater knew that Polysperchon had neither the physical courage nor energy of mind that would be needed to keep peace in Macedonia after his death. But Polysperchon had some experience in government, having been left in charge of Macedonia during Antipater's visit to Asia; and he was generally liked, being the head of no particular faction. For a little while at least things would go quietly under him, and this was as far as Antipater's interest in the future went. Most people, in their concern for affairs after their death, do not think beyond a week, a month or a year—perhaps they anticipate unconsciously the exact length of time for which they will be remembered. A few meddle tyrannically in the lives of those who survive them, thus obliging people to remember them beyond the natural period.

Cassander was enraged that Antipater had not appointed him regent. He was in Greece at the time of his father's death; he immediately began working to win the discontented factions to his side and to form alliances with the Greeks. While in Epirus, Olympias had corresponded with the Greek cities, intriguing against Cassander and promising them many rewards and advantages if they supported her when she made her long-postponed attempt to drive all her enemies from power. She had most success with Athens, which, weary of the indignities it had suffered, thought that it might receive more gracious treatment from a woman than from any of the Macedonian men of consequence. But there were other women who had a hand in Macedonian affairs: chiefly, for a time, Eurydice. After Antipater's death she threw off restraint and sought help everywhere for her plan to make her husband King. She was able to form a large party—for where a witless king rules there are more opportunities for power than with a king of strong mind. Eurydice's influence became so great that Olympias continued to put off her return to Macedonia, and Roxana was obliged to flee to Epirus with young Alexander. Cassander was meanwhile building up a party of his own, though giving a little help to Eurydice. He had with him the more experienced generals and officers, who thought that Eurydice and Olympias must both fail. Eurydice relied largely on a rabble held together by the excitement of being led by a woman; and Olympias would have to make her way back with the help of a foreign army, which would perhaps not remain loyal to her for long. Many of the Greek cities now pledged their support to Cassander—finally, even Athens.

In Asia, Eumenes alone supported Olympias. This was the same Eumenes who had been Alexander's secretary; he had abilities also of a military kind, but did no active soldiering until after Alexander's death, though then an old man. He wrote to Olympias and Polysperchon, begging them to attempt nothing until affairs in Asia were more peaceful—he was then engaged in a struggle with Antigonus, who was a supporter of Cassander's. But Olympias would wait no longer. 'I am so spent,' she wrote, 'that if I do not act now I shall die. I have fought during my whole life, and, though I have won no victories, defeat has come to have a look of victory to me. I do not expect victory of this attempt. Why indeed should I desire a success that would give this hateful foreign woman, my son's concubine, power over myself and over Macedonia? Let it be defeat—let it be only a taste of that of which I have tasted much: to me it will mean that I still live. My life has been used in destroying myself, and I know no other way of living. If I wait any longer I shall die: thinking that there is nothing left of me to be destroyed.'

In 317 Olympias and Polysperchon, with an army of Epirots, faced Eurydice and her soldiers on Macedonian soil. But the

sight of Olympias, attended by her women in Bacchanalian
style, was so terrifying to Eurydice's men that they immediately laid down their arms. Roxana wished to present
Alexander to them, but Olympias would not permit this.
Eurydice and Philip were put in chains. When Olympias
heard that many were shocked by her cruelty, she had Philip
stabbed before Eurydice's eyes and a sword handed to her
with which to kill herself. But first Eurydice bound her
husband's wounds with strips torn from her dress, that he
might not die like a slaughtered beast; and then she asked
leave to send a last message to Olympias, before she used
the sword on herself.

'We are all accursed. I am the grandchild of the great
Philip, and this is his son. But you were his wife: your
death will be the darkest. We have not lived our own lives—
we have been creatures in hell—we die without knowing how
we might have lived had we not all been mad.'

And then Olympias turned to punish whoever had been
of Eurydice's party and whomever she suspected to be of
Cassander's. Many were banished, but still more killed.
Among those on whom her vengeance fell was Nicanor,
Cassander's younger brother, who had come away from
Greece to work secretly against her. Polysperchon was horrified by these reckless murders, which seemed to be inspired
by a lust of ruin rather than by policy. But his fortunes were
now fatally entangled with hers; even if he had dared to
desert her, he would have been marked everywhere as her
accomplice and found a home in no party. When Cassander
invaded Macedonia and the spirit of revolt spread, Polysperchon resigned himself to the necessity of defending the
unlucky cause of Olympias to the last.

The cause of Roxana and her son had been swallowed up
in that of Olympias; but her ambitions were of a simple
kind, possible to fulfil, while Olympias was moved by purposes
outside the range of common events and therefore had an

unearthly indifference to consequences. During the time that the two women spent together they spoke little, and Olympias was aware that Roxana's reserve was due to envy. It pleased Olympias that her son's wife should admire her for her crimes : that Alexander had chosen such a woman proved him her son. Nevertheless she hated Roxana, feeling certain that she had connived at his death. The story told to Olympias was that Alexander had died after a fever. But since his death she had solved the mystery of the disappearance of the poison-cup, having learned from her spies that Antipater had sent the slave who disappeared at the same time to Aristotle. She had also discovered that Cassander had visited Aristotle on his way to the East, and that Cassander and Roxana and Perdiccas had been present when Alexander died; and the description of the strange flush that had lingered on Alexander's face after his death persuaded her that he had drunk from the cup.

Aristotle she thought more villainous than the others, even because he could have had no such interest in killing Alexander as theirs. Moreover, Aristotle had once been entrusted with the task of instructing her son, in order to save him from being as great a fool as his father. Instead of showing Alexander his failings, in order that he might be on guard against them and avoid doing what he could only do in a fool's way, Aristotle had made him believe that wisdom consisted in the concealment of foolishness. The result was that Alexander had deceived no one but himself—for only a wise man can conceal well—and thus had been treated either with contempt or fear. If he had not cut himself off from her influence, she could have helped him to make himself so feared that he would have been safe from contempt. Perhaps the end would not have been different—but his life would have seemed less disgraceful. She blamed herself first, for having chosen such a father for her son; but after that she blamed most of all Aristotle. She spoke of him always with a vehemence that led people to regard her hate of him as an insanity, and her insinuation that he had played a part in Alexander's death as a delusion. Rumours of his complicity spread, but as they were said to come from Olympias they were discounted. The accusation went into history as something creditable to Aristotle because the authority could be proved untrustworthy.

When Cassander invaded Macedonia, Olympias fled to the eastern coast and secured herself, with Roxana and Alexander, in the city of Pydna. The Epirot army that had accompanied her into Macedonia had by now returned to its native land. The King of Epirus, her cousin, tried to organize a force to go to her rescue; but the soldiers mutinied and he was dethroned and banished from his kingdom. Polysperchon collected an army to resist Cassander, but when the two forces confronted each other most of Polysperchon's soldiers went over to Cassander. Yet Polysperchon did not abandon Olympias's cause, doomed though he knew it to be, until he heard that she was dead. The rest of his life was spent in vain intrigue and warring in Greece. In the end he made peace with Cassander; his fortunes had fallen so low that he was content to accept an unimportant command.

Cassander besieged Pydna, to which Olympias had fled. Olympias refused to surrender, though provisions were low and her soldiers desperate, holding out for many months. Finally, the horses of her small army had to be slaughtered for food; and the elephants she had taken with her—a whole brigade, a present from Alexander—were fed on sawdust, so that they grew ill and died. Polysperchon was loyal, but powerless to help her. Then came news from the East of Eumenes's death: he had fallen into Antigonus's hands and been murdered. He of all Alexander's generals had remained most loyal to her family, though a Greek. She regretted him; but had he been truly loyal, she felt, he would have been more violent on her behalf and on Alexander's during his life.

And indeed in these times there was nothing to trust in except violence.

In the spring Olympias's starving soldiers deserted—sorrowfully and openly. She was almost happy that the terrible end was near. All her life she had burned to do violent things against others, and she had done many. Yet she had never reached the dreamed-of extreme. She saw now that this must be in violence endured, not inflicted. And suddenly she became gentle with Roxana, feeling that she would be lost in her own fate. The message of surrender had already been sent to Cassander. He had replied by an offer to send the two women and young Alexander to Athens in a galley; for, if he took them into his power, he must either imprison or kill them, and the Macedonians would then have an excuse for rebelling against him, since the house of Philip was still regarded by many as sacred. Roxana longed to take advantage of his generosity, for her son's sake, but Olympias sent Cassander a disdainful challenge to come and fetch them, accusing him of cowardice.

Cassander, embarrassed by his charges, sent Roxana and Alexander to Amphipolis, to be kept in honourable confinement; and her spirits were so low that she accepted this as fortunate. Olympias embraced her at their parting, saying: 'I leave you with pity, Roxana, for I think you will live yet a little longer.' This was in 316. Roxana lived till 311, when Cassander, having made peace with all his enemies, felt safe enough to order her and her son to be assassinated.

There was little murmuring against the imprisonment of Roxana and Alexander, since their hold on the popular imagination was not strong. But, in disposing of Olympias, Cassander had to be circumspect. Although her crimes were known, there was a perverse reverence for her in every Macedonian heart. She was not the only great personage who had committed crimes; and she had been frank in her hatreds, as many around her had not. Cassander solved the difficulty by arraigning her before all those who had a reason for demanding her death—the kinsmen of people whom she had had murdered. But, although many denounced her, the judges appointed by Cassander did not dare to speak the final condemnation. She stood before them smiling, fierce, contemptuous; she was very old, but straight, clear-eyed, immovable. It was not because of her age that they hesitated to condemn her, but because she was stronger than they, and they felt impotent under her gaze. And yet she wished for death, and they wanted her to die. The suspense was agonizing to all. What would break it? Cassander stirred unquietly in his seat.

Then, swiftly, without changing her expression, Olympias took a knife from the folds of her dress. She held it in her hand for a moment, looking at it as if she meant to use it on someone in the court; and indeed, had she attempted to do this, there was none who could have resisted, so heavy was the spell in which she held them.

'I wished to know glory in my time—and now at last I shall know it.'

The knife slid across her throat. She seemed to die even as it touched her, falling instantly: when they reached her she was dead.

Had Olympias been a woman of great virtue, as well as of great energy, what could she have done with her virtue in that age, in those circumstances, except hide it away? Something she kept hidden away in herself, something that would not be still, that she tried over and over again to destroy: was it, perhaps, virtue? At any rate, there was a zeal in her for noble things. Finding nothing on which to spend it, she turned it into a rage against herself and her times—which were those not only of her son Alexander but of his tutor, Aristotle.

III

NEW WAYS IN JERUSALEM

I

THE ANCESTORS OF MARIAMNE

WHEN, on the death of Alexander the Great, Perdiccas became regent, he was supported by another of Alexander's generals, Seleucus—a proud man, who helped others in their schemes but confided his own to no one. It was Seleucus's secret ambition to be a king in the East, with Babylon for his capital. Ptolemy already ruled in Egypt; but no other general of Alexander's had yet found a sure home abroad. The rival generals would in time exhaust and destroy one another, Seleucus felt. In the meantime he would aid the victor of the moment, and be ready to desert him when his luck began to turn. Thus, Seleucus looked on quietly while Perdiccas was killed in his tent. In 321, Antipater of Macedonia rewarded Seleucus's discretion by making him satrap of Babylonia.

All this it is important to know if we would understand what Palestine was at the time of King Herod the Great, and what had happened by then to the Jews. For Seleucus was the founder of the kingdom of Syria; and it was from the tyrannical and corrupt Syrian monarchs that the Jews wrested a worldly portion of their own.

When he was secure in Babylonia, Seleucus gave support to the general Pithon, and then to the powerful Antigonus in his war with Eumenes, Alexander's former secretary. But soon Antigonus grew alarmed at Seleucus's popularity in Babylonia and became his enemy. Seleucus then worked with Ptolemy of Egypt against Antigonus, and succeeded in re-establishing himself at Babylon in 312—which we may count as the foundation-date of the Seleucid monarchy. The next year Antipater's son Cassander and Ptolemy made peace with Antigonus, to whom the rule of Asia was now left. But Seleucus nevertheless held his own in the part of Asia that he had chosen for himself, extending his conquests as far as the Indus. Then Seleucus took part in a new coalition against Antigonus—who met defeat and death at the Battle of Ipsus in 301. Between Seleucus and Ptolemy there was now fierce rivalry. To spite Ptolemy, Seleucus married the beautiful Stratonice, daughter of Demetrius, Antigonus's son and heir; this woman he later gave for a wife to his own son Antiochus, who was to inherit his empire—the largest that had been formed out of the confused realms of Alexander. When Seleucus was about to invade Greece, in an attempt to make himself King of Macedonia, he was treacherously killed by Ptolemy's eldest son.

Throughout his reign Seleucus laboured to introduce Greek culture into his kingdom, founding many new cities and populating them with Greeks and Macedonians. This, too, bears upon the later story of the Jews, since the advance of Hellenism touched them closely, uniting them as they resisted it and later causing disruption among them as some yielded to it. The most important of Seleucus's Hellenic foundations was Antioch, on the northern coast of Phoenicia: this became the capital of Syria, and a place of magnificence and prosperity.

It was not the murderer of Seleucus who became King of Egypt after the first Ptolemy, but his beloved youngest son, Ptolemy Philadelphus, whom he had by the wife that was dearest to him—Berenice, a woman of Antipater's family. And this also has a bearing upon the later story of the Jews; for the name Berenice—originally Macedonian, then Egyptian—was a favoured one among them for daughters.

Nor must it be thought that in the times after Alexander all the Jews were concentrated in Judaea. In Egypt were to be found numerous colonies of Jews, descendants of those

who had fled there when Nebuchadnezzar captured Jerusalem. In Babylon lived a large, stable Jewish community,
descendants of those who had preferred to remain behind
when Cyrus of Persia made himself patron of the return to
Jerusalem. And all over Syria, and in all the market cities
of the eastern Mediterranean, were colonies of industrious
Jews who maintained the ancient Law while adapting themselves in worldly matters to the ways of the people with
whom they lived. There was far more steadfastness to the
Law among the Jews of the Dispersion than among those who
were governed from Jerusalem.

The first governor in Jerusalem, after the Jews had been
re-established there by Cyrus, was Sheshbazzar. He was of
the royal Jewish line; but the successors of Cyrus adopted
the policy, of appointing Persians as governors. If, sometimes, they appointed a Jew, they were careful to choose one
who was not of royal blood. In 445 the Jew Nehemiah, who
was cup-bearer to the Great King and much esteemed by him,
begged to be allowed to go to Jerusalem to revive the ancient
spirit among the Jews: for they had let the walls collapse
and neglected the sacred beauties of the city and fallen into
shameful indifference to their inheritance. Nehemiah,
appointed governor, repaired the walls and built up again
the gates that had been burned down; he also made many
new laws, for the greater dignity of daily life in the Jewish
community. By the time that Alexander defeated the
Persians, the leadership of the Jews in Jerusalem had for a
century been in the hands of their own high priests.

Of all the foreign peoples with whom they had to do,
the Jews loved the Persians best, and the Persians returned
this warmth. The Romans valued the Jews as allies and
advisers, because of their worldly shrewdness; but the Persians
found that admirable in them which made others impatient—
their rapt sense of the divine being. The Jews have gentle
hearts where they feel gentleness of heart. The name of Cyrus

remained delightful to them, almost as lovingly spoken as a prophet's. And they even thought kindly of the harsh Xerxes, who allowed himself to be dissuaded from a murderous persecution of the Jews by his favourite concubine, Esther— a Jewish woman. (The story is vague, the facts having melted into the feelings with which it was repeatedly told by the Jews to their children. It occurred perhaps a little before the time of Nehemiah. Esther was probably a descendant of a Jewish family that had been carried off to Babylon by Nebuchadnezzar; and Haman, the wicked adviser who would have destroyed the Jews, was, it is said, a Macedonian.)

The Jews were at first little affected by the change of rule in Syria that resulted from Alexander's victories. Instead of a Persian governor there was a Macedonian governor, but they continued to enjoy the same privileges as before. After Alexander's death, Syria was one of the prizes for which his generals competed. When Antigonus fell, Ptolemy of Egypt secured the southern portion to himself. Although Seleucus moved his capital from Babylon to Antioch, having in the westward extension of his empire gained northern Syria, it was not until a century later that the whole of Syria came under Seleucid rule.

Under the Seleucid kings the Jews were for a while left to follow their own traditional ways of life. But certain Greek customs were nevertheless adopted by the educated classes; for instance, even the priests came to approve of the pleasures of the gymnasium and to indulge in them. Antiochus IV was the first Seleucid king who attempted to make the Jews desert Jehovah for the Greek gods. In 168 he occupied Jerusalem and rededicated the Temple to Olympian Zeus.

Now, at Modin, a town in the northern part of Judaea, there lived a priest of the noblest Jewish blood, named Mattathias. He belonged to the Asmonean family, and it was by his piety, carried on in the patriotic labours of his sons, that the Jews were brought to look upon themselves as a reborn nation; and it was a descendant of this family, Mariamne, whom Herod the Great took for his second wife.

When Mattathias heard how the Jews were being persecuted, he was very angry and spoke with defiance against the Syrians, which reached Antiochus's ears. 'Antiochus has dreamed evil dreams,' he told him, 'and comes to Jerusalem to seek a Daniel. But he has outraged the god who might give him a Daniel.' Antiochus sent an ambassador to Mattathias, who said: 'The King would know what you mean by this name of Daniel.' To which Mattathias made this reply: 'When Solomon set riddles to Hiram of Tyre, the heathen did not beg the Jew to supply him with the answers as well. If Antiochus cannot guess the answer and will not pay a handsome forfeit in order to know it, let him be circumcised and initiated into our secret lore.'

Then Antiochus sent an army against Mattathias and his sons and followers. They fled to the mountains, and were pursued. Many battles were fought, in which the Jews were cruelly cut down; and when captured they were forced to make idolatrous sacrifices. But Mattathias held up their courage with fierce exhortations to faith in the Law. Before he died he said: 'I am the scapegoat that has gone into the wilderness for the glory of God and the purification of his people, that they may be victorious in battle against the heathen!' He knew that many Jews were being tempted into profane rites by the threats and promises of the Syrians. There was no prophet to lead them; they must use the means of war against the Syrians, since their faith was not a strong enough arm by itself. Therefore he spoke to them in soldierly as well as priestly language, and recommended his sons to them.

Judas Maccabaeus, son of Mattathias, was a resourceful fighter and a zealous Jew; with his brothers he organized the patriots into a skilful, quick-moving army. There were many proud victories over the Syrians, but just before his death the narrower patriots deserted him because he made an

alliance with Rome. Judas fell in battle and his brother
Jonathan took over the command; and after Jonathan, another
brother, Simon; and after Simon, his son John Hyrcanus.
By this time three Samaritan districts had been added to
Judaea, and the port of Joppa gained, among other places,
and colonized with Jews. John Hyrcanus added the remaining
Samaritan districts and subdued the Idumeans to the south of
Judaea; these people were not abhorred by the Jews, being
descended from Isaac, and when converted became pious and
patriotic. Constant rivalry for the kingship had greatly
weakened the Seleucid government, which was now unable
to restrain the nationalistic fervour of the Jews. After the
Idumeans, the people across the Jordan were brought within
the Judaean fold. And the Itureans of Galilee also were
subdued and converted; these belonged to a race of moun-
taineers that lived by brigandage and was spread from the
Lebanon to the region of Damascus. Another strange race
blocked the expansion of Judaea to the south and south-east—
the Nabateans, a merchant people whose centre was Petra.

The Jews who had remained loyal to the old ways and
supported the sons of Mattathias were the inspiration of the
Pharisee sect, that later fought so stubbornly against com-
promises with the heathen world. The sons of Mattathias
had done no worse than ally themselves politically with
Rome. But in time the religious strictness of the early
Asmoneans was relaxed—even the names used in the family
were foreign. John Hyrcanus was succeeded in the
ruling office by his elder son Aristobulus, the first of the
line to take the title of King; then came another son,
Alexander. Alexander hated the Pharisees, and was encouraged in his savage persecution of them by the Sadducees:
these were the sophisticated Jews, who looked down on the
Pharisees as troublesome bigots. But his wife Alexandra
sympathized with the Pharisees and denounced her husband's
treatment of them. After his death, taking the rule into her

own hands, she devoted herself with vigorous piety to their rehabilitation. She was a woman of unflinching will, of the kind that grows stone-like in old age and lasts on beyond her time by suppressing every feeling that might bring back the weaknesses of life. She was the grandmother of a woman, also called Alexandra, whose will was as strong as hers but who wasted it in passion. The second Alexandra had a daughter, however, who knew how to make herself stony, even when she was young: this was the Mariamne already spoken of, whom Herod adored.

The old Alexandra's first son was called Hyrcanus: him she allowed only to be High Priest, though he might have been King if he had dared to oppose her will. Her other son, Aristobulus, began to covet the royal office for himself: why should he not have it, since his brother had relinquished it? Many supported him in his ambition, and soon his mother heard that he had placed himself at the head of an army. But she did not show anger or feed the vanity of the rebels by seeming to oppose them. 'I will give a few fortresses into your control,' she said, 'and let that content you.' Then, as if Aristobulus had done nothing against her, she sent him on a confidential mission to Damascus; which he failed to conclude well, as she had anticipated. When he returned she did not scold him, showing him that she had not expected him to succeed. He was so chagrined by his incompetence that during the rest of her life he gave her no further trouble. But his supporters were ready to follow him in battle against Hyrcanus so soon as the old Queen was dead.

Before Alexandra died she was visited by the chief man of the Idumeans, Antipater. He was a Jew, the Idumeans having been converted two generations before, and she received him kindly. He applauded her stern measures against foreign innovations; his own countrymen practised their adopted faith with old-fashioned strictness and dwelt far enough away from the centres of progress to have avoided contamination

by Greek ideas and manners. Their principal contact was with
the Nabatean traders who passed continually through their
territory in transporting merchandise from Arabia to the
Palestinian ports: with these people all converse was on the
subject of business matters and money. Antipater himself
had grown very rich through his dealings with them. His
wife, Cyprus, was a woman of Petra, the Nabatean capital;
she had renounced her native faith on her marriage and helped
him to bring up their children as good Jews.

Antipater's design in coming to Alexandra was to make
her look favourably upon a plan he had formed of assisting
Hyrcanus, after her death, to maintain himself against his
brother Aristobulus. Hyrcanus was known to be excessively
affable: he would without doubt give in to Aristobulus and
even remain on friendly terms with him—unless someone
frightened him into resistance. Antipater saw here a chance
for his own advancement. If Alexandra approved of his
interest in Hyrcanus's cause, his fortune was made; Hyrcanus
would be obedient to anyone who had been chosen by his
mother to protect him. Alexandra consented to the plan on
the condition that Antipater should swear to make Hyrcanus
deal always tenderly with the Pharisees, and so deal himself,
and his children after him if they came to have a share in the
affairs of the kingdom. Antipater swore what she wished.
'Should you or any of your blood break this oath,' Alexandra
said terribly, 'God will send a cold madness into your head,
as he did with my wicked husband Alexander.'

But when Alexandra died and the army of Aristobulus met
the army of Hyrcanus at Jericho, Aristobulus was victorious.
This defeat Hyrcanus took for an ill omen. It was at Jericho
that the Israelites, led by Joshua, had won the great victory
that began their establishment in Palestine; and Hyrcanus
had observed the same rites that they had used. He had
circled the enemy with his army day after day, priests following behind with their trumpets. Aristobulus, he thought,

remembering the old story, would not expect battle before the seventh day, and by then his troops would be distraught with pious fear and surrender when attacked. Antipater raged against the simplicity of Hyrcanus: 'If Aristobulus remembers the old story,' he said, 'he will also remember that those within the walls were lost because they grew dazed from watching the Israelites go round and round until the seventh day—and he will fall upon you suddenly in the midst of your winding dance.' And so it happened.

Hyrcanus would have abandoned the struggle, but Antipater humoured him with talk of the life of leisure and holiness he would be able to lead when he was High Priest at Jerusalem again: promising that he himself would relieve him of all the cares of government. Antipater obtained help for Hyrcanus from the King of the Nabateans—to whose advantage it was that his Jewish neighbours should be at peace. However, Aristobulus was able to continue the war against his brother until Pompey, having deposed the last Seleucid king, annexed Syria to the Roman Empire: then Pompey laid siege to Jerusalem, to which Aristobulus had retreated, and captured it for Hyrcanus, who was made High Priest of Judaea and the surrounding districts.

The Roman rule now lay upon the Asmonean kingdom. Taxes were levied, and Aristobulus and his two sons were taken by Pompey to Rome to decorate his triumph. Yet Pompey had been kind. He had forbidden his soldiers to plunder the Temple, and listened patiently to Hyrcanus's scholarly explanations of Jewish customs; and he had also paid the expenses of the many thank-offerings that were burned on the altars in celebration of the delivery of Jerusalem from strife. Antipater was at first dejected by this loss of national sovereignty. His own part was now more difficult than he had imagined: he would have to ingratiate himself with the Romans and at the same time make Hyrcanus a symbol of internal strength and unity. As the management of the Jews was the more delicate and difficult task, he decided to win the confidence of the Romans first and use them to support his domestic policies.

The Pharisees, whom Antipater had sworn to respect, were angered by his apparent acquiescence in Roman rule. He had extracted a pledge from the Romans not to interfere with the ancient customs of the Jews; but the Pharisees remained suspicious. Moreover, there were many of all parties who saw in Antipater's management of Hyrcanus an attempt to usurp the royal power that had belonged to the Asmoneans. Hyrcanus had only a daughter. The captured Aristobulus had two sons, Antigonus and Alexander: here at least was some hope for the continuance of the old royal line. Most active against Antipater was this daughter of Hyrcanus, Alexandra. She had been married to her cousin Alexander, Aristobulus's son, while the old Queen still lived, before war between the two brothers had broken out. From the beginning her sympathies had been with her husband's family. She despised her father for his softness, and had come to loathe piety because he made it seem the pastime of a foolish man. Therefore, when her husband escaped from Rome, she was among the most active in the secret rallying of supporters; and she even formed a plot to kill her father along with Antipater and his sons.

Antipater defeated Alexander, with the help of the Romans —to whose decision he left Alexander's fate. Then Alexandra went to the Roman commander dressed as an old woman, pretending to be Alexander's mother, and by her pleading procured his pardon: had she gone to him as his wife she would have been imprisoned too for her part in the uprising.

'Why do you make yourself so ugly?' asked her little daughter Mariamne, when she saw her mother dressed in this strange way.

'Because I have a great favour to ask of a cruel man, child,' her mother answered, 'and must make him pity me.'

To this Mariamne said: 'If I had a great favour to ask of a cruel man, I should make myself as beautiful as possible and speak to him very proudly.'

'And what if he refused to grant your favour—would you still be proud?'

'Even prouder!' cried Mariamne.

'You'll grow up to be a woman of stone, like my grandmother Alexandra,' said her mother bitterly.

The next year Aristobulus and his other son, Antigonus, escaped from Rome and came to Judaea, where the rebel forces again took up arms. But again they were defeated—though Aristobulus and his two sons still survived.

2

CLEOPATRA AND CAESAR

It was at about this time that Pompey's governor in Syria was induced by a huge bribe to help Ptolemy of Egypt regain control of his kingdom, from which he had been expelled for his profligate behaviour and insane extravagance. Antipater assisted the Romans in the expedition by which Ptolemy was re-established in Alexandria; and in this way the Jews were partly responsible for the accession to the throne of Egypt of that Cleopatra who later caused so much trouble in the world—and to themselves as well. From the time of the first Ptolemy, all the kings of Egypt had been of the legitimate line of descent. The Ptolemy who was Antipater's neighbour was the first bastard of the Ptolemaic family to rule the kingdom. When he died, in 51 B.C., Cleopatra, who was his daughter, succeeded him. By her father's will she was obliged to marry her brother Ptolemy on becoming Queen, and for a time they ruled together. She was then a very young girl, but had already begun to look upon the world as a mean, dark place, in which fortune and brightness were to be had only by seizing from others what one could and keeping it in one's hold as long as possible. Believing that there were not enough desirable things for all to have a share in them, she made up her mind that the happiest person was the one who was the cleverest thief. She worked with vicious fanaticism to have what she coveted; thinking that none knew so well as herself the joy of possessing and none therefore deserved so much. When she had won her way she softened as a goddess to mortals—pouring out affection and benevolence with an abandon that was unmatchable and frightening, but irresistible. Then she was happy, and felt virtuous.

Cleopatra hated the Jews because, she said, they knew only one kind of happiness and virtue, which was to cast out evil from their lives but take nothing in its stead lest that too be evil. The Romans she liked better, though she thought them without passion, deliberate even in their rashest acts: she liked them because they were not afraid of ruin and so not afraid of triumphs. This was the woman with whom Alexandra, Hyrcanus's daughter, became friendly, hoping to turn her against Antipater. First she wrote to her secretly, giving information about Antipater's relations with the Romans that she judged to be of interest to her. Then she sent Mariamne to stay with Cleopatra for a time, since Antipater wanted her for his son Herod, and she wished to cheat him of the prestige that he would gain by an alliance between her family and his. This visit took place several years after Cleopatra's accession, when Caesar was in Egypt and they lived together as lovers. She had forced her love upon him when he intervened in the war that had broken out between her brother and herself, and influenced him to enter the war on her side. Her brother was killed and she became the full sovereign, yet Caesar lingered on, hoping that it would be thought at Rome that his purpose was to make a docile ally of the Egyptian Queen. But Rome and the world soon knew that he was in love with Cleopatra.

Caesar was a reserved, disbelieving, obdurate man, and Cleopatra had conquered him by loving him for what others found repellent. 'In you, Caesar,' she told him, 'I have something that, being not sweet, will not corrupt—but, like a sour metal, will only tarnish.' And in Cleopatra Caesar had something of another world, something hellish it might be, a stranger—but, because a stranger, one with whom he could yield to weariness of himself and yet feel that in his own world he had lost none of his secrets. When he left Egypt and was parted from her for a little while, he forgot what she looked like and thought of her as someone he had never seen, though always known. It was, indeed, difficult to make a memory of her face, which continually changed from one face into another—sometimes that of a lustful child, sometimes soft and silvery with repose, as when she was pleased at a cruel act done, that would not need to be done again; often stiff with contemptuous amusement at her own follies, as when she had Caesar and herself borne through Alexandria on a platform that rose above the house-tops, and there threw off her wrapping of golden tissue and stood naked. Nor did she have the look of any race—not of the Egyptians, whose queen she was, or of the Macedonians, from whom the Ptolemies were descended, or of the Syrian Greeks, with whom they had intermarried (the first Egyptian Cleopatra was a Syrian princess).

Before Mariamne set out for Egypt she thought she would not like Cleopatra; her mother praised Cleopatra as a woman who treated her enemies as she herself would have liked to treat Antipater and his family and supporters. Mariamne was then about twelve years old, but the misfortunes of her family had already taught her much about the crimes that people commit against one another in their divisions and resentments. She had sworn to herself that when she grew up she would try not to commit crimes against those who committed crimes against her. She would hate them, but do them no harm; she would not twist her face into ugly looks, as her mother did when planning revenge, or shriek horribly when she spoke of her enemies. She would be proud, and let nothing upset her. And if Cleopatra tried to make her talk of her grandfather Hyrcanus and her other grandfather Aristobulus and all the quarrels in the family, she would tighten her lips and say nothing, and perhaps that would make Cleopatra send her home again.

But Cleopatra turned out to be a different sort of person

from what Mariamne had expected. She did not seem at all interested in talking of quarrels, only in being happy; she showed Mariamne all her beautiful clothes and clapped her hands with pleasure when Mariamne took presents from her. And she kissed Mariamne a great deal, which she would not have liked had not Cleopatra behaved as if she were a little girl herself. And once she said, when Mariamne caught her with an angry look on her face and turned away: 'Ah, little Mariamne, come back—I've stopped thinking of what angered me. Look—it's gone!' And her face was sweet and smooth again. 'Yes, I know,' she said, drawing Mariamne to her, 'I am a very wicked woman and I have done very wicked things in my life, and I dare say I shall do things as wicked again. But the wickedness is only my crossness with people when they won't be happy along with me. Then I kill them —if I can—and then I am happy again.'

Mariamne looked at her disapprovingly and would not smile. So Cleopatra began searching among her things for a present, to make Mariamne forget what she had said about killing people. Then Caesar entered the room. 'She won't speak to me, because I told her I sometimes killed people.'

Caesar went over to Mariamne kindly. 'I'm afraid we all do,' he said, taking her hand. 'I've killed a great many more people than Cleopatra has.'

'Yes, but you don't make a joke of it, as Cleopatra does.' Mariamne said this so mournfully that Caesar could not help reproving Cleopatra a little. 'You should not have spoken of these things to her.'

'But she knows I'm a very wicked woman,' said Cleopatra, still rummaging among her things and not looking up, 'and loves me nevertheless. So do you—nevertheless. That's the best kind of love. Here! For you, Mariamne. You must wear it and try to look like a very wicked woman yourself: they won't think you're beautiful, otherwise.'

It was a bracelet of soft gold, in the shape of a serpent.

Cleopatra wound it round Mariamne's arm—because she was small, still a child, it reached above her elbow. Mariamne kissed Cleopatra for it. 'But I won't be wicked,' she said. 'I'll be good, and they'll be afraid of me for that.' She played with the bracelets on Caesar's arms. 'You don't wear these to show you're wicked, do you?'

'In Rome they give bracelets to generals for outstanding valour. I dislike wearing them, but people think you are over-proud if you don't. Would you have one of mine for a present?'

'I should love one! I'll wear Cleopatra's to remind me to be good, not wicked like her, and I'll wear yours—well, to help me to be not too proud. But I'm afraid I shall be. Mother says it's my great-grandmother Alexandra's blood in me.'

When Mariamne was gone, Cleopatra and Caesar sat down together. 'The poor, queer little Jewish girl,' said Cleopatra.

'I think she's lovely!' Caesar said.

'So do I!'

Then they talked of themselves. The little Jewish girl had shed some of her sanity over them: they talked together almost as husband and wife—or, at least, like two ordinary, sensible lovers, not like mad great people. Caesar was soon going away to war, and then he would have to go to Rome. He had been made Dictator: he would not be able to live with her in Egypt again. She must come to Rome, after their child was born. He had been there since the autumn of 48—it was now the spring of 47.

Soon after Caesar's departure Cleopatra sent Mariamne back to her mother. And in a little while a boy was born to Cleopatra, whom she called Caesarion. When Caesar had prepared a house for her, she went to Rome, bringing Caesarion; and remained there until Caesar's death, in 44, faithfully loved by him to the last. Cleopatra was disliked and feared at Rome, and those who dared to speak against her to Caesar were always urging him to send her back to Egypt. But he would say: 'That would be a bad thing for Rome, for it is she who cleanses me of all that is wild and evil in me, by loving it.'

In the conflict between Caesar and Pompey, Antipater, Hyrcanus's vizier, had supported Pompey: Caesar's victory was a great surprise to the whole world. Pompey had long been regarded as the leading Roman of his time. Perhaps this was because his campaigns were in the East and therefore seemed grander achievements than Caesar's works in Gaul; moreover, Caesar's ways were simple and soldierly, while Pompey delighted in the hero's part. At Rome the senatorial party had been pro-Pompey, and when the war between Pompey and Caesar started and Caesar marched from Gaul into Italy, Pompey had all the resources of the state at his command. But the senatorial party was itself unpopular throughout Italy, and with the army. Town after town received Caesar with jubilation; soldiers who were called upon to join Pompey's forces deserted to Caesar. Pompey was forced to withdraw to Greece—his wife Cornelia he sent for safety to Lesbos. The final battle between Caesar and Pompey took place on the plain of Pharsalia in Thessaly, in August 48. Pompey, defeated, went first to Lesbos, to fetch Cornelia and his young son. His plan was to take refuge in Egypt and wait there until his friends should have collected a fresh army. It was now that Antipater dissociated himself from Pompey, refusing to let him enter Judaea.

Cornelia, Pompey's wife, was a beautiful and learned woman. On the journey from Lesbos to Alexandria she tried to dissuade him from his resolution to face Caesar again. 'Let us settle quietly in Alexandria and devote ourselves to study and the education of our son. The great library of the Ptolemies is there, and scholars from all over the world visit this place: we could hold ourselves fortunate in sub- stituting the society of the wise for that of the great.' But

Pompey was too distracted with rage at his defeat to be soothed by this argument. He sent a ship ahead to announce his arrival, reminding the advisers of the boy-king (Cleopatra's brother, Cleopatra having just been deprived of her share in the rule) how he had helped his father to regain his throne. The Egyptians resolved not to meddle in the dispute between Pompey and Caesar. As Pompey's ship neared the port they sent a boat out to meet him, as if in friendship. Pompey went down into it with a few attendants, understanding that further boats would be sent for his wife and son and the rest of his suite. When he rose to step on shore he was stabbed from behind; and Cornelia saw him fall.

Caesar, arriving in Egypt in pursuit of Pompey, was shown the head of his vanquished enemy. They had once been friends, and Pompey's first wife was Caesar's daughter Julia, now dead. Caesar wept. Pompey's only fault had been that he believed himself destined to greatness, and lived his triumphs as if they were prophetic of still more glorious ones. 'Yet is my way better?' Caesar asked himself, thinking how he accepted his triumphs coldly, suspicious of what might come next. 'Who is not a worse man than his fellow?' He had the body of Pompey decently burned and carried the ashes to Rome with him, where he gave them to Cornelia.

It has already been told how Caesar, soon after his arrival in Egypt, became involved in Cleopatra's dispute with her brother. This little war in Egypt gave Antipater his first chance of showing friendship to Caesar: by helping the Roman reinforcements to reach Caesar quickly. In the course of the siege of Alexandria the royal library was partially burned, and the loss of so many valuable manuscripts distressed Cleopatra. The library had been begun by the first Ptolemy and increased by each of his successors, growing to hundreds of thousands of volumes. We shall see how Mark Antony consoled Cleopatra for this loss.

Antipater suffered no disadvantage from Caesar's conflict

with Pompey; but for his enemies of the Asmonean family it had fatal consequences. Caesar allowed Aristobulus, Mariamne's grandfather, to fight for him in Asia against the Pompeians, and both he and his son, Mariamne's father, Alexander, were killed by them. When Caesar first saw Mariamne, on her visit to Cleopatra, he felt a pang of guilt, that her father and grandfather should have been killed in his cause. The Asmonean party now had only one leader, Mariamne's uncle Antigonus, her father's brother.

Caesar recognized Antipater's abilities as an administrator and increased his powers in order to ensure peace in Judaea; to Antigonus's claims he paid no attention. Antipater now governed Judaea in his own right, not merely as Hyrcanus's vizier; and, because he felt that the Asmonean cause was crushed, he was no longer anxious that a betrothal should be arranged between Mariamne and his son Herod. At the time of Caesar's appointment of Antipater to the governorship, Herod was twenty-five, and had already been married for several years to a woman of a noble Idumean family. The Idumeans were Antipater's strongest support, being his own people. Rumours of the proposed betrothal had already reached Doris, Herod's wife, and there had been a hostile murmuring against it among the Idumean nobility, though Mariamne's extreme youth made it probable that the marriage would be only a formal one, to be dissolved at political convenience.

Antipater thought that Mariamne would very likely be betrothed to someone of Cleopatra's court and stay in Egypt for the rest of her life. Alexandra might follow her to Egypt; Hyrcanus had surely not much longer to live; the remaining Asmoneans could be easily dealt with. Alexandra had a young son, Aristobulus, who might be a danger when he grew up—but someone could be bribed to put him out of the way. The death of the old Aristobulus and Mariamne's father, Alexander, further simplified the situation for Antipater.

And thus it was that little attention was paid to Mariamne's sudden return from Egypt to Jerusalem; and Alexandra herself considered it wise to make her enemies forget about her and her family for a while.

Having been flatteringly confirmed by Caesar in the powers he had assumed, Antipater now bestowed important offices on his sons. His eldest son Phasaël he made special overseer of the Jerusalem district: Phasaël was slow and pious and would get on well with old Hyrcanus, whose conscientiousness as High Priest and dreamy innocence of character had made him much loved in the capital. Herod, his next son, he made Governor of Galilee, which was the most troublesome district of the Judean realm—the native brigand bands kept up a constant warfare with the Jerusalem authorities. The Galileans were not only brigands but fierce zealots, though converted to the Jewish faith not much over fifty years before. It was said in Jerusalem that the Galileans were the beggars of the earth, whose one virtue was that they despised rather than coveted the good things that others enjoyed. In becoming Jews they turned their faith into a hate of other Jews—even as in their cult of brigandage they preyed upon themselves rather than upon strangers. To say of someone that he was 'as poor as a Galilean' meant not that he was an unfortunate man, humbly without substance, but a vain and debased person, who would make no effort to live with the dignity possible to a human being. And those who had emigrated to Galilee from other parts of Judaea, or from Syria, were equally poor-spirited: people who had heard that in fertile Galilee one could live cheaply, with little labour.

Antipater chose rightly in appointing Herod to pacify the Galileans—for Herod was ruthlessly disdainful of all that was barbarous and backward, having already formed the aim of lifting the Jews to such a state of worldly grace and grandeur as Solomon had intended for them. Herod was the son whom Antipater wished to succeed him in authority.

However, Herod's success in subduing the Galilean brigands made new difficulties for Antipater. Members of the defeated bandit-families went to Jerusalem and appealed for compassion, making it seem that the campaign in Galilee had been one of rich against poor; and Antipater's opponents were quick to make use of the indignation of the lower classes, fanning it with attacks upon Antipater's deference to the Romans. Hyrcanus, understanding little of what was going on, was persuaded by members of the Holy Council that Herod had broken the ancient Law in his treatment of the Galileans. Although Hyrcanus was too dependent on Antipater to attempt to use his right as High Priest to punish Herod for impious behaviour, his clumsy interference added to Antipater's embarrassment; Antipater could control but not suppress him, since the old man's Asmonean blood gave a sanction to his rule with which he did not dare to dispense.

These troubles were still unresolved in 44, when Caesar was murdered.

3

THE YOUNG HEROD

In the difficulties arising out of the Galilean campaign Herod had been supported by Caesar's legate in Syria. Now Cassius, one of Caesar's murderers, arrived to take over the rule of Syria. Antipater and Herod hastened to protest their friendship for the Republic; they promised Cassius to collect seven hundred talents for him in Judaea—he was greatly in need of money for bribes, to make himself popular in the East. Antipater used the occasion to mortify his enemies, appointing them to help him collect the money and thus involving them in the resentment that the emergency-tax would certainly arouse. Herod took revenge on the people of Galilee by exacting a hundred talents from them, although such a large amount was out of proportion to the wealth of the district. Even the more prosperous places had difficulty in meeting the demand, and in four capital cities many were sold as slaves to make up the deficit.

The chief of Antipater's enemies at the time was a man called Malichus. His slowness in producing the amount assigned to him for collection so infuriated Cassius that he was in danger of arrest and execution. Old Hyrcanus, whom, meanwhile, Antipater's enemies had been constantly exhorting to assert his authority, took courage to plead with Cassius for Malichus's life, sending him a hundred talents of his own. Malichus was saved, but Antipater was now resolved that Hyrcanus must be removed at the first opportune moment.

Hyrcanus was indeed guiltless of any desire to weaken

Antipater's power, which was the source of his own freedom from royal cares. But this made it the easier for Antipater's enemies to use him: by associating the harmless old man's name with their activities they could make it seem that they worked only for the honour of the Asmonean line. In the next year, 43, Antipater was poisoned while dining at Hyrcanus's house. Although Hyrcanus was generally believed to have brought about his death, it was Malichus who had managed the affair, by a secret arrangement with Hyrcanus's butler. Hyrcanus himself was panic-stricken. Who would look after him so well as Antipater had done? Could he rely on Herod—or would Herod believe him his father's murderer? Most of all, he feared being made the centre of a conspiracy for the restoration of the Asmoneans. Antigonus was still alive, and there was also his grandson Aristobulus, Alexandra's child and Mariamne's brother. Hyrcanus begged Alexandra to give no encouragement to the conspirators. 'These are new times,' he said. 'We cannot expect to keep up the old ways in everything. New times, new blood. God will be well pleased if we do but continue to offer the oblations proper for the Sabbaths and the holy festivals and give the burnt-offerings in the ancient style, dividing the meat and salting it as prescribed. It is these things that are dear to the Lord, not worldly pride of blood and the succession of kings. Did not the prophet Samuel warn the people of the iniquity of kings, when they clamoured for one? Therefore let us leave those matters to the Romans.'

Alexandra promised not to meddle in public affairs for the time being—but because she felt that it was best to wait, to see what Herod would do. Should Herod prove as able a man as his father, they must use other means against him than open warfare. Mariamne was growing extremely beautiful; if Herod became fascinated with her, the Asmoneans would have a weapon at the very bosom of their enemy. To her father Alexandra said: 'You are a selfish old man and care for nothing but the security of your priestly emoluments. How do you think it is for me? To see my father become the fool of an Idumean upstart, and my husband sacrificed to the Romans because of him, and my husband's father also, your own brother and my uncle? And my children, who should be the pride of Judaea, true Maccabees, sturdy and fair, living like bastard outcasts? Is Israel dead?'

Antipater, before he died, said to Herod: 'When you must be stern, keep kindness in your heart, though hidden. And when you can be kind, be so; but always changing, as the moment requires. And deal leniently with the Pharisees, as I swore to the old Alexandra. Perhaps they have the right on their side. They at least wish to be always in the right, which few enough desire. And of all our peoples, deal most severely with the Galileans, who would make it a mean thing to be a Jew, our faith the faith of the mob, and every hovel a temple. It is their heathenish arrogance to have religion always on the lips, and to fancy that God walks among them whispering epigrams in their ears like one of those vile rhetoricians for which their city of Gadara is notorious. There is not a brigand of Galilee who does not have heavenly visions and mouth revelations to his followers, and every Galilean woman with child dreams of bearing a new deliverer of our people. We Idumeans have never known these madnesses.'

Herod did not wonder that his father should have used his dying breath in denouncing the Galileans, since it was they who first stirred up trouble after Caesar had appointed Antipater governor of Judaea in his own right. The prestige that Malichus had acquired as leader of the nationalist, anti-Roman party could be traced to the mothers of the executed Galilean bandits who had been bribed to wail in the Temple day after day and thus turn popular feeling against Antipater and his sons.

As soon as Antipater was dead, Malichus asked Hyrcanus to bestow upon him the civil authority—which as High Priest he had a traditional authority to do. Hyrcanus consented to this, fearing that Malichus would have him killed if he made objections. But he was sure that Herod would eventually rule in his father's place. What would happen to him then? Herod believed him to have had a part in Antipater's death; and the support he had given Malichus would be taken as proof of his guilt. Once again he appealed to his daughter Alexandra, begging her to allow him to offer Mariamne to Herod at the first sign of Malichus's collapse. Herod would no doubt be delighted, at the beginning of his rule, to ally himself with the Asmonean family; and then he could not be harsh with his new wife's old grandfather. Alexandra consented to this plan, since it matched her own, and now told Mariamne what she intended for her. 'By this marriage,' she said, 'you will probably save your grandfather's life. Yet I would not ask it of you for that reason alone—he has lived a cowardly life and deserves a coward's death. But as Herod's wife you will have ways of avenging the wrongs that our family has suffered and of redeeming our fortunes.'

'If my marriage to Herod will really save my grandfather's life,' Mariamne answered, 'I shall be glad to marry him for that reason alone. Yet, when I become his wife, I will be a true one. I will love him for what is good in him, and try to help him to resist badness; and, as he is cruel and bad, I will accordingly hate him. But I will not carry on any war against him except my own.'

'We shall see about that,' said her mother spitefully. 'The mother of Herod's bride will be a person with whom both Herod and she will have to reckon.'

Mariamne had seen little of Herod up to this time. She remembered that he was thin and sharp-eyed; that his face wore a troubled yet not unkind look; and that he spoke softly—not from timidity, but as if holding back his feelings, in suspicion. 'I hope he will love me,' she told herself.

Hyrcanus was in an ecstasy when he heard that Alexandra

would consent to the marriage. Herod had by now defeated
the supporters of Malichus, and Malichus himself was dead.
Alexandra's brother-in-law Antigonus, who had been living
with the Prince of the independent Itureans, had invaded
Judaea and attempted to rally the scattered forces of Malichus;
but him too Herod had defeated, with the help of his elder
brother Phasaël. While Herod was proceeding in triumph
towards Jerusalem, Hyrcanus wrote to him in an affectionate
style, swearing that he had yielded to Malichus only through
helplessness, protesting his devotion to the dead Antipater and
all his family: he would wish to see the bond between the
two families made permanently secure by a marriage between
his lovely grandchild Mariamne and the son of his old friend
Antipater. Herod did not trust Hyrcanus. But he felt that
for a little while at least it would be well to continue him
in his office of High Priest: too many changes at the beginning would make the people nervous and hostile. As for
Mariamne—he had heard that she was beautiful, and he was
weary of his wife Doris, a stupid and narrow-minded woman
unfit for life at the capital. He had a son by her, who might
become an enemy of the children he would have by Mariamne;
but he trusted to Mariamne's Asmonean blood to justify his
disinheritance of Doris's son. His betrothal to Mariamne
would, he felt, soften the populace toward him. He would
enter Jerusalem with Mariamne at his side, and the sight of
the daughter of the Asmoneans would warm their hearts.

Herod wore a scarlet robe, and Hyrcanus, greeting him,
put garlands on his head. A few noticed that his robe was
caught with a buckle of gold, such as kings used, but because
of the royalty of Mariamne this seemed proper. Mariamne
wore the serpent bracelet that Cleopatra had given her, and
a dress of the rare silken stuff, mixed with threads of gold,
that the women of the island of Cos were skilled in weaving.
The dress was a betrothal present from Cleopatra, who had
also sent a chest full of garments of the finest Egyptian linen.

To Mariamne Cleopatra wrote: 'I shall not wish you happiness, for you frown upon what I call happiness. I wish you therefore a life that you can live nobly. For myself, since Caesar's death I have become more wicked than ever, doing mad things to make me forget him. But I have not yet found a mad enough thing to do: for I remember him. Surely you must hear evil tales of me in Jerusalem. They are probably all true, those you hear. Yet do not believe that I am happy in them. I am surrounded by contemptible beings. I succeed in destroying a few, but that gives me no pleasure. These are not words to address to a good-hearted girl on the eve of her betrothal. Read them, however, as words of affection. If you were here, I should embrace you dearly and weep a little over you and pity you for your goodness. Instead, I give you leave to pity me for my badness. There is a fire in me that burns up the badness —but it burns only when I love someone. You would not call this love, or perhaps you would say that it was evil to wish to love so much. Do you still keep Caesar's bracelet?'

Cleopatra was soon to forget Caesar: for Antony. In 42, at Philippi in Thrace (to which Philip the Great of Macedonia had himself given this name), Antony defeated Brutus and Cassius, the murderers of Caesar, in two successive battles. The young Octavian, Caesar's grand-nephew and adopted son, had an equal share in the command; but the victory was chiefly Antony's work. Since Caesar's death, the political situation in Rome had been confused and dangerous. Antony had been devoted to Caesar, and at the time of his death was Consul with him. Without concealing his grief and horror at the murder, he had managed by delicate political manœuvres to make peace with the senatorial party, which was responsible for it. Then Octavian had challenged his power, and it was not until late in 43 that they were reconciled. Cicero was executed at this time by Antony's order: he had killed Antony's stepfather, and in his orations made violent attacks on Antony himself. Antony had led a disorderly but not an evil life. He had served in many campaigns in the East, and with Caesar in Gaul, and his record was an honourable one. He was handsome and high-spirited—a favourite in gay company, and sometimes the prey of flatterers and seducers. But his vices sprang from warmth of heart, not from vileness of mind; wishing only to love much and be much loved, he did not trouble to measure between love and love. He had divorced his first wife, Fadia, because she became indifferent to him from an excessive affection for their children. His second wife, Antonia, he had divorced because she let the most depraved man in Rome make love to her—Dolabella, whom the sanctimonious Cicero had once defended when he was on trial for his life.

After his second divorce, Antony had consorted with the well-known actress Cytheris, who drove off the parasites and debauchers that had attached themselves to him, and was a loyal and loving friend. Then he married again. And then, when Antony went to Asia after Philippi, to collect money with which to pay his soldiers, he was sought out by Cleopatra, who provoked him to love her in every way of love, both bad and good. From the moment he first saw Cleopatra he began to be a dying man.

Herod did not marry Mariamne until several years after their betrothal. The change of government, with Antony as the new master, precipitated new disorders in Judaea. The enemies of Herod sought to turn Antony against him, pointing out how uncertain he and his father had been in their Roman policy, changing their allegiance with every new leader. But Antony had troubles enough with the remnants of Cassius's garrisons in the East; moreover, his impatience to go to Cleopatra in Egypt made him anxious to avoid entanglement in the internal affairs of Judaea. Herod was obviously the strongest man there, strong enough at any rate to keep all the hostile factions in check if Antony gave encouragement to none of them. Herod for his part swore to serve Antony as his father had served Caesar. He also sent him a present of money, saying at the same time: 'Whenever you are in need and call upon me, I shall help you to my utmost—so long as you succeed in retaining power: no honest man would promise more, unless he were the friend of your heart. I claim no such right, only the humble one of being the friend of your office.' Antony was so charmed by this frankness that he appointed Herod and his brother Phasaël governors of Judaea: this was in 41.

But still the marriage between Herod and Mariamne was put off. This was the more remarkable in that by now Herod loved her passionately, even reverently. One reason for the delay was that he wanted to make himself worthier of her: until all was peaceful in Judaea he would have no time to acquire the refinements that he thought proper to him as her husband. And another reason was that he was too harassed by political cares to be able to fix a sure time for the marriage. The third, and perhaps the strongest, reason was in Mariamne herself: that, wishing to be honourable with Herod, she was glad to have the marriage delayed until she should truly love him. And meanwhile her beauty increased. She was different in appearance from the women of Judaea, having a golden touch in her skin and hair that was sometimes seen in the women across the Jordan. There was indeed a tale in the Maccabean house that its furthest ancestors had lived in Gilead, before settling at Modin. But her grandfather Hyrcanus, who doted on her, said that she shone with the colour of David, and claimed that in his pious researches he had traced their line back to Jesse of Bethlehem, David's father.

Once, chiding her for her primness with Herod, he said that she should use the arts of Rahab on him, the woman of Jericho who was David's ancestress and her own. For Hyrcanus was very anxious for the marriage to take place.

This nonsensical talk greatly angered Mariamne. 'Perhaps it is a grandfather's privilege to talk in this way,' she said. 'But the High Priest of Jerusalem should surely not permit himself such looseness of tongue.'

Hyrcanus was not offended. Chuckling and patting her fondly, he said: 'The very words my mother Alexandra would have used!'

In the year 40 the Parthians began causing trouble both for Antony in Syria and Herod in Judaea. They invaded Syria, and Antony had to tear himself away from the dazzling life that he was leading with Cleopatra. But he achieved little, interrupting the campaign to go to Rome; for certain difficulties had arisen between himself and Octavian. Herod was thus left to deal alone with these wild Easterners.

At Rome Antony was persuaded by his supporters to strengthen his position by marrying Octavian's sister Octavia. Now, before Antony left Italy for the war in Greece in which Brutus and Cassius were defeated, and while he was still under the influence of the actress Cytheris, he had married a woman called Fulvia, who had been twice married before and had lived in a passionate, reckless way but was of loyal and generous heart. Cytheris had urged the marriage, feeling that Antony would be protected by it from hurt if she found it convenient to ally herself with another man. Fulvia's own garish past would make her indulgent to Antony's waywardness; a more respectable woman would have ruined him, driven him back to his old debaucheries.

Fulvia became an ardent defender of Antony's interests, watching over them with an almost maternal jealousy. While Antony was in Egypt her conduct was rash, and unguarded. She entered into a plot against Octavian; but she acted from devotion—and in full awareness of Antony's relations with Cleopatra. At last she was obliged to flee from Italy, and Antony met her at Athens—this was at the time when the Parthian trouble had aroused him from his rapturous idling at Cleopatra's court. Antony was extremely vexed with Fulvia for having meddled so dangerously in his affairs; and she, grieved at having failed to serve him well and at his anger with her, became suddenly old and ill. He took her back to Italy with him and cared for her kindly, but she lived only a few months. It was shortly after her death that he married Octavian's sister Octavia.

Octavia was beautiful and sober-minded; for a time Antony found it restful to be with her, a relief from the feverish atmosphere in which he had lived with Cleopatra. But he knew that he must sooner or later return to Cleopatra. The dissolute women of Rome were like wine to him, darkening the nightmare of life; but a good woman, he told himself, was cruelly like water, awakening him to life and to a painful lucidity. From Cleopatra alone he had what utterly comforted: pure poison, something that put him into a long black sleep.

In 39 Antony returned to the East, the Parthians being still active; but he left the prosecution of the war against them to Ventidius, because he could endure to be away from Cleopatra no longer. Octavia set out with him on the journey, thinking that she might keep him from going to Cleopatra and work upon his mind to defend the honour of Rome in the East. At first Antony seemed glad of her presence, hoping indeed that she would keep him away from Cleopatra for at least as long a time as would be required to suppress the Parthians. But he grew irritable with her, and her patience made him ashamed—until they both agreed, sadly, that it was best that she should leave him to proceed alone.

The trouble which the Parthians caused Herod was serious. In 40, the year before Antony's return to the East, they gave support to Antigonus, Mariamne's uncle, who still survived and had not yet given up hope of regaining the rule of Judaea for the Asmoneans. Antigonus invaded Judaea, having

arranged with the Parthians that they should come to his help
after he had succeeded in entering Jerusalem. It was the time
of the feast of Pentecost, the harvest festival, when the two
offering-loaves were waved before the Lord and given to the
priests, and burnt-offerings laid upon the altar, of lambs of
the first year and other appointed beasts. And it was also
the time of hospitality, when the stranger was admitted to
the family meal. On this custom Antigonus based a cry that
appealed to the populace. As his soldiers approached the
city gates, he made them shout 'Admit the stranger'—
which was a way of saying that the sons of Antipater had
made a stranger of Antigonus the Asmonean.

Herod succeeded in driving Antigonus and his followers
into the precincts of the Temple; but, as the populace was in
an uncertain mood, he consented to Antigonus's proposal that
the Parthians be called upon to settle the dispute. Phasaël,
Herod's brother, offered to go to the Parthians, taking
Hyrcanus with him. They would not dare to touch a priest,
Phasaël said, and Hyrcanus's presence might restrain them
from committing violence on himself. Herod he would not
let go: 'Our father would have wished me to die, rather
than you.'

Then the news reached Herod that the Parthians were holding Hyrcanus and Phasaël prisoners; and, as by this time
Antigonus had succeeded in making his cause popular, promising the liberation of Judaea from Rome, Herod thought
it best to withdraw for a while. Mariamne's mother, Alexandra, would have had her break her contact with Herod and
remain in Jerusalem in Antigonus's protection. But Mariamne
loved Herod all the better for his bad fortune and insisted
upon following him; and her mother, not wishing to leave
Mariamne to become an instrument of Herod's designs against
her house, unwillingly accompanied them into exile. They
went to Idumaea, where Herod lodged them in the fortress of
Masada in his brother Joseph's protection. This Joseph was

a somewhat foolish and untrustworthy person; but Herod had few now in whom he could trust.

In the fortress were Mariamne and her mother and young brother Aristobulus, and Herod's mother, Cyprus, who was very old, and his sister Salome, with whom Mariamne now came into close contact for the first time. Salome was opposed to Herod's marriage with Mariamne, believing her in league with her mother to destroy the family of Antipater. And she envied Mariamne her beauty, being herself thin and swarthy and sharp-featured. Mariamne soon became aware of Salome's hostility. Alexandra urged her to attempt to win Salome's affection by gifts and flattery and humouring. But Mariamne was merely courteous when she could be, and silent when she could not. So began Salome's denunciations of Mariamne to Herod as an overbearing woman who looked down on their family.

Herod at first attempted to get help from the Nabateans, pointing to his own Nabatean blood (through his mother) and the kindness which he had always shown the merchants of Petra. But the Nabateans were pleased that he was in this plight, for he had a great deal of money invested with them. And at the same time he heard that the Parthians had killed Phasaël and sent Hyrcanus back to Jerusalem, where Antigonus had cut off his ears in order that he should be unfit for holy office and therefore no longer useful to Herod. Antigonus was Hyrcanus's own nephew. Yet perhaps he thought himself merciful in doing him no worse injury, since the long enmity between Hyrcanus and Aristobulus, his own father, had broken up the family and made it the prey of usurpers. After mutilating Hyrcanus, he gave him back to the Parthians; who, having no interest in the old man, sent him to live in Babylon. The Jewish community at Babylon received him with honour; he soon settled down to a comfortable life of study and prayer, and held himself happier than he had ever been in Jerusalem.

Herod now resolved to go to Rome and impress upon Antony and Octavian and the Senate the danger to Roman prestige that Antigonus's control of Judaea meant, because of his relations with the Parthians. Passing through Egypt, Herod visited Cleopatra, who was curious to see the man to whom Mariamne was betrothed. Herod was not handsome, but he moved with a brisk grace that pleased Cleopatra: to reduce such a man to languor would be a triumph indeed. Caesar had been strong, but his energies were corrupted by an inward disgust for the times to which he belonged and for himself also as a true man of his times. Antony was an even more typical Roman than Caesar—more shameless in his despair of being a better man than he was. Herod, however, was of another race; he was perhaps a weaker man than either, yet he seemed of newer blood. The legends of the Jews were very old, and their religion taught them to regard their whole story as in the past, with the present an inglorious sequel. But Cleopatra felt that the Jews had not yet begun to live their real story. It was as if Herod had secrets in him that he himself did not know. Could she steal them from him?

They talked together about the situation in Judaea, and about the state of Rome. Cleopatra pretended to regard Antony as lost to her; and she tried to dissuade Herod from his intention of going to Rome. Herod had only his friendly relations with Antony to rely on, and Octavian, she said, was vexed with Antony because he did not get on well with his wife, Octavian's sister. Why not, she urged, stay in Egypt? She would give him an important command. They would reconquer Judaea together—rule it together. Cleopatra did not feel herself disloyal to Mariamne. She thought that Alexandra would certainly not permit Mariamne to marry a man whose fortunes had sunk so low. Nor could she believe that Mariamne loved Herod. He was shrewd, serious, perhaps of good heart; but there was a narrowness in him, a fear of something—his voice was strangely soft for a man of so many harsh traits. But, although she could not believe that Mariamne loved him, she knew—even from his voice—that he loved Mariamne. It was in trying to destroy this love that she was wicked, for in it was all Herod's hope.

4

KING HEROD AND QUEEN MARIAMNE

HEROD hurried away from Cleopatra, embarking at Alexandria for Rhodes. There he stayed some months, communicating with Antony and lavishing gifts on the island, which had been plundered by Brutus and Cassius in the recent war. Where did Herod get the money for this? Some he had brought with him from Idumaea, and he was able to borrow more from the wealthy Jews of the island on the strength of the very friendly letters that Antony sent him from Rome. But the larger part of his resources was from a more mysterious source, of which few knew: jewels and precious ornaments from the tomb of David.

One of the vaults had been opened by an Asmonean high priest of an earlier period; three thousand talents were extracted, with which to bribe the Syrians, who were besieging Jerusalem. Then, at a time when money was sorely needed, Antipater had once persuaded Hyrcanus to go with him to the tomb: it was when Antipater had been confirmed in his authority by Caesar and wished to make him a rich present. The people of Jerusalem were led to believe that the reason for Antipater's visit to the tomb, in Hyrcanus's company, was to swear there an oath of loyalty to the Jews—which indeed he did, to soften the effect of his having sworn allegiance to Rome. But while they were there, attended only by a few priests in Hyrcanus's confidence, a second vault was opened, and from this came the jewelled things that Herod wore in a belt under his robe, bequeathed to him by his father: for not all had been used in purchasing

Caesar's present. Much more treasure yet was said to be stored in the place where David's bones rested—but this was well concealed in the earth, difficult to find. 'I felt that I should be struck dead if I attempted to reach that,' Antipater had said to Herod. 'But one day, if you become King, and require treasure for a work of glory, it would not be improper for you to search for it.' The thought weighed heavily on Herod. Even the jewels about his waist, which he had not himself taken, burned deeply into his body. Nevertheless he used them.

'There is a curse to lift from Judaea,' he told himself, 'a curse of fear. Is it that we keep the Lord too much to ourselves? Surely we would be a happier people if we did not make a secret possession of our sacred knowledge. And perhaps the most fear-ridden one among us is destined to accomplish this—even I, as King of the Jews by the favour of Rome.'

Throughout the months of waiting at Rhodes for a proper time at which to present himself in Rome, Herod was in an exalted mood. He had recognized that there was more contempt than love in Cleopatra's efforts to seduce him, and this added to the warmth of his resolve: he would be such a King of the Jews as even Egypt must honour, as it had honoured Solomon. But Solomon had married an Egyptian princess—Taphnes, daughter of Pesibkhenno: he would not have any woman that was not of his own people. Herod kept strictly to the written Law, and to the practices fixed by the Pharisees; nor would he have lain even once with Cleopatra, or at any time companied with a whore.

At last Herod sailed for Rome. He was introduced to the Senate as a champion of Rome against its enemies in the East, and his father's achievements were cited. Then Antony praised him, so eloquently that he was granted the title of King. When he left the Senate, King of the Jews before the world, Antony and Caesar escorted him to the Capitol, for the offering of sacrifices in celebration of the event; and Consuls and other important personages preceded them on the way. If Herod had come defeated and forlorn, begging the Romans to restore him to his former position in Jerusalem, Antony might have ignored him. But he showed a fiery will, such as the Romans liked to see in a man, with a quick scorn on his lips for those who had brought about his exile. Moreover, the ship that bore him to Italy he had had built for him in Rhodes and fitted in kingly style; and it was loaded with luxuries from the East, like a ship of Solomon's returned from Ophir.

'I passed through Egypt on my way to Rhodes,' Herod told Antony, 'and spoke with Queen Cleopatra there. She would have had me linger with her a while, for she finds life wearisome without you. But I thought that you would have preferred her to endure your absence unconsoled, since impatience seems to ripen her charms and put a glittering bloom upon them.' Herod smiled a little at Antony as he said this, and Antony, looking away and closing his eyes for a moment, smiled also.

A week later Herod returned to the East. His first act was to collect an army to relieve Masada, where Mariamne and his family still were: it had been besieged by the forces of Antigonus and had suffered distress from shortage of provisions and water. Herod succeeded in raising the siege, but the meeting with his relatives was not a happy one. Alexandra sneered when he told them that the Romans had made him King of the Jews. His brother Joseph, who had not managed things well, excused himself by complaining of the quarrels of the women. His sister Salome charged both Alexandra and Mariamne with contemptuous behaviour toward his whole family during his absence. Alexandra replied by accusing her of unkindness to Mariamne, his chosen bride.

They had assembled in the principal hall of the fortress to greet Herod. When Mariamne, unwilling either to answer or endure Salome's insults, rose to go away, the effect was as a solemn renunciation of Herod and his people: he sat king-like in a central chair at one end of the hall, and in leaving them she had to turn her back to him and walk thus a long distance to the door. Alexandra did not stir, waiting to see what Herod would do. Salome looked triumphantly at her brother, pleased that he should witness how Mariamne behaved to them. At first Herod did not know how to interpret Mariamne's withdrawal. Then, suddenly, it seemed to him that it might mean the end of their betrothal. He rushed after her, and they stood talking near the door, the others not hearing what they said.

'You do not hate me because of them?' he asked anxiously. 'If you can only be patient a little longer, I shall be King in Jerusalem and as my Queen you will rule them.'

'Yes, I will be patient now—and after our marriage also,' Mariamne answered. 'But I have no desire to rule your family. Moreover, nothing would stop Salome from trying to injure me.'

'Only love me, do not hate me because of them!' Herod begged.

'If I hate you it will be because of yourself alone. You need fear no trouble from me because of my mother's ambitions, nor because of any unkindness of theirs.'

'But will you love me?' Herod asked with unhappy insistence. 'You know I love you extremely. I am a shell of a man at present, as I am no more than a shell of a king—empty except for two passions: a passion to be dear to you, and a passion to endear the Jews to the world. Let me succeed in the first, and the other will surely prosper, and I shall be a whole man.'

'I had rather you were half a man, and good in that half. That would be enough for me to love. I cannot promise that I will love the whole.'

'You shall, you shall,' Herod whispered excitedly as she

245

passed through the door, feeling that she had promised him enough for all his desires.

The number of those collected in the fortress of Masada, besides soldiers and retainers, was eight. There were Mariamne and her mother, Alexandra, and her young brother Aristobulus, a very beautiful boy; Aristobulus was angelically learned in the holy wisdom, in which old Hyrcanus, his grandfather, had tutored him. Then there was the aged Cyprus, Herod's Nabatean mother; she was in her dotage, querulous, and believed everything against Mariamne that Salome told her—but she died before they left Masada. And Salome herself; and Herod's brother Joseph, whom he had left in charge of the fortress; and a younger brother, Pheroras, the most pleasantly favoured of the family in appearance but somewhat shallow and selfish. Lastly, there was another Joseph, Herod's uncle—the younger brother of his father.

This Joseph was a mild, small-minded man of an amorous disposition. During the time when all resided together in close company in the fortress, he had made advances to Mariamne, of which she took no notice and which indeed he did not mean to be regarded seriously. But Salome thought them provoked by Mariamne; and in spite she resolved to marry Joseph, her own uncle. Joseph was not displeased to be Salome's husband. She had no bodily charms except lustrous black hair—which seemed, because of her embittered character, a sinister thing rather than a beauty. But she was young, and Joseph middle-aged; the marriage flattered and invigorated him.

It was in the year 39 that Herod cleared Idumaea of his enemies and raised the siege of Masada. Then he went into Judaea and camped outside Jerusalem. Here there were Roman troops, with whose help he should have been able to capture the city. But the Roman commander had been bribed by Antigonus to remain inactive; and so Herod went into Galilee, which was now in a turbulent state again, the brigand bands more daring and vicious than ever before.

Having tracked the brigands down and dislodged them from their caves, he executed the most powerful of their leaders. It was difficult, however, to know whom to punish of the population; the simplest-seeming country people might be secretly in league with the chief brigand of the region or with a rival band. When he returned to the south he left a small force behind to keep watch and suppress any new outbreak of brigandage. But he was soon called back and obliged to pacify all Galilee again. He was very angry with the Galileans, angrier than if they had acted as allies of Antigonus. There was no political motive behind their unruliness; there was no motive at all, only a hatred of well-being. 'Perhaps these people should never have been made Jews,' Herod said to himself. 'As heathen they would be easier to reduce—somehow through their knowledge of the Lord they have acquired an intimacy with Satan.'

Antony had by now come to the East, to direct operations against the Parthians. Cleopatra went to Antioch to greet him on his arrival, but stayed with him only a short time, knowing that this fresh sight of her would haunt him during the campaign and make him uneasy until he saw her again. The campaign was a difficult one, for many petty rulers in Syria had been encouraged to rebel by the Parthians. Antony set out for the most remote place of trouble—the town of Samosata in Commagene, to the extreme north of the province, where the local king had renounced his allegiance to Rome.

Ventidius had been ordered by Antony to send two legions to Herod as soon as he had sufficiently humiliated the Parthians. In time the legions were sent, but under so feeble a commander that Herod had little advantage of this help. He decided that he must make a very strong appeal to Antony, and used a way that he had seen his father use with success: he would give help to Antony, who had so far been unable to make the king of Commagene surrender, and thus Antony would have to show enthusiasm for his own cause.

Arriving at Antioch with a small force, his best soldiers, Herod found assembled there a well-equipped Roman army whose officers had put off answering Antony's summons, the difficult journey to Samosata seeming less urgent than the pleasures of Antioch. Herod addressed the officers as an Eastern king and ally of Rome and made them feel ashamed: in a short while he had led them to Antony's assistance, Samosata had fallen, and all the legions in the East were at his service for reward.

Before going to Syria Herod had divided the soldiers he was leaving behind between his brothers Pheroras and Joseph. Some he left in Samaritis in Pheroras's charge; the rest with Joseph in Idumaea. He had told Joseph to avoid serious engagements, but Joseph had disobeyed him and attacked Jericho. In this battle Herod's army had been destroyed, and also the Roman forces that Joseph had called to his support; and Joseph himself had been killed. This was the second brother that Herod lost through the rebellions of the Asmoneans.

Alexandra, during Herod's absence in Syria, had decided that her brother-in-law Antigonus would now triumph over the Idumean usurpers and Rome. She therefore quarrelled so violently with all the members of Herod's family as to make the marriage between Herod and Mariamne seem impossible; and, much against her will, Mariamne was obliged to leave Masada. Alexandra brought Mariamne and Aristobulus to Samaria, which had been a neutral city since Pompey took it away from the Jews and conferred independence on its natives. But Mariamne, loyal to her betrothal, secretly sent a message to Herod on hearing that he had returned from Syria; in this she told him that, in spite of her mother's break with his family and of anything he might hear against herself, she was ready to marry him when he wished.

First of all, on his return, Herod dealt once more with the Galileans, who were again waging brigand-wars among themselves. He might have left this until later, for the doings of the Galileans did not much affect his conflict with Antigonus. But he was easily enraged by them, and it had become a point of honour with him to keep them within bounds. Then, with two of the Roman legions that Antony had allotted to him, he moved on into Samaritis, driving the enemy before him. Soon the entire army that Antony had put at his disposal would reach Judaea, and then he would march on Jerusalem. Meanwhile he went to Samaria where Mariamne was; he had received her message and was resolved that they should be married immediately.

Alexandra was so angered by Mariamne's determination to marry Herod that she left Samaria and went to Jerusalem, to the protection of Antigonus—who was delighted to receive her, feeling that her desertion of Herod's cause would bring him many new supporters. She thought that Mariamne would follow her; Mariamne remained, however, sad to be married among strangers, yet preferring this way to a ceremony at which her mother would have conducted herself scornfully toward Herod's relatives and they resentfully toward both herself and her mother.

The occasion of their marriage was perhaps the only time when there was an equal love between Herod and Mariamne. Herod seemed to be thinking of Mariamne alone—as if the capture or loss of Jerusalem had nothing to do with the joining of their lives. For a little while he did indeed forget Jerusalem. The winning of Mariamne was the first desire in his heart; and in her good-will toward him she allowed herself to believe it the last as well, and to hope that through his love of her she could help him to renounce all that was vain.

Herod took for himself and Mariamne one of the elegant new villas in the Roman style which had been built since the Romans became patrons of the city. The hill of Samaria is somewhat lower than the surrounding hills, which recede gently from it and frame it reverently. It is a place not only of great beauty, but of great strength also, having served as a

fortress in the early days of Israel. First, it was destroyed by
the Assyrians. Then, after four centuries of quiet, Alexander
the Great captured it, killing many of the Samaritan inhabitants
and sending the Jews who still lived there to a near-by district.
He repopulated it with Macedonians from Syria. It remained
in possession of these new colonists until the close of the
second century B.C., when John Hyrcanus the Asmonean
drove out the inhabitants for their cruelty to their Jewish
neighbours and once again destroyed it. So it stood, a half-
ruined place, until Pompey gave it back to the Samaritans.
At the time of Herod's marriage to Mariamne—in the spring
of the year 37—it was still only partly rebuilt. In the weeks
that they spent there together they came to cherish it—
wandering among the ruins in which the springs ran to waste
and lamenting the sorrows of Israel along with those of Judah.

'One day,' Herod said, 'I will make Samaria as glorious as
Jerusalem—the second capital of my kingdom. But first I
must beautify Jerusalem, and make the Temple shine again.'

Mariamne shook her head reprovingly, for he had promised
not to speak of such projects while they were in Samaria.
Even the idea of rebuilding Samaria seemed to her a dangerous and unlucky one. Here Jeroboam had in pious pride set
up a rival kingdom to Judah and the line of Solomon; and
his own line had soon been dispossessed; and then had come
the Assyrians and after them centuries of desolation. 'Do not
awaken the sorrowful past,' she said, 'and let us make no new
sorrows, to embitter the memory which the future shall have
of us.' And, as for glorifying the Temple, she said: 'Leave
that to a happier time, there has been too much shedding of
blood in our own. Did not David forbear for that reason,
which was revealed to the prophet Nathan by an angel? And
so long as Nathan was with Solomon, Solomon also forbore.
And when Solomon did at last rebuild the Temple, afterwards
the new glory of Judah soon faded.'

Herod only said: 'Perhaps you are right, Mariamne. Yet

the Jews have waited so long for peace and glory. Is it never to come?'

'Let us try only for peace,' Mariamne answered, 'and leave the bestowal of glory to the Lord.'

Then, finally, the Roman legions arrived in Judaea and all was ready for the siege of Jerusalem. A curious thing happened on Herod's last day in Samaria. Just as he and Mariamne had left their bed-chamber the floor fell in behind them. The cause was a sudden collapse of part of the terrace on which the house had been built: once the hill had been channelled with trenches, for the management of the waters in which it abounded, and the new house had been put up without sufficient study of the foundation-soil. Herod treated their escape gaily. 'This is surely a sign to me,' he said, 'not to forget my intention to rebuild Samaria—and one day it shall be done.' But Mariamne was uneasy, regarding the incident as an omen. 'Perhaps it marks the end of our happiness—where it began.' She felt now that Herod would certainly take Jerusalem. They would live as royal beings, and her mother would come to her again, and Herod would bring his family from Idumaea; and Salome would renew the old quarrels. As she looked back on Samaria from her carriage, she wondered how much would have happened by the time Herod had built it up again. The new Samaria and the new Jerusalem seemed both to lie beyond her own lifetime.

In July of the same year Herod was able to send the Romans away: his reign in Jerusalem was secure. He dealt severely with the prominent families of Jerusalem that had supported Antigonus, expropriating their wealth and executing many of their members. These executions left forty-five free places in the Sanhedrin, the religious council: which he filled for the most part with Pharisees, because of his oath to his father to favour them and also because it was important to have their support at the beginning of his reign. It was three years since Herod had been declared King of the Jews at

Rome; but only now could he regard himself as King, when he sat enthroned in the Palace of the Asmoneans and had the Temple in his control. He felt most bitter against Antigonus for allowing the Temple to be stained with Jewish blood—for he had not been able to restrain the Romans from carrying the battle into the very holy of holies. Remembering his talk with Mariamne at Samaria and what she had said of the prophet Nathan's warning to David, he did not yet dare to undertake the pious work to which, above all others, he dreamed of giving his name.

Alexandra, with her usual alertness, had abandoned Antigonus as soon as she realized that he could not escape Herod's vengeance. Herod had sent Antigonus to Antony, who was in Antioch, preferring not to punish him himself. Antony was about to go to Rome for a brief visit, and planned to take Antigonus with him, to show him in his triumph. But Herod pointed out the danger of this: if Antigonus were allowed to survive, a prisoner in Rome, he would somehow contrive to escape and make trouble again, as he had done before. Moreover, Herod sent Antony at this time a big present of money for the help he had given him: Antony could not refuse a reasonable request to so generous an ally, and so Antigonus was quietly executed. There were now only two surviving male members of the Asmonean line: old Hyrcanus in Babylon, and young Aristobulus, Mariamne's brother. Alexandra did not much mourn the death of Antigonus, since she could now press Herod to make Aristobulus High Priest—Hyrcanus, being mutilated, could not resume the office.

Mariamne urged Herod to send for Hyrcanus. He was her grandfather, and a gentle, untroublesome person. His presence in the Palace might soften the daily antagonisms; and there was no reason now why he should remain in far exile in Babylon. Herod sent an affectionate and flattering letter to Hyrcanus, on a tablet of brass, addressing him by the name of father and promising him the honourable reception in Jerusalem that his former services to Judaea and his high rank merited. Hyrcanus was happy enough in Babylon. But the thought of seeing his grandchildren again delighted him. He felt, also, that he would be safe from implication in dangerous plots and yet have great importance in Jerusalem as the head of the Asmonean family and the Queen's grandfather. Although he did not look forward to seeing his scornful daughter Alexandra, he told himself that she would now have to treat him more respectfully.

5

CLEOPATRA IN JERUSALEM

ANTONY longed to see Cleopatra again, and wrote to her to come to Antioch: he was about to leave for Italy, to discuss certain difficulties that had arisen between Octavian and himself. On this visit she won a promise from him that he would divorce his wife Octavia while in Italy and marry her on his return. 'Then we will separate the East from Rome and rule it together, and make it the divine half of the world.' But in Italy Antony could not bring himself to speak of divorce to Octavia—partly because it would have angered Octavian, but chiefly because she was kind, uttering no complaint and seeming to understand that his passion for Cleopatra was painful and terrible to him. When he set out for the East she accompanied him, as before: this time at his request, in a last hope of saving himself from Cleopatra's magic. But once more he sent her back again before they came into Eastern waters. On her return to Rome her brother began to be indignant with Antony. But, defending him, she said: 'We are all leading lives different from those we would lead if we could start again. Antony seems more perverse than the rest of us because he rushes on faster to his end. But I am not sure that we who go more slowly, trying to give our lives a natural look from day to day, are really the more virtuous in that.'

Again, upon his arrival, Cleopatra hurried to greet Antony. He was planning to invade the Parthian Empire and inflict upon the Parthians a final punishment from which they would be unable to recover; and a great army had been assembled and splendidly equipped for this purpose. But he lingered with Cleopatra, letting nearly the whole year pass. Sometimes they were at Antioch, where Cleopatra held court as if she were the Queen of Syria as well as of Egypt; sometimes they went on journeys together, like monarchs inspecting their realm. And all the while Cleopatra kept urging Antony to grant her territories for the enlargement of Egypt—since it was easier to get them by gift from Antony, for their future empire, than it would be to win them later from Rome itself. Thus she added to Egypt the region of the independent Itureans to the west and south of Damascus. She also pressed for large parts of the Nabatean kingdom, but this would have involved Antony in a difficult war—and he had not yet lost all sense of his obligations to Rome. However, Antony presented her requests to the Nabateans, and, being themselves anxious to avoid a war, they yielded certain valuable lands to the east of the Red Sea. Finally, Cleopatra begged Antony to make Herod yield a part of Judaea to her. This fever of acquisition came of her desire to reconstitute the Greater Egypt of her ancestors.

Antony wrote frankly to Herod about her demands, not as one giving an order but as one asking for advice. He felt that Herod would understand that he loved Cleopatra and wished to please her; that he was reluctant, nevertheless, to lose the friendship of the King of the Jews; and that Cleopatra, as Queen of Egypt, with a powerful army at her command, could cause trouble both to Rome and Judaea if she were crossed. In this dilemma Herod acted so discreetly that he was able to relieve Antony of anxiety without losing much himself.

Herod wrote to Antony saying that he would make a gift to Cleopatra of the rich district of Judaea that she desired, in memory of her kindness when his enemies had driven him from Jerusalem and in token of the affection which existed between her and his beloved wife Mariamne. If Cleopatra would honour them with a visit on her way back to Egypt, they could then decide together as to the manner in which this property should be conveyed to her. When, toward the close of 36, Antony at last set out to invade the Parthian Empire, Cleopatra began her return journey to Egypt; and she stopped at Jerusalem, as Herod had asked, to make arrangements about her new property, and to see how Herod and Mariamne were getting on together, and also to have some talk with her old friend Alexandra, Mariamne's mother.

As she approached Jerusalem, on her left the valleys of Jehoshaphat and of the Kedron, and the valley of Hinnom on her right, she looked at the city with a shudder of distaste. It was now the rainy season, and all colour had gone from the hills. This was the bloodless grey that she associated with the faith of the Jews—a god of clouds, frowning and solitary, hidden from the living and dead alike. At the fork of the valleys stood the mountain home of Herod and his people, and all the hills round about seemed to watch it with a fierce, gloomy love, as if they knew of outrages from which they could not save it. 'The hearth of God', the Jews called it. But Cleopatra could only feel it as the home of a homeless people. 'They will not taste of a fruit if they know there is a worm in it.' As she said this to herself she thought of Herod, who had refused her love, and set her mouth in a thin, smiling line. Surely that had been from fear: now he could not dare to be afraid of her, nor yet could he dare to deny her exquisite courtesies and compliments. But she had not made up her mind how she would behave to Herod— much would depend on Alexandra and Mariamne, and his own manner to her.

The nearer she drew to the city, the higher seemed the eminence on which it was built; and, though she had resolved to despise it and everything and everyone in it, she could not help feeling an uncomfortable stir of awe as she passed through the northern gate, that had been newly gilded for her coming. To the west the city rose steadily to an abrupt height, and on that side only a few severe buildings stood. The approach to the Temple and the Palaces was through the eastern part, on the hill of Moriah, separated from the upper city by a sharp ravine. The street along which her carriage and train of camels proceeded was a spacious thoroughfare, with fine colonnades on either side, where the road was raised for pedestrians. In ordinary times people of the lower classes were not permitted to walk here, but on this day everyone was driven off the central way, which was left clear for Cleopatra and her train and those who had gone out to meet her.

The procession passed outside the Temple, where the priests were waiting. They greeted Cleopatra respectfully, but also as if standing guard lest she should attempt to enter: 'The doors of the Lord are closed to the heathen,' they seemed to say. And then she was conducted to the Palace of the Asmoneans, which stood upon a cliff where the upper city rose sharply above the lower: facing somewhat to the south, somewhat to the east, with a few gardened terraces softening the edge. The house was of cedar, even as King David's had been, but the tower that protected it was of stone; and from the cellar of this tower a winding tunnel led into the subterranean parts of the Temple, where the treasure-stores were and the reserves of water.

Herod had not gone out to meet Cleopatra himself: he waited for her with Mariamne and Alexandra at the Palace. And this was the first thing that annoyed her—besides the feeling that the very sight of Jerusalem forced upon her, of being looked at by hidden, disapproving eyes. The members of Herod's royal council had greeted her at the gate; and within the city the members of the Sanhedrin had approached her slowly from the heights and then turned again to escort her past the Temple to Herod's palace. With the men of the Sanhedrin came Hyrcanus: he was the first who smiled to her. 'I am the father of your friend Alexandra,' he said, as if to put her at her ease; and she liked him for this, and smiled back sweetly, which ravished him. At the Temple itself, the High Priest had stepped out from the other priests and gone before her to the Palace: as occupying the second office of importance in the kingdom, it was his task to present Cleopatra to Herod. This was Ananel, a very modest man and a conscientious priest, whom Herod had appointed on his return to Jerusalem. He came from Babylon, and had been loyal to Herod throughout the rebellion; and since his appointment had discouraged disputes and rivalry between the religious factions. Alexandra frowned as she watched him lead Cleopatra up the Palace steps, down which Herod was slowly descending to meet her: for she coveted his place for her young son Aristobulus.

After embracing Mariamne and Alexandra, and being greeted by Salome and Joseph and Aristobulus and Pheroras, Cleopatra retired to rest in the apartments that had been prepared for her. And here Alexandra came soon afterwards, secretly, lest Herod should be angered at her being the first to speak in private with the Egyptian Queen. Cleopatra listened sympathetically to Alexandra's complaints. 'Come with me to Egypt,' she said, 'away from this desolate place.' For it seemed to her that no one could be happy in Jerusalem. And Cleopatra meant her invitation sincerely; she was generous in hospitality, and would have liked to have a friend near her while Antony was away, there being no one in her court with whom she could be safely intimate. But Alexandra was thinking of hereditary glories denied to her and hers, glories that could have no other setting than Jerusalem. This Cleopatra could not have understood. Nor could she have understood that being in Jerusalem made Mariamne's difficult life with Herod endurable to her—Cleopatra had known from one glance at Mariamne that she was not happy.

'Tell me!' Cleopatra said to Alexandra. 'Surely Jerusalem has declined sadly since that Arabian queen came to visit

Solomon? For, by all the tales, she was mad with pleasure to be in it.'

'I know nothing of that,' Alexandra answered. 'But it has certainly fallen from greatness since the usurpers stole it from my family.'

'But are there perhaps secret beauties underground, within the hills on which it is built? Come, I would not betray your confidence, you know!'

Alexandra shook her head. 'There is only what you see.'

'But the Temple? Is there not something terrifying and wonderful in the place you call the holy of holies?'

'There is a golden altar, and the candlestick of light, and the table of the shewbread, and precious pouring vessels and vials, and censers and crowns and ornaments of gold and silver.'

'Nothing more? What of your Lord—does your Lord not come there?'

'In the holy of holies our Lord is reverently invoked; more I cannot tell you.'

And Cleopatra felt that the secret of Jerusalem was being kept from her.

After Cleopatra had rested and eaten, Herod and Mariamne took her to see the chief sights of the city. She was shown the sepulchres of the kings, cut deep into the eastern side of Moriah, and the principal city gardens, which were also on this side, facing the valley of the Kedron; and the precious spring near the village of Siloam, which was also here. Then, going northward and turning a little to the east, they conducted her through the groves of the garden of Gethsemane, a place of which they were very proud: it lay at the foot of the Mount of Olives, the most fruitful hill of any thereabouts. But Cleopatra thought it a mean place, by contrast with what she had expected to find at Jerusalem. What was the secret? What was being held back from her? Could Mariamne perhaps be prevailed upon to talk more freely than Alexandra —or Herod himself?

In the evening Herod and Cleopatra withdrew from the others to discuss the property that had been ceded to her. Now, this was in the district of Jericho, and consisted of rich palm-groves and balsam-gardens: Herod would certainly lose by its transference to Cleopatra. But he had thought of a way of redeeming the loss—if Cleopatra could be persuaded that she would gain by it. He had come to her apartments for this talk, and was sitting at the foot of the couch on which she was reclining. She studied him as he spoke, thinking more of the changes in him since she had last seen him than of her palm-groves and balsam-gardens. He was no handsomer—and even leaner. But he was really a king now, and what had before seemed mere slyness and mistrust had become a majestic reserve. There were clearly purposes in him of which he told no one, and which he never put aside. What had they to do with the secret of Jerusalem? What part did Mariamne play in them?

He was speaking of the difficulty that she would have in managing these new groves and gardens of hers, in the heart of a country not her own. The people of the region might, in ignorance, be hostile, and resent his own efforts to protect her interests. Suppose he administered the property on her behalf, guaranteeing her a yearly income of two hundred talents? Then the inhabitants would not be troubled by foreign collectors; for all they knew, the money might be a private gift from himself to her, in token of the friendly relations existing between the two countries. Cleopatra nodded carelessly in consent—to-morrow the pact could be inscribed on a tablet. Her private feeling was one of relief. By such an arrangement she would be saved the trouble of supervising the region herself; and Herod would be every year recognizing her superior authority in paying this tribute, itself a pleasant addition to her revenues.

Then Herod went on, in his low, cautious voice: perhaps he might assist her also with the lands that the Nabateans had ceded to her. He had indeed conferred with them on the matter, and was prepared to guarantee her a further two hundred talents yearly income from these lands; he would come to a separate arrangement with the Nabateans, to protect himself against loss. And again Cleopatra nodded. She knew that for herself the double bargain was a good one. Herod's motives in proposing it were not clear. He was obviously a shrewd driver of bargains—but was there not something else behind this? Could this be the Jewish way of love-making?

Herod had of course weighed his own advantages carefully. In intervening thus between Cleopatra and the Nabateans, he would have a hold on them that would be useful in the future; if he did not succeed in collecting from them every year all the money which he had promised on their behalf, he would acquire a power of influencing their policy toward both Judaea and Rome. As for the lands near Jericho: he had for some time been intending to increase the revenue they yielded by introducing a more succulent date, and by sending travellers to all the cities of the East to make the Jericho balsam even more famous than it was, as an unguent for wounds and a cure for disorders of the stomach. Pompey had brought its fame to Rome, carrying a jar of it in a triumphal procession. And Herod saw that the very yielding of the gardens to Cleopatra would make the balsam more talked of everywhere. 'Let me send you some of these plants,' he said, 'for your own gardens: their fragrance is worthy of you. With great care a few might be kept alive in your climate—in our country it is only in the plains of Jericho that they flourish. And it would be proper that you should accept these as a gift from me, for it is said among us that an earlier king of our people had the plant as a gift from a foreign queen.' This reference to Sheba's visit to Solomon made Cleopatra dare to take Herod's hand.

'Let there be affection between us, Herod,' she said. 'You

are as cold with me as if I had evil designs against you—yet I swear I want nothing but happiness between your country and mine. It seems to me that you Jews care nothing for happiness, and despise those that do. Come! Be easier with me.' But Herod sat rigid, and a fine sweat appeared on his forehead, whether of fear or anger she could not tell. Cleopatra sprang up from the couch and brought a large basket near, fastened with a silver lock and strengthened with silver rods. Then she reached for a flute that lay on a little table and sat down on the couch again. She began to play, with a softness that made Herod want to run from the room and at the same time paralysed him.

Something in the basket stirred; Cleopatra opened the lid and continued playing. The head of a serpent rose from the shadowy depth of the basket, higher and higher, in a tremulous perpendicular. Then the head slanted smilingly, and the body circled after it like some twisted tree of Africa waking from its sleep. The serpent slid upon Cleopatra's lap; she stopped playing and began to hum—two notes, over and over. The head shot up, to the level of her eyes, and Herod saw the fangs flash. She stopped humming, holding the serpent's look with her eyes alone. Suddenly Herod gasped out in horror. Cleopatra seized the asp by the tail and whipped it away from her, letting it drop then into the basket, which she closed and fastened again.

'That might have meant my death,' she said. 'I can only hold him so when there is absolute silence: I thought you realised that.' Herod continued to stare at her. 'Was it so frightening? But the asp is a sacred emblem of immortality! Surely, then, it is fitting that a queen should know how to master it?'

Cleopatra was by now growing angry. But she must not let Herod see this. She began to laugh, hoping to break Herod's taut poise and bewilder him into surrender. She knew that she was behaving foolishly now, but could not stop herself. Running to another basket, a lidless one, she bent over it tenderly. And just then Alexandra entered, followed by Mariamne and Salome.

'We have come to bid you good night, dear Cleopatra,' Alexandra said. 'Perhaps you have finished your talk with Herod by now?' Alexandra concluded from Herod's strained look that Cleopatra had defeated him over the bargain that she knew he had been planning, and the thought pleased her. 'What have you been doing to turn my son-in-law so pale?' she asked tauntingly. Herod sent Mariamne a beseeching look, and she decided instantly that his paleness was not due to his having had the worst of the bargain.

Cleopatra continued to laugh. 'I have been showing Herod my pets. I never travel without my asp and my cat. The asp is for immortality, as I have just been explaining to Herod, and the cat for the Moon, the Great Mistress of the Future.'

By now Cleopatra's cat had come out of its basket and jumped on to the couch. It was black, golden-eyed, slender and small-headed; it sat high, its long straight front legs close together, as in the sacred images of cats. Only the very tip of its long tail twitched a little: the rest was indeed still as an image. It seemed posed to be so looked at, absorbing the gaze of the four women and Herod without allowing itself to be aware of them.

'You have no cats in Jerusalem, I suppose?' asked Cleopatra. 'You do not look into the future here?' Herod shuddered. Mariamne's face flushed sternly: she was ashamed of Herod's behaviour, but she was also coldly enraged with Cleopatra for attempting to work her strange arts upon the King of the Jews and the husband of her friend.

Salome said: 'There are wild-cats, I have heard it told, in the eastern part of our country. But no, there are no pet cats in Jerusalem—and recently we have had too many troubles to be able to think of such pretty distractions.' This was insincerely spoken, with a hateful glance at Mariamne. And

Mariamne, enraged with Cleopatra though she was, could not but smile that she should be accused of being the cause of there being no cats in Jerusalem.

'Why do you smile, Mariamne?' Cleopatra asked.

'There is no need to explain that,' Mariamne answered, looking at Cleopatra fully and unsmilingly. 'Cleopatra! You have come here as our royal guest, and my husband is honoured to be your host. And I looked forward to seeing you myself, for I remembered your kindness to me, and Caesar's, when I visited you, and your sending me lovely gifts on my betrothal to Herod. Yes, I thought of you with love, as a woman who did wicked things but with the delight of a child, not caring whether they were wicked or good, thinking only of pleasure, and then vexed with herself because the wickedness always spoiled the pleasure. Either you have changed, or I was too young to understand you then. But I see you now as a woman who wills beforehand to be wicked.'

Salome and Alexandra both turned upon Mariamne, for once united in feeling: 'How dare you speak to the Queen so!'

Herod, shaken out of the trance of horror, went up to Cleopatra and spoke in his natural voice: 'Forgive her. She is with child, and speaks wildly sometimes.' To all the women he said: 'Be so good as to leave us: we had not yet finished our talk. You are all over-excited by the extraordinary honour that the Queen has paid us in visiting us. To-morrow there will be time for more intimate interviews.' For he was now anxious lest Mariamne's outburst should make Cleopatra less complaisant in the matter of the palm-groves and balsam-gardens and the Nabatean lands.

But Cleopatra hissed back: 'Leave me alone with Mari-amne!' Herod and Alexandra and Salome withdrew, unwillingly, all intensely displeased with her, and each for a different reason. And the cat sat on motionless, except for the twitching of the very tip of its tail now and then.

Cleopatra tried gentleness. 'Why do you judge me so severely? Why should you think I am even more wicked than I was?'

'Herod's face told me that you had frightened him, and I was angry, because you should have known that he is not a proper subject for your arts: I do not say this merely because I am his wife. And something in the eyes of the cat made me see you as a huge heathen goddess, forgotten, no longer worshipped—and she has forced herself into your little body in order to make men look at her, and fear and adore her. . . .'

Cleopatra cried: 'Stop! I'll kill you!' She had seized a dagger from the couch—being accustomed always to have some weapon near to protect herself from a treacherous slave or courtier.

Mariamne was too shocked by her own strange language to take notice of Cleopatra's threat. 'What terrible things I have said. The cat has put a spell on me. It's the cat—the cat!'

'Stop! I'll kill you!' There were two screams—and the second was nearly lost in the first. The first was Cleopatra's: she had thrown herself at the couch and now lay crumpled on the floor. The second might have been hers also, or it might have been the death-screech of the cat as she plunged the dagger into it.

Mariamne would have fled from the room. Cleopatra rose and held her back. 'You can't leave me,' she whispered, tearing Mariamne's net head-dress in the violence with which she caught at her. 'In Egypt those who do what I have done are put to death: no one must ever know of this. My life shall now be an unlucky one, whether it is known or not. But because of this I shall be free of all prudence, and so truly happy.'

'What is it you wish me to do?'

'Get me spices and salts and all that is necessary for embalming. For I must take it back with me and bury it at

Bubastis, as is our custom. But no one must know how it died. I must do the work with my own hands. Go, get me these things somehow. I do not blame you. If it should ever happen that I harm you in some way, it will not be in revenge, but because I have given myself utterly to wickedness. As you said: I shall will beforehand to be wicked in what I do. I am beginning to feel happy again already. This accursed city—I did not think it would give me so sweet a thing as entire freedom from goodness!'

When at last Mariamne reached her bed-chamber, she found Herod pacing the floor nervously in his sleeping-wrapper. He stared at her dumbly: fearing to ask what had happened—noticing that her head-dress was torn and that the fringe of her robe was blackened as if she had been walking in the cellars.

Mariamne spoke first. 'Cleopatra leaves us early in the morning.'

'Then the bargain is off! I should have humoured her—then this would not have happened. But I knew she wished me to lie with her, and the thought filled me with revulsion. Oh, Mariamne, what have you done? You could have humoured her more easily than I. She will now try to turn Antony against me, and persuade him to give her other districts of Judaea. And your mother will encourage her in this, for my ruin; and my sister will lay the blame of it on you and spread rumours of this.'

'You do not speak as a king should, nor as I should like to hear my husband speak. The bargain is not off: Cleopatra's secretary stays behind. I have sworn to her that I would say nothing of what happened between us. It did not concern you—and indeed, if you heard it, you might laugh, though I could not.'

Herod sighed with relief and looked more tenderly at Mariamne. 'I'm sorry that you should have been upset. She's a heathen beast—and every word you said of her was true.'

'I was angry with her for having tried to play with you: I could see that she had. But I think also that you should have conducted yourself toward her with more grace, instead of shivering in outraged virtue. You make virtue seem a craven thing. After all, you knew what sort of woman she is. I am weary of you all.' And Mariamne withdrew to an inner chamber, to be undressed by her maid.

Herod, waiting in bed, thought to himself: 'Sometimes what Salome says of her seems the truth. She is an Asmonean, and will perhaps always despise me as a commoner. But it will be better when the child is born. If it is a boy, he shall be my heir—and then she must surely love me for all I do, since I shall be working only for the glory of the kingdom which will be his.

Soon after this a child was born to Mariamne, a boy. They called him Alexander, after Mariamne's father. And this angered Salome, who would have had Herod give him a name used in their own family. She was also angered by her husband Joseph's increased affection for Mariamne and his delight that there should be an infant in the Palace—they had no child of their own yet, and she was beginning to regret that she had married so old a man. It was at this time that she made up her mind to rid herself of Joseph by setting Herod against him.

6

THE LAST SCION OF THE ASMONEANS

ANTONY did not succeed in humiliating the Parthians, and returned from his expedition to the East in great dissatisfaction with himself. He knew that the cause of his failure was his impatience to be back with Cleopatra: he had relied on his old good luck and brilliance in the field, but the campaign had been difficult and intricate, requiring a patience that he had long lost. Now gossiping tongues would wag more maliciously than ever against him in Rome, and Octavia would grieve quietly for his sake—it was this that made him most uneasy. But Cleopatra went to Antioch, where he rested after his return, and persuaded him that the reason for his defeat was insufficient support and encouragement from Rome: when their interests were united they would manage things better. She gave Antony money to distribute to his troops, which renewed their loyalty; and advised him to try one more campaign yet before breaking finally with Rome. The Armenian King had not helped him against the Parthians as he had promised: here was an excuse for invading Armenia and extending their empire northward from Syria, beyond the Taurus mountains.

Meanwhile, in return for her generosity, Antony gave Cleopatra the jurisdiction of further lands on the eastern borders of Syria. And there was another favour that she asked of him at this time: she longed to possess the royal library of Pergamum, to replace what had been lost of her own during Caesar's siege of Alexandria. She pressed Antony to obtain this for her now, while he could still act as the representative of Rome in the East. He immediately sent agents to Mysia, to take possession of the library and to present to the city a large sum of money, which he had from Cleopatra, lest a complaint be made about the matter to Rome. The existence of a rival library at Pergamum had long irritated the Ptolemies; consequently, in acquiring it, Cleopatra ended an old story. When the volumes reached her, she had them searched for certain missing manuscripts of Aristotle, but none were found. The second Ptolemy had bought a collection of Aristotle's works from a family in Mysia, the descendants of a relative of Theophrastus, to whom Theophrastus bequeathed the volumes and manuscripts that Aristotle had left him in his will; and it had long been thought that the most precious pieces of the collection had been held back and secretly sold to the King of Pergamum.

'Perhaps it is just as well,' Cleopatra wrote to Antony about this matter. 'For the scholars who flock to my library to study the works of this philosopher will continue to delight themselves with fancies about the missing treatises—whereas surely if they were discovered they would be found to be little different from the others, and Alexandria would be the poorer in clever discourse and speculation. For myself, I am content that there should be no more of the works of Aristotle, for I have always thought him like a man who made laws for a kingdom, and had none; and as for his notions of virtue, those too seem to me to be like rules for being thought virtuous while acting with smallness of heart. My own heart is large, as you know, and so by Aristotle's measure I am a monster. I think that if I were determined to be virtuous I should become a Jew: Jews at least make it so difficult a thing to be that it would be worth the attempt, if one's heart were stiff as well as large. Though I hate these people, I cannot help admiring them for their extremeness in reverencing what they call the Law: I would do nothing myself except extremely. All the truly serious philosophers, such as Pythagoras and Plato, have borrowed from the Jews their idea of a supreme truth—in combating the looseness of Homer, in whom there is neither thought nor mention of Law. But this Aristotle has cut up truth into mean morsels, for the convenience of mean appetites. I have been very wicked in my life, but always with sincerity, and so am not to be deceived by those who make a learned hypocrisy of virtue.' Then she went on to speak of affairs at Jerusalem.

Alexandra had written to Cleopatra, begging her to persuade Antony to make Herod appoint young Aristobulus to the office of High Priest, in Ananel's place. The letter had been brought to Egypt by a distinguished musician in Alexandra's service; her excuse to Herod for sending him was that Cleopatra desired to improve her own musicians in playing on the harp. When the musician returned to Jerusalem, he bore a letter from Cleopatra, in which she advised Alexandra to send a portrait of Aristobulus to Antony, and also one of Mariamne.

Antony, having set out for the Armenian campaign, had gone only as far as Laodicea. Reports had reached Cleopatra that he was spending all his time there dallying with women. But she was not incensed with him because of this—she knew that without such distractions he would sink into a dull despair and lose all. Indeed, when he left for the Parthian campaign she had paid several courtesans of good character to accompany him, and also two boys of beautiful figure and soft ways. Her plan now was to tempt Antony to send for Aristobulus and Mariamne : she would rather have him amuse himself with one or the other or both than with the women of Laodicea, who, according to the reports, were robbing him of money as well as energy. Herod was so greedy for power, she felt, that, though he loved Mariamne, he might not dare to incur Antony's enmity by refusing to send her to him; and he might be pleased to have the boy out of the way. She had not told her whole plan to Alexandra, in suggesting the presentation of the portraits, but merely said that they might make him look the more favourably on her petition. What was in Alexandra's mind in sending Antony the portrait of Mariamne as well as that of Aristobulus, we cannot be sure.

And this is how Cleopatra wrote to Antony: 'My friend Alexandra, Herod's mother-in-law, has informed me that all is not well in Jerusalem; and I know that it would be an annoyance and even a danger to you, if trouble broke out there now requiring your attention. Apparently the supporters of the old Asmonean line are greatly dissatisfied in having a foreign Jew for High Priest, when there exists a proper candidate in the person of young Aristobulus, Alexandra's son, now of age. Yet some of these fanatics who wish the foreign Jew removed are anti-Roman in sentiment, and I am not altogether sure to what degree they ought to be encouraged. Perhaps it would be best for you to see the boy for yourself and discover what his own sentiments are. I have heard, by the way, that he is amazingly beautiful. His sister Mariamne, Herod's wife, is also very beautiful, though of a cold and haughty nature. Perhaps it would interest you to see the pair of them, since you are so long held up in Laodicea and time must go wearily there. The mother could escort them to you, so that Herod need find nothing improper in the visit. And I should be amused to learn that you had successfully besieged the virtue of the proud Jewess, who leads a very drab life in Jerusalem and might be overborne by the magnificent entertainment you would undoubtedly provide for them.'

Shortly after this letter reached Antony the portraits of Aristobulus and Mariamne arrived, brought by the same musician who had visited Egypt. However, although Alexandra had arranged all this very secretly, Herod learned of the sending of the portraits from a slave of hers, called Aesop, whom he had charged to report to him anything of a mysterious kind that went on in her palace—Herod had recently assigned to her a separate dwelling, because he could no longer endure the quarrelling between her and Salome. He said nothing about the matter, not wishing Alexandra to be aware that she was watched, but felt certain that he would in time hear something from Antony which would throw light on Alexandra's action.

Soon Herod received a letter from Antony, in which he wrote that reports had come to him of discontent in Jerusalem with the present High Priest, and of a desire in many that the office be given to Aristobulus, who had a blood-right to it. 'I do not wish to interfere in your conduct of affairs in Judaea,' Antony wrote, 'but I think it best that you should know what is being said abroad: it would do neither of us any good if complaints were made in Rome. Perhaps it would be wise to send the young man, your brother-in-law, to me. Then, if there were any difficulty with Rome over the matter, I could say that I had talked with the candidate of your enemies and found him unsuitable. But, should this suggestion give offence, disregard it. At all times, however, I should be delighted to welcome any member of your family —and yourself especially. It would not be fitting that you should leave your kingdom just now to visit me, if what I hear of affairs in Jerusalem be true. Yet your wife and mother-in-law might with propriety pay me a visit on your behalf, bringing Aristobulus with them: which would remind the unruly kings of the East that Rome has powerful allies near at hand, and also increase your own prestige.'

Herod smiled sourly to himself as he read this letter. He was not angry with Antony, whom he pitied deeply, as a man who would before long be lost. And he felt no new anger against Alexandra, though she seemed ready to sell her own children: he had always known that she would commit any crime to do him harm. As he read, he guessed that Cleopatra herself was behind Alexandra's plan, and quietly came to a decision. But he would keep the story from

Mariamne, who was again with child and might be distressed if she knew the truth. The next day he announced Aristobulus's appointment as High Priest in place of Ananel. Alexandra was astonished at Herod's sudden change of policy, and because he gave no reasons grew suspicious. Then Herod invited Aristobulus to live in his own palace, instead of with his mother: which added to her nervousness. To Antony Herod wrote: 'Judging that you wished me to do so, I have made Aristobulus High Priest: it is therefore impossible that he should visit you.' Of Antony's reference to Mariamne he made no mention; but he did not forget it.

Herod, who had previously paid little attention to Aristobulus, now discovered a warm affection for him. He was very like Mariamne and indeed beautiful, and in a way not disgraceful in a boy. He was also learned in all that his office required: Hyrcanus had continued to instruct him after his return from Babylon. And his mind was innocent of his mother's plots and hates. Mariamne was pleased with this new fondness between Herod and Aristobulus. For there was nothing in it of scheming or ambition—Herod's feelings for Aristobulus were such as she would have liked him to hold for their own child. Salome loathed to see another Asmonean become so dear to Herod, and blamed Mariamne afresh for turning Herod against his own family.

Then came the Feast of Tabernacles—the first great feast at which Aristobulus officiated. All Jerusalem was charmed by his grace and dignity; Herod was overjoyed with him. When the Feast was over, he took the whole family to Jericho to celebrate Aristobulus's success and gave a banquet there in his honour. But Alexandra remained mistrustful, and Salome's disapproval was so severe that she refused to go with them to Jericho.

After the banquet they rested, the afternoon being extremely hot. Then, towards evening, Herod went with Aristobulus and a few others to the fishponds, all playing together like boys, splashing and ducking one another merrily. But Herod soon tired and, having put on his robes again, lay down upon a marble bench in the garden near the pools. He was thinking that perhaps they might all live happily together now if Salome could be reconciled to Mariamne and her family, when frightened cries rose from the pool. And the cause was, as he soon learned with horror, that Aristobulus had been drowned.

Alexandra was of course grieved by the death of her only son. She was quick, however, to make use of her loss against Herod. To Mariamne it seemed that she almost rejoiced to have, at last, something heinous of which to accuse him. Those who were at the pools swore that Herod was not near when Aristobulus died; Herod himself said nothing, being sorrowfully aghast at what had happened. Mariamne was sure that he had done Aristobulus no harm. But she felt that they were all behaving grossly and selfishly: her mother making use of the occasion for ugly vengefulness; Hyrcanus sobbing like a child and behaving during the seven days of mourning as if no one lamented Aristobulus so much as himself; Herod consoling himself by giving Aristobulus the most expensive and ostentatious funeral possible; Salome silent with satisfaction. Only Joseph, Salome's husband, behaved easily, perhaps because he had little reason to feel strongly about Aristobulus's death. During these days Mariamne grew tolerant of his doting affection for her, which up to now she had found repulsive and annoying. The whole family thought Mariamne heartless because she did not wail over Aristobulus's death. Soon after he was buried her second child was born; he was named Aristobulus.

Herod summoned all who had been in the pond with Aristobulus and questioned them separately in private. There were seven. Six swore that the seventh had been far out in the pond with Aristobulus, apart from the rest; that it had seemed to them that in ducking Aristobulus he had held him longer under water than was safe. Then there had been a great splashing about, so that they could not tell what was happening. And then the seventh had cried out that Aristobulus had disappeared. The seventh would only say that Aristobulus had suddenly gasped, clutching his heart as if it ached, and fallen into the water: when he pulled him out he was dead. Herod threatened the man with torture if he did not say more. Thereupon he confessed that Salome had engaged him to kill Aristobulus at Jericho.

When Herod challenged Salome with the man's story she spoke out freely and indignantly. Yes, she had caused Aristobulus's death. Herod was blind, she said, bewitched by Mariamne. He did not see that in elevating the heir of the Asmoneans to the priesthood he was preparing for his own downfall: the love that Aristobulus had inspired in the populace would soon have been used by Herod's enemies against himself. Salome was so eloquent in her denunciations and professions of loyalty that he was half-persuaded that she was right. When she pointed out how little Mariamne had said about Aristobulus's death and swore that her restraint must cover a hostile design, he was tempted to agree that Mariamne kept her feelings too much hidden.

While he was still in the doubtful state of mind produced by his talk with Salome, he received a letter from Antony, who was still in Laodicea, summoning him to give an account of Aristobulus's death. Clearly, Alexandra had been at work. He was obliged to answer Antony's summons. He appointed Joseph to be regent during his absence, and told him to make the protection of Mariamne and her children his first care. But, guessing that Cleopatra was leagued with Alexandra against him, he feared that he might be going to his death. He therefore made Joseph promise that, in the event of his being killed by Antony, Mariamne also should be killed: for he felt sure that Cleopatra would rejoice to see Mariamne made Antony's whore, his camp-woman. 'Breathe this to no one,' he said, 'and, if I return alive, speedily forget it. You cannot doubt that I love Mariamne madly. I shall die more easily knowing that she will not survive me to be thrown to Antony by Cleopatra for a plaything. I have good reason for supposing this to be Cleopatra's intention.'

It was during this period that Herod began to spend hours studying himself. He felt that he was made up of many opposite things, which perhaps would never mix happily together. Once he had known only two parts in himself: his love for Mariamne and his desire to make Judaea great. These had seemed simple things to reconcile, though Mariamne had not thought so. But now even his love for Mariamne was broken into conflicting feelings, and his hopes for the future of his kingdom were crossed by continuous vexations with the Jews themselves. The Jews wished for greatness, yet suspected everything that might be an instrument for achieving it. No sooner had he brought about something fortunate than, suddenly, prophecies began to circulate about a holy man that would arise to save them. From what? From success in what they most vaunted: the glory of their faith and of their land. There were waves of religious frenzy and restlessness, as if the Jews were tired of being Jews in the old way. And yet, when he tried to give them new ways, they turned against him. 'Oh, my poor people,' he would say to himself. 'When they left Egypt they started on a long journey, of which the goal will perhaps not be seen in my lifetime.'

On arriving at Laodicea, Herod found Antony preoccupied with military affairs and less concerned about the death of Aristobulus than he had expected. His wife Octavia, distressed by the scorn with which Antony was being talked of in Rome, had persuaded her brother Octavian to let her go to him with money and fresh troops: only a victory in battle, she felt, could restore to him some of his former self-respect. She had no hope of winning him back, or indeed of his ever fully regaining the fame he had lost. But, seeing him exposed to the unkind gaze of the world, she could not restrain an impulse to cover him—as if to let him die in decency. So in Rome, during his absence, she had insisted on being regarded first of all as the wife of Antony, maintaining in cheerful style the house in which they had lived together, though Octavian continually urged her to leave it. And the children that she had had by him, two girls, she loved equally with the children of her first marriage; and she had also taken into her home his younger son by Fulvia, who had died shortly before his marriage to herself.

In permitting Octavia to go to Antony with help, Octavian made it clear that this must be his last chance, and also her last attempt to revive in him a sense of his responsibilities. When he heard that she was on her way to him, Antony was not annoyed, for she had written that she came as a friend only, without making any claims upon him as his wife.

Octavia had sent the troops ahead and they had already arrived in Asia by the time that Herod had presented himself in Laodicea. She had gone no farther than Athens, waiting for a final summons from Antony: she carried with her not only money for the Armenian campaign, but a letter from Octavian, which he wished her to put into Antony's hands herself. At the last moment Antony felt that he could not bear to see her again. Yet he did not want to hurt her by an abrupt refusal.

Herod easily persuaded Antony that he had played no evil part in the death of Aristobulus; and in this city of strangers, with Cleopatra, far away, plotting things that he only half-understood, Herod seemed to Antony the only friend he had in the world. 'Go to Athens, and speak with Octavia for me,' he said. 'She knows that you are loyal and can be trusted to bring the money to me safely. And there will be less offence to her and to her brother if my message is brought by a king and sworn ally of Rome. Say to her that it is more for her sake than mine that I beg her not to come to Asia. I will try to fulfil my duty to Rome, and you can tell her of the preparations for the campaign that you have witnessed. But it would cause her unnecessary grief to see me as I am now. I am so different from my earlier self that the very look of my face has altered. It is strange even to me: how much more so would it be to her?

'Sometimes, when I start to speak or smile, my old ways come upon me—and then suddenly I say to myself, "No, I am different," and I do differently. And the reason? I don't know. Cleopatra alone knows the reason. Of all the men of my day, I had the greatest talents. (This I say with my intelligence, not with my vanity: there could be no vanity left in me now.) Perhaps it is that Cleopatra alone understands how much death is in me. Nor would she love me so much, I think, if I were not fated to ruin.'

Herod was greatly embarrassed by these confidences, but also deeply affected: as Antony spoke, he wept. How could the heathen talk so lightly of ruin, look towards it with a shrug? Perhaps misfortune lay before him also. But to live thus already in one's future: it was like a live man meddling with the secrets of death. A fright seized Herod, for himself. Might the Lord save him from the miseries of the heathen. Might he never lose the protection against mortal horrors that he had in being a pious Jew. For in the temple of the heathen there was no inner veil, and no mercy seat, and all their altars were earthly. Antony may have thought that it was because he still ruled the East in the name of Rome that Herod consented to go to Athens; and perhaps Herod would have done nothing for him had he been a fallen man already. But, although the errand was to Herod a political favour that he could not as Antony's subordinate refuse to grant, it had for him a solemn personal meaning; all the way on the journey to Athens he thought broodingly of his own life, and swore to himself that he would try to hold back from headlong courses.

Herod's interview with Octavia was short. She showed no surprise at Antony's message, treating him courteously but somewhat haughtily. She was not unlike Mariamne in her bearing. Both were beautiful women, and virtuous as well. Was there an ill omen in this resemblance? Were such women given to men not for love but to be mirrors of their failings? When Herod set out from Athens for Jerusalem he was more uneasy in mind than he had been at the start of his journey.

7

UNCLE JOSEPH

BECAUSE Herod had been so long absent, some people began
to say that Antony must have killed him; others, having
heard rumours of his journey to Greece, said that he had fled
from Antony's anger and would probably not dare to return
to Jerusalem. Little by little, everywhere in Judaea, all the
factions hostile to Herod drew closer and conspired to drive
out Herod's uncle, Joseph, who was temporary ruler of the
kingdom, and make old Hyrcanus king. Their plans were
confused, for Hyrcanus had not long to live and there was
no adult of royal blood to succeed him. Some would have
waited until a successor to Hyrcanus had been decided on.
Alexandra, however, urged them to act quickly, lest Herod
should be alive after all and return before they had achieved
anything. If they drove out Joseph without delay, she argued,
they would be able to overcome Herod on his appearance;
then a husband could be found for Mariamne, to be regent
after Hyrcanus's death until Mariamne's eldest son, Alexander,
should be old enough to rule. Alexandra herself was inclined
to believe that Herod still lived; but there was such a
strong general belief in his death that Doris, his first wife,
had begun to seek support for the claims of Antipater, her
son by Herod.

Joseph had for a long time ignored the disturbances in
various parts of Judaea and the signs of conspiracy in Jerusalem.
He could be loyal on Herod's behalf, but not astute; moreover, he had been giving more thought to Palace affairs than
affairs of state. Having no happiness with Salome, and de-
lighting in everything of domestic interest, he had made

Herod's and Mariamne's private problems his own. Mariamne was perfection to him, and for her children he had a reverent love that he could not have had for any that Salome might have borne him. He regarded Herod as unworthy of Mariamne; but, as he thought that no one could possibly be worthy of her, he was anxious that she should be fond of Herod, who was at least ready to admit his unworthiness.

Mariamne no longer shrank from Joseph. They were both lonely, and she had come to look upon him as something of a child. Moreover, he served as a shield from Salome's hatred of her. Salome now had an equal hate for both; but Joseph treated her accusations and reproaches jokingly, while Mariamne could do no more than make herself seem indifferent to them. And there were many other annoyances in the Palace from which Joseph protected her.

There was, for instance, the light behaviour of Pheroras, Herod's young brother, with the Palace women. To Mariamne's disapproval Pheroras would only have responded with defiance, and even more shocking behaviour. But Joseph laughed at his doings as one might at a boy's foolish escapades; so that Pheroras grew ashamed, keeping his love-making more discreet. Pheroras had been married to the sister of Doris, Herod's first wife. She had died soon after their marriage, however, and Herod had not yet been able to find him a wife that pleased him. His flirtatious ways Herod and the rest of the family ascribed to his being more handsome than was becoming in a man. 'He is more like a Greek or a Roman than a Jew,' Joseph said to Mariamne. 'Now, you would not have Herod more handsome than he is, would you? For if he were, he would be less attentive to your own beauty.'

'I wish Herod were not so attentive to my beauty,' Mariamne answered, 'and made less difference between us in the qualities that it is proper for everyone to have. He looks upon me as a being of superior beauty and virtue and sets me apart from himself: it is because of this that I am cold to him, not because it is not in me to love more warmly.'

Joseph scarcely understood her. How could a woman complain that a man loved her too well? It must be that Mariamne thought him not passionate enough. So he swore that no man ever loved a woman with so strong a passion as Herod loved her. But she kept shaking her head, it seemed to him in disbelief. And then Joseph was tempted to tell her of the secret order that Herod had given him before he left for Laodicea: that he should kill Mariamne if Antony killed him, to save her from falling into Antony's hands. This was all he told her: he could not have explained to her Herod's reasons for believing that such events might occur, since Herod had not told him that Alexandra had sent Mariamne's portrait to Antony. Mariamne did not ask for an explanation. From the moment that Joseph confided Herod's order to her she avoided him, and refused to leave her chamber. Joseph became desperate, afraid that she would do something violent, afraid of what she would say to Herod when he returned and of Herod's anger when he knew that his order had not been kept secret. If only Mariamne would let him speak to her: he could persuade her that Herod meant the thing to be done only in an evil extreme, for her own sake, because he loved her so fiercely.

What did Mariamne think, how much did she understand? Did she altogether hate Herod for this, or could she imagine that there could be great love behind such a purpose? She felt no fury against him, certainly, and she was sure that she was in no danger of dying in just this way. But Joseph's secret left her with a taste of sickness that she could not get rid of—as of tasting life itself, her own life, and finding it something foreign and unclean. Not Herod, but she herself was mad: mad to be alive at all in a world that she could not believe in. She thought of Cleopatra: was it feelings of this kind that drove Cleopatra to be so wicked? 'Or am I merely stupid,' she asked herself, 'should I think that all that happens around me is reasonable?' Most women have at some time asked themselves this same question, or felt a hesitation of the same sort: between an obstinate amazement at what happens around them, and the temptation to find excuses in their own simplicity for its strangeness to them. Exactly how Mariamne answered the question we could never say.

There are clues to many things in the past, and with the air that the people of other times once breathed, also, we can swell trifling relics of them into a near semblance of what was. But we cannot make the portrait or the story exact. Of those who are only recently dead, even, it is impossible to say: 'This is exactly what they were like, how they felt and thought.' The dead have left their living selves unfinished— many words unsaid, many questions unanswered, some question unasked. We try to round out their stories for them, put into their mouths the words they might have spoken, answer questions they would have wished answered. If they could read what we write of them, they would probably be able to say no more than 'No, I do not think I could have done that'; or 'Yes, I might well have spoken in that way.' Our likenesses of them cannot be more exact than their memories of themselves—if they remember. The shape of history—the living shape—is a haze; we must be careful not to make the light too clear—or the things we try to see by it will vanish.

Mariamne sat in her chamber during these weeks wishing that she could either hate Herod for what she had learned, or else forgive him and say to herself that his prudence deserved the name of love. Perhaps from day to day she both forgave and hated him. But she must also, at this time, have stopped feeling that she had any real part in Herod's story; from now on the stony look, that Alexandra said she had from her great-grandmother, spread from her eyes to all her features.

Salome was sure that Mariamne was plotting murder against Herod and his whole family, and she had also persuaded herself that Joseph had been bewitched into pledging his assistance. Joseph, indeed, went about like a man writhing with guilt. But the reason was that it pained him to have distressed her, and also that he had at last realized the danger they were all in from the rebels, who were now everywhere active and had already seized some of the most important fortresses of the country.

Joseph finally decided that their only hope of safety was to flee for protection to the camp of the Roman legion at Jerusalem. But Mariamne refused to leave her chamber or hear his pleadings, and he did not dare to go without her. And now Herod returned. By the time that he reached Jerusalem he had gathered his troops and suppressed his enemies; at Jerusalem he found all quiet again, except for the troubles within his family. Salome was the first to see him. She told him of Alexandra's part in the rebellion and of the intimacy that had grown up between Joseph and Mariamne during his absence; and how for many weeks before his arrival Mariamne had remained secluded in her chamber, as if for shame.

When Herod entered her chamber Mariamne let him embrace her, but she made no response. He searched her face. 'Why have you no word of welcome for me? Are you not pleased that I have returned alive, and put our country in order again? What is it, Mariamne? Why do you love me the less as I love you the more? Do I grow repulsive to you because I grow powerful? Is it for myself alone that I work? But you make it as if I did, by your coldness, by your refusal to share in my achievements. And so perhaps I have become a king like any other, feeding alone on the glory I harvest: as you behave to me, so also do my people.' And still she did not speak. He turned away, then suddenly turned towards her again. 'And what of Joseph?'

She raised her eyes and looked at him expressionlessly. 'And what of Joseph?'

'I do not want to accuse you of anything unspeakable. Do not drive me to do so.'

Mariamne's words came slowly. 'Even if I were a bad woman, I should not choose so foolish an accomplice in sin, a man with such a loose tongue. For as he brought me your secret, so would he have brought you mine.'

Herod was horrified: Joseph must have told Mariamne of his order to kill her should there be any danger of her falling into Antony's hands. Must they not have grown very intimate with each other if Joseph had taken her into his confidence to such a degree? He did not dare to justify himself to Mariamne—because he did not dare to press her to say what more had passed between Joseph and herself. They both looked away from each other, and each felt the other's pain without being able to relieve it. Herod drew himself up and tightened his mind around the thought: 'I am the King.'

He immediately held a secret session of his council and denounced Joseph for having failed to defend the kingdom properly during his absence, and also for having violated a confidence of the most solemn kind. He described the nature of the order, without mentioning Antony's name, and also challenged the council to say if there could be any doubt of his love for the Queen, and if it was not the cruel duty of a king and a husband to provide for the honour of his wife in the last emergency, even at the price of her life? Tears filled the eyes of every member of the council, and Joseph wept loudly; but Herod's eyes were dry. The council condemned Joseph to death.

After the execution of Joseph, there was a strange kindness between Mariamne and Herod, though fewer words and gestures of affection than ever before. She could not forget Joseph, or how he had died, and why; but she could not blame Herod, feeling that life at the Palace would have been intolerable if Joseph had lived on among them. And she guessed, from Salome's new air of triumph, that she more than Herod was responsible for his death. Herod, she realized, had suffered much in being driven to punish this fond old man, who was his father's own brother. It was as if both now saw that, dreadful as was the execution of Joseph, worse things yet must happen in their lives, which nothing could prevent but greater closeness of love; and Herod was at last learning that this could not be, and Mariamne softened toward him as he seemed to accept their failure with each other in a quiet, kingly way.

She did her best to be a correct wife to him, and he tried to please her by showing her courtesy rather than love. Alexandra was temporarily kept under guard in her palace, for her part in the recent rebellion, and so they were spared the embarrassment that her visits usually caused. Salome, moreover, now married to an Idumean noble, Costobar, was so busy initiating her new husband into her hates and policies that she relaxed her persecution of Mariamne. Costobar was well suited to be her husband. He had been Herod's governor in Idumaea, but Herod had taken the office from him because he had been found to be intriguing for help from Cleopatra to make Idumaea independent. Herod had at first intended to punish him. But, when he saw that Salome had a passion for him, he thought that the marriage might make a friend of Costobar and also distract Salome from her preoccupation with Mariamne and Alexandra.

8

CLEOPATRA AND ANTONY

By this time Antony, in a flare of his old brilliance, had defeated the Armenians in battle and carried off the Armenian King in triumph: not to Rome, but to Alexandria. By this time, too, Cleopatra had given way to every freakish impulse—it was said of her that her slaves went mad, one after the other, because she never stopped laughing. She proclaimed herself to be the Goddess Isis, and the Queen of Queens, and celebrated a marriage with Antony by which he was supposed to be transformed into the God Osiris; and their two children were called the Sun and the Moon. It was just before this ceremony of deification that Antony sent Octavia a bill of divorce. Her brother had already made her leave Antony's house in Rome, and angry letters had begun to pass between him and Antony. Octavian had the highest honours paid to his sister, to keep the Romans in mind of the injuries that she had suffered from Antony; when a portico commemorating a victory over the Dalmatians was erected, it was named after Octavia. But Octavian was more outraged by Cleopatra's assumption of the rule of lands belonging to Rome than by Antony's insults to his sister. Moreover, the ceding of land to Cleopatra had not stopped—thus, when her intrigues with Costobar were broken by Herod, Antony consoled her with the cities of Gaza and Joppa. And most scandalous to the Romans, whom Octavian had gradually worked up into a war-fury against Cleopatra, was that she went attended by a Roman guard.

In 32 Octavian declared war on Cleopatra. Since Antony still remained, in name at least, the Roman ruler of the East,

287

Herod did not dare to desert him. He had yet to see how
the conflict between Rome and Egypt would be decided, and
what part Antony would play in it. Herod could not recognize a change in the political situation in the East before it
was a military fact. And there was also a small chance that
Antony himself might turn against Cleopatra if he saw that
she could not resist Rome: then any assistance that Herod
had given Antony would be regarded as evidence of his
loyalty to Rome. Hence, when Herod wrote to Antony
assuring him of his support in the coming conflict, he was
moved by other reasons besides fear of Antony's immediate
power. There was also a reason that he could scarcely have
defined to himself—a superstitious sense of connexion with
Antony, as if he were an evil counter-part of himself whom
it would be bad luck to abandon utterly yet. Herod was by
now convinced that neither would ever succeed in being any
happier than the other, though one of them might perhaps
be more fortunate. These were the two most curious men
of their time.

Antony was extremely pleased by Herod's offer of support.
But Cleopatra said that Herod was not to be trusted; her
real reason for urging Antony not to accept help from him
was that she could not bear the thought of seeing Herod
again. Antony, feeling that Herod might be offended by a
complete rejection of his offer, begged him in kindly language
to subdue the Nabateans, who were in revolt. The campaign
was to Herod's interest also, and he immediately started to
make war on them. But even this minor help from Herod
Cleopatra found distasteful. She sent an army to molest his
men.

It was the summer of 31. Octavian had organized the
Roman fleet for an attack on Cleopatra, and in the early
autumn he arrived in Greece with an army, landing in Epirus.
Cleopatra and Antony made their own fleet ready and sent
it north, travelling themselves by land across Greece, stopping

on the way at important cities to receive homage and bestow gifts as if they were the unchallenged sovereigns of the world. The two fleets met off the promontory of Actium; soon Cleopatra saw that the battle was going against her, and sailed away, begging Antony to follow. When the sea-battle was wholly lost, Antony fled after Cleopatra, leaving his land-forces to surrender.

Herod had just been defeated in battle by the army that Cleopatra had sent to molest him in his war with the Nabateans, when news of Actium began to spread over the world. Antony's defeat encouraged the Nabateans, and the Jews for a time lost heart; and then an earthquake shook Judaea, killing thousands and ruining many places, which the people looked on as a warning from God. Herod was about to leave Judaea with fresh troops to continue the war against the Nabateans. When he saw that they hesitated, he addressed them solemnly and warmly: his words were carried all over Judaea, and the gloom lifted. It was said that Herod spoke on this occasion like a prophet. Perhaps now the yoke of Rome would be thrown off, and Herod would himself be the promised king that was to liberate them.

The holy man Menahem, who belonged to the Essenes, a sect stricter even than the Pharisees, said that in Herod's reign the Jews would surely pass from the second quarter of their time into the third. This many took to mean the passing from old sorrows into a just enjoyment of divine favours. They reasoned: 'Two quarters make a half, and two halves make a whole. In earlier days we suffered because the Law was not yet delivered, and we could but guess at it: that was the first quarter. Then the Law was delivered, and we suffered for the better learning of the Law: this was the second quarter, which is now drawing to a close. And the third quarter must be a rejoicing in our possession of the Law. And the fourth quarter must be the peace that is too holy to imagine, but the Lord's to bestow.'

Much talk of this sort went round; and much foolish talk always. And even the people who were indulgent to foreign customs and despised all religious doings of an old-fashioned kind—those who were called Sadducees—could not help feeling that a portentous moment in time had been reached. Antony's authority was gone; under his rule contact with Rome had slackened, and nothing new had happened in Greece and the whole East for a long time. But Octavian was marching through Greece and western Asia, the order of things had changed. The world was on the verge of new prosperity, new fashions, new ideas, a new marriage between East and West. So spoke the Sadducees.

But in the address that Herod had made to his troops he spoke more of God than of the world. 'You have no reason to tremble,' he said, 'since you go forth against barbarians who have no conception of God. I have strengthened our kingdom with many new resources, but everything that I have done and that you have helped me to do would be valueless, and doomed to crumble like the works of the heathen, were it not for the foundation on which we build, the rock of the Law.' Some said that Herod spoke in this way because of the Pharisees, whom he was always anxious to appease and among whom Alexandra had many friends. But he also spoke ecstatic words of which the Pharisees did not approve: saying that the Jews must use against their enemies not only the weapons in their hands, but the faith in their hearts also, and confound them with their own blindness as Elisha cast a mist round the enemies of Israel at Samaria. Yet perhaps by talk of this kind he meant no more than that they should conduct themselves in a glorious style, that would impress Octavian—in whom Herod was now as greatly interested as were the Sadducees.

Octavian paid a short visit to Italy before proceeding to the final attack upon Antony and Cleopatra. Before he left the East, Herod had subdued the Nabateans, and with such speed and thoroughness that Octavian saw that he must be careful not to treat the King of the Jews as an enemy; which was the very impression that Herod hoped these victories would make on him. Now Herod sent no more offers of help to Antony, planning to present himself to Octavian as soon as he returned from Italy. Antony and Cleopatra, he knew, were preparing to meet Octavian at Alexandria. But their fleet was even weaker than it had been at Actium, and their cavalry was made up largely of Armenians, who would perhaps desert at the first opportunity. The infantry was more to be trusted, but it was officered by friends of Antony who had long been disgusted by his subservience to Cleopatra. Herod was not in any doubt of the issue; nor, perhaps, were Antony and Cleopatra.

Meanwhile a new tragedy had been added to the fate of the Asmoneans. During Herod's war with the Nabateans Alexandra had again been active. News of the victories of these Arabs over his troops, and then of Antony's defeat at Actium, had given her fresh hope: Herod must now fall. Besides secretly spurring on his enemies at Jerusalem, she once more teased Hyrcanus to offer himself as king in Herod's place. 'If you fail, Herod will forgive you as he has so often done before. And if you succeed you will have a chance in your last years of wiping out the inglorious memory that you would otherwise leave behind.' But Hyrcanus resisted, begging Alexandra to let him live in peace what was left to him of life.

'Moreover,' he said, 'I have a feeling that this time Herod would not forgive me, should we fail. We have tried his patience much.' And he reminded Alexandra how Herod had not hesitated to kill Joseph when he thought him treacherous—a man of his own blood. But Alexandra would not rest. She composed a letter to Malchus, who governed the Nabateans, to be signed by Hyrcanus: in which Malchus was complimented on his victories over Herod and asked to give

Hyrcanus refuge in Petra until Herod's complete ruin should have been brought about. 'Then,' the letter ran, 'I shall return to Judaea as King, and a lasting friendship will exist between you and ourselves.'

For a time Hyrcanus refused to sign the letter, but Alexandra persisted; and so it was sent. But then Hyrcanus, unable to rest, confided in Mariamne what he had done, thinking that perhaps by now she herself had turned against Herod. Mariamne did not scold him: she knew that he would not have done such a thing of himself. She wept over him and embraced him. 'Oh, Grandfather, why have you not died sooner? For Herod must now kill you.'

'But need he know? Who would tell him? Suppose our party is victorious before he can return to Jerusalem?'

'I will tell him. He is my husband, and the father of my children, and he is also the King.'

'But your Asmonean blood? Have you not some loyalty to that, although you have none to me?'

'You and my mother wished me to marry him, and I thought that this would end the struggle between our family and his, and so did he. But my mother planned to use me against Herod, and indeed she has done so, though not in the way she meant. For I have not loved him, perhaps because of my proud blood, and thus in my heart I have been against him. Is that not a great enough injury: would you have me betray him as well as hate him? Yes. I think I hate him. But not cruelly. I hate him only for his successes—and for that part of him which is gaudy-minded and in love with worldly power. It is this part that turns his love of me into a heathen lust.'

'But he still loves you, dear Mariamne, your influence with him is still great. If you feel that as his wife you must tell him what I have told you, can you not at the same time persuade him that this whole affair was your mother's work? Her he would not dare to kill. Yet it may not come to this. He may fall before you have a chance to tell him.'

'He will not fall. Have we not just heard how he spoke to his troops before renewing the war against the Arabs? A man about to fall does not use such language. He spoke with the pride of one who knows his strength. And I would love Herod if he had more pride yet. But there is something heathen in his soul—he would lose all pride if he were once brought very low in fortune. The pride of a true Jew is most sure in humiliation.'

Hyrcanus was not listening. Was this the sweet girl whom he had always loved so dearly? What had happened to the old ways of the Jews, that the life of a grandfather should be made a cold matter of honour and philosophy? Yes, she had wept a little. But she had not torn her hair or her garments.

He crept away for comfort to Alexandra—she at least was a Jewish woman in the old style. Then he thought: No, she will be angry with me for telling Mariamne. And then he tried to persuade himself that Mariamne would not, after all, tell Herod—perhaps she was only trying to frighten him. So he went back and talked to her again, saying that although he had put his name to such a letter he would of course not act upon it, not even if Herod were defeated and all Judaea rose against him. 'I shall go back to Babylon, where I was so happy, and no one shall ever again attempt to make use of my right to the kingship.' But Mariamne shook her head sadly, refusing to promise anything.

When Herod returned from the Arabian war, Mariamne told him what she knew. Soon afterwards his spies intercepted Malchus's reply to Hyrcanus—in which he promised him a refuge should there be any chance of overthrowing Herod. Herod then said to Mariamne: 'You should not have told me this, perhaps, for my enemies are not strong enough to be able to use Hyrcanus against me. Now there is no other course for me than to put the poor old man to death.'

Mariamne answered: 'A wife who does not love her husband must be the more scrupulous in such matters.'

Hyrcanus was executed; being equally guilty with him, Alexandra did not dare to provoke an outcry against his death. At this time Mariamne gave birth to her fourth child, a second daughter, but could not bear to look at it. Herod named the child Cyprus, after his mother—the elder daughter being Salampsio.

Soon Herod set out for Rhodes to greet Octavian, who had now returned from Italy. He left his brother Pheroras in charge of the kingdom, although he had little confidence in him, as a sign that in the event of an accident on his journey he meant the rule to stay in his family. Herod by now had built up a powerful army, and he disposed his forces carefully about the kingdom. His instructions for keeping order in Galilee were especially severe. 'There is something for which I cannot forgive the Galileans,' he sometimes said. 'It is as if, in spite of being Jews, they were the greatest enemies the Jews had—and yet it is a long time since they have given me any trouble.'

Mariamne and Alexandra he sent to the fortress at Alexandrium, under the protection of his treasurer, a man called Joseph, and Sohemus, an Iturean officer. But his children and other relatives he sent to Masada, in Idumaea. To Sohemus he gave the order that, should anything happen to him on his journey, both Mariamne and Alexandra were to be killed. His fear now was not that Mariamne might fall into the hands of someone who would use her shamefully, but that on his death, as the mother of his heirs, she might be induced to work with Alexandra against her family. And he felt also that life would be even more hateful to her after his death than while he was alive.

Although Mariamne did not love him and there was, he knew, something against nature in his love for her, they were bound as neither could have been bound to anyone else.

Whom else could Mariamne have married, and hated less—and who else, married to her, could have adored her for the pride that made her hate him? And who but Mariamne would have understood that, in trying to advance his people in a way of which God would approve, he felt himself a cheat? And yet where among them was a better man? With God's help he might succeed. If he failed, the world would go its way without new help from the Jews. And what could the heathen do of themselves but again and again rise to mortal grandeur, their judgement and their dignity proceeding from themselves, and again and again be threshed? Must the course of time be so long? And then—these were his thoughts as he sailed towards Rhodes—he seemed to see the pale, motionless lips of Mariamne and to read the answer on them: The course of time is long. The bond between them was of such unspoken things.

At Rhodes, Herod was well received by Octavian. He did not try to excuse his devotion to Antony—even saying that he had loved him, and now pitied him. Octavian was pleased that Herod did not waste his time with fawning explanations, as many former supporters of Antony were doing. Moreover, Herod made him a present of some jewels, the most magnificent that Octavian had ever seen. These were the last of those that Herod had inherited from Antipater, and that Antipater had taken from the vault in the tomb of David. Herod, being at last rid of the secret belt in which he had carried them, felt lightened. Returning to Judaea, he looked toward the future with keen excitement. Octavian had treated him as an independent king, and spoken highly of the Jews. He was sure that Octavian would rule long in Rome. There was no madness in him, no flame, but this was as it should be: fire was safe only with the Jews, and only they understood its true meaning. Then he thought of the rebuilding of the Temple—he could begin that now. The perpetual fire of faith would again be rekindled on a new altar before the

Temple. Also, he thought of another work to which he had long pledged himself: the rebuilding of Samaria. This would be for Mariamne's pleasure, after the rebuilding of the Temple. But, as it happened, he began the rebuilding of Samaria first.

On her return to Jerusalem Mariamne was markedly distant in her manner with Herod and yet more active and punctilious in her government of the Palace household than ever before. But he had no time to study this change, since he was busy collecting money and provisions to help Octavian in his march across the desert to Egypt. When Octavian arrived at Ptolemais, Herod entertained him warmly and royally. Mariamne accompanied him on this occasion, and Octavian was so impressed by her queenliness and beauty that Herod felt almost grateful to her for not loving him—as if she would have been a less wonderful wife to have if she had been a fonder one.

Octavian made a successful crossing of the desert with his army, having had Herod's advice and assistance in the difficult problem of the water-supply. Before he reached Alexandria Cleopatra sent him a message, with her sceptre, offering to surrender and to swear allegiance to Rome. She told Antony that this was a ruse to delay Octavian. And she was in utmost uncertainty now, for the Alexandrians were turning against her, and Octavian was urging her to destroy Antony. Antony would have fled to Rome: there he might be able to find supporters again. But Cleopatra forbade the fleet to carry him. 'I have no more hope for myself than for you,' she said. 'We have ignored the world around us and lived in defiance and despite of it: let us not weaken now, for we could live by no other spell.' She would not allow the Alexandrians to go out to meet Octavian, lest the city take on a desolate, war-pinched look. Nor would she listen to any of Antony's plans for the defence of the city. In these days she would see no one but her magicians, and she fed both Antony and herself on drugs that made them drowsy and light-minded and unashamed of what they did. It was even said, later, that they lay together in the Temple of Isis, in the presence of the slaves and magicians who had accompanied them there, and that their children looked on.

Meanwhile the fleet and the cavalry had deserted to Octavian. Antony's own infantry held out the longest, but at last they too surrendered. The campaign was ended, except for the capture of Antony and Cleopatra. When Cleopatra heard that Octavian was about to enter Alexandria, she set out for a tomb that she had had built for Antony and herself just outside the city, begging him to accompany her. There, she said, the magicians would give them a drug that would make them as dead for a whole year, though it would seem to have been a short sleep when they woke: they would arise like gods and the whole world would fear them. But Antony let her go alone, shaking off the spell for a while: he could not believe in Cleopatra's talk of the miraculous drug and thought that she meant to poison them both, should Octavian discover them. He tried to gather together the few soldiers who remained in the city. If Octavian found that he had not lost all honour, might he not forgive him as a love-mad man and take him back to Rome to be reconciled to Octavia? Then a slave came to him, saying that Cleopatra was dying. He ran dazedly to the tomb, the slave panting after him. Cleopatra lay as dead; and Antony, remorseful that he had for an hour been disloyal to her, threw himself groaning on his sword.

Cleopatra's talk of the miraculous drug had not been a pretence. Her magicians had told her of it, and while she was waiting for Antony in the tomb she had ordered them to give her just enough of it to prove that it was not a poison. She began to revive soon after Antony had stabbed himself. When she first saw him he was still alive; he was lying on the floor of the tomb, looking up at her, and as she moved and rose from the low slab on which she had been reclining his eyes started. She knelt beside him and took his hand gently. 'Explain, explain!' his eyes seemed to say.

After Octavian had brought Cleopatra from the tomb to her palace, his first care was to remove all poisons and daggers from her reach, for he thought that she would rather die than be carried captive to Rome. She was strongly guarded, but otherwise treated with all the respect and reverence to which she had been accustomed. Even Octavian, in visiting her, behaved with as much courtesy as if she had still been the reigning queen of Egypt. And he did not speak of Antony, or the change that his conquest of Egypt would mean for her, but of Julius Caesar, who had loved them both. (Octavian was the son of Atia, who was the daughter of Caesar's sister Julia.) 'I was a petulant boy, a weakling, but fortunate in a wise grandmother and mother and above all in a wise uncle. For usually, as we grow up, men help us to unlearn what our women teach us; but in Caesar, who took over my education, there was much that was womanly—and now I am fortunate in a wife who has all a woman's prudence, but the hot will of a man also.'

'And thus you have been spared from the dangers of living your own life? Even the wise Caesar did not enjoy such safety.' He knew that she meant to challenge him to love her as Caesar had; and she was still beautiful, and the forlornness of her situation made her seem sweetly pitiable. But he went on talking quietly of Caesar.

'I know that he loved you, and can even understand why. But why did you love him? There was nothing desperate in him, or reckless—which is what I think you love in a man?' In his look she read what she had read in Antony's eyes as he died: 'Explain, explain!' And, unable to bear the memory, she turned her face away and did not answer.

After a time Cleopatra's manner changed. She began to speak herself of going to Rome, and with apparent cheerfulness, telling her slaves what to prepare for the journey and what to take along as presents for Livia, Octavian's wife. Deciding that she was perhaps weary of Egypt and genuinely looking forward to new life in Rome, Octavian gave her complete freedom—doing all he could to make her feel that she was departing like a queen, even letting her ride beside him in a procession through the streets, as if she were his royal hostess.

On the day on which they were to leave, when Octavian's guard came to Cleopatra's palace to bring her and her belongings to the waiting ship, she was found dead upon her couch. Beside the couch, open, stood the silver-bound basket in which her favourite serpent lived; and near her on the couch lay a flute. Perhaps she had played to the serpent and drawn it to her, and then hummed to it, and then held it with her eyes only, as on the day when Herod watched. Perhaps in the serpent's eyes also she had read the challenge 'Explain, explain!' and had wilfully broken her magic.

9

THE SILENCE OF MARIAMNE

ON hearing of Antony's defeat and death, and the death of Cleopatra, Herod went to Egypt to congratulate Octavian—whom we shall now call Augustus, the name in which he was soon to be perpetually confirmed. In return for Herod's help and courtesies, Augustus now gave him back all those districts and cities of which Antony had deprived him for Cleopatra's sake; and he was also granted free sovereignty over Samaria, and over certain other cities—such as Gadara in Galilee—which had up to that time enjoyed a partial independence. After this Herod went with Augustus as far as Antioch, where the two men appeared in public together as equals. When Herod returned to Judaea, he carried with him Augustus's benevolent wishes for the prosperity of his country, and also a pleasant message of greeting for Mariamne.

Soon afterwards Augustus left for Rome. With him went the two children of Antony and Cleopatra; whom Antony's wife Octavia took into her charge upon their arrival. And Egypt was now Augustus's.

To Mariamne Herod said: 'We are at a new start—not only Judaea, but the whole world. And Cleopatra is gone: Egypt is dead, and all its vileness and hers.'

Mariamne answered: 'It is an end, I agree. But that is something sorrowful. And the sorrow must be felt and tasted before there can be a new start. Life does not move so quickly, the past is not so easily forgotten. For myself, I cannot so easily forget Cleopatra, as the ancient Jews did not forget the savoury things of Egypt, the fish and the cucumbers and the melons and the leeks and the onions and the garlic. Do I not still wear the bracelet she gave me, though she behaved so badly to us when she was in Jerusalem? She saw that the world was evil and yet craved for happiness in it, which she thought to get by being evil herself. And she had no more happiness than I have had—who chose the other way. There was something that was the same in each of us: we were alike in that we hated the world, and yet saw that it could not have been otherwise. And we both tried to love in spite of this hate: perhaps she was more successful than I. Therefore do not talk lightly of a new start. Evil as the old things were, they were all that we had. And if you feel that they are gone now, be sorrowful—for it will be a long time before new things come to replace them, and we cannot say how much better they will be.'

'When you talk like this, on and on, as if I were not standing here listening, you seem like a dead woman.'

'And am I not? Do you not yourself behave as if there were little difference to you between my being alive and my being dead—since you give orders for my death and then permit me to live, as if it did not much matter one way or the other? Nor, indeed, does it.'

Thus began for Herod the months of agony which ended in the trial of Mariamne.

Already Salome had accused Mariamne of adulterous relations with Sohemus, who had guarded the fortress in which she stayed while Herod was away. But the only evidence that Salome had been able to produce was that Mariamne had shown approval when Herod rewarded Sohemus with a governorship; and Herod, remembering painfully how his uncle Joseph died, and Hyrcanus, had been reluctant to start an inquiry that might lead to another death. He had felt, also, that any further discord between Mariamne and himself would end disastrously for them both, since they had reached the limit of patience with each other. Now, however, he could not doubt that she knew of his order to Sohemus, and therefore suspected—as before, in the case of Joseph—that something wrongful had taken place.

Salome was delighted when he came to confide his fears to her. Acting on her advice, he said nothing of the matter to Mariamne for a long time. First he interrogated all the slaves and attendants who had been with Mariamne at Alexandrium; but none of these would say more than that she sometimes spoke with Sohemus, never in her own chamber. Then he summoned Sohemus himself, and accused him of having told Mariamne of the secret order. Sohemus would only say that Mariamne had somehow guessed it and asked him if it were not so, and that he had found it impossible to lie to her. Herod did not wish to hear more; Sohemus was condemned to death by Herod's council, on a charge of treacherous indiscretion.

Here for a time the affair rested. Mariamne knew that Sohemus had been executed for treachery, and she guessed that Salome had been again at work. And she was aware that every time Herod looked at her now he was calculating something with himself—as if he were measuring whether he hated or loved her, and could not decide. Finally she left the Palace and went to live with her mother, saying to Herod: 'I think my presence maddens you, and that you will be calmer if you do not see me.' Salome said that Mariamne had gone in order to conduct some love-affair out of Herod's sight, or to meddle in some plot of her mother's.

Between Salome's husband, Costobar, and Alexandra there had grown up a friendship; and he had, moreover, long regretted his marriage with Salome. His frequent visits to Alexandra's palace were now used by Salome as a further ground of accusation against both Mariamne and Alexandra. If Herod had at this point divorced Mariamne, Salome would perhaps have been content. But he held back fearfully from punishing her, scarcely knowing with what to reproach her.

Salome contrived to make Mariamne seem guilty of a dreadful intention. When Herod heard Salome's story, he felt a blaze of relief within him, for these had been months of chilly terror and suspense: he must now act, in spite of himself.

This was Salome's story. Mariamne, she said, had come one day to the Palace, as she frequently did, to see her children: sometimes now they were with Herod, sometimes with Mariamne. Hearing that Herod was suffering from frequent headaches, she went back to her mother's palace and fetched a medicine. This she gave to Herod's cup-bearer, telling him to put a little in his master's wine but to say nothing of the matter to anyone. The cup-bearer, knowing that there was some trouble between the King and the Queen, feared that the medicine might be a poison: instead of doing as Mariamne had asked, he brought the flask to Salome, to ask her opinion and advice. She had taken the flask to the court-physician, who had found it to contain a deadly poison.

'I am lost!' Herod cried.

'No, you are not lost,' Salome answered, 'and you have me to thank for that.'

Mariamne was tried before Herod's council, and Alexandra along with her. The trial lasted many days, into a second and a third week; for Herod kept pleading with Mariamne to speak in defence of herself, which she refused to do. He would grow exasperated with her and threaten to close the trial, leaving her to be condemned by her own silence. Then, the next day, he would once more exhort her to save herself. He had their children led into the council-chamber, thinking that the sight of them might move her. And he called on the witnesses over and over again, in the hope that, realizing how black a story their testimony made, she might be provoked to tell her own. There were four witnesses: Salome, the cup-bearer, the court-physician, and a eunuch of Alexandra's, who had been brought by torture to say that he had himself poured away the usual contents of the flask, which had always contained a common household-remedy, and held it while Mariamne poured into it a new potion that she had mixed.

Throughout the trial Alexandra had also pleaded with Mariamne to speak, protesting tearfully that she knew nothing of the potion and that, although Herod had often doubted her loyalty, she had never acted with any other idea than that of protecting their common interests. She had been mistaken, she said, in presuming to make his interests her own : but perhaps this zeal for the kingdom could be excused in one whose family had for so long served it and in whose veins ran the blood of Judas Maccabaeus—as it did in the veins of Herod's own children. Salome sneered at her for fawning upon Herod. Whenever her mother spoke Mariamne clenched her hands, but there was no other sign to show that she had heard. Finally Herod forbade Alexandra to speak, since her conduct brought shame on Mariamne.

Then a day was decided upon that should be the last. The members of the council were growing restive, thinking that Herod pressed leniency too far. He knew that they meant to condemn Mariamne, and also that they understood this to be his real wish : to them it had seemed that he prolonged the trial only in order that it should not be said that Mariamne had been dealt with unjustly.

'Could the council not be requested to condemn her to perpetual imprisonment, rather than death ?' he asked Salome on the night before the last day.

'Do not forget that she is one of the Asmoneans—for whom the populace has a superstitious affection. If it were known that she were alive, there would be no peace in the kingdom until she was set free.'

'But perhaps after a time I might release her and send her away from Judaea to live in exile. Would not the world think better of me, then ? And what of my own heart ? Her death will destroy it.'

'Rather be without a heart than suffer the woes that your love has brought upon you, and upon all of us.'

But what taught Herod most clearly that it was too late to change the course of the trial was the look on Mariamne's face as she waited for the session to begin: she was smiling in a way that he knew the others could only read as guilty defiance, though for him it was a smile of unasked forgiveness. And he noticed that she was dressed in precious clothes—the robe that Cleopatra had sent her when they were betrothed; but she was wearing, instead of Cleopatra's bracelet, the golden band of a general that Caesar had given her. Her death was certain now: Herod felt that she would kill him if he tried to deny it her.

When the condemnation was spoken Alexandra cried: 'It is just! She has been an ungrateful daughter and an ungrateful wife as well.' Mariamne flushed. Herod jumped up and clapped his hand over Alexandra's mouth; when he turned round, Mariamne had already been led away.

Then the madness began. Every night he paced the corridors of the Palace, calling her name. He convoked his council and abused it for not inquiring what Salome had done with the flask between the moment when she took it from the cup-bearer and the moment when she put it into the hands of the physician—a whole day. Did he wish to accuse Salome? they asked. 'I accuse myself,' he wept. Then a pestilence broke out in Jerusalem, and Herod went among the people at night in disguise, whispering to everyone, 'It is God's punishment for the murder of Mariamne.' One night he was recognized and brought back to the Palace.

'You must go away for a time and compose yourself,' Salome said.

'Yes,' Herod answered, 'I shall go away. I shall go to Samaria.'

In Samaria the madness cooled and Herod came to think of Mariamne as someone who had died very long before.

It was at Samaria that they were married, and he had said then that he would one day revive the glory of Israel's ancient capital. And this was how it came about that Herod beautified Samaria before he began the rebuilding of the Temple.

10

HEROD IN ALL HIS GLORY

WHILE Herod was busy with his plans for Samaria, news came to him of trouble in Jerusalem. A fresh rebellion was on the way, fomented by Alexandra: she had tried to persuade the commanders of the city's fortresses to turn against Herod and recognize her as regent. He hurried home, and had Alexandra immediately executed. Thus died the last surviving member of the old royal family.

Herod felt that a new era had truly begun for himself and Jerusalem and the world. It seemed to him that the past could now be forgotten—save for Mariamne. He remembered how she had said that there must be long sorrow before forgetting came. But she had also spoken of the sweet memories that the Jews kept of Egypt. So, of his past, which had belonged to Mariamne, he would remember her beauty; and he would think of her coldness to him as a heavenly taste of good that he had enjoyed in the midst of evil—the evil that was now disappearing. 'And I will be a virtuous as well as a strong king,' he swore, 'I will slowly win my people to the pleasures of the outer world, and the world to the truths that my people hold in trust from God.'

To the heathen cities in his own kingdom, and also in Syria and elsewhere, he did many kindnesses and made many presents; and in the larger Jewish cities he introduced theatres in the Roman style, and Roman and Greek entertainments. The more pious of his subjects protested against the foreign modes that Herod planted among them, the Pharisees in particular. But Herod went on confidently, feeling secure in his own piety and in his power to reconcile Jewish and heathen traditions by an equal liberality toward both. His friendship with Augustus he counted as the first and most necessary victory; his own people would yield in the end, when they understood that all he did was for their honour. At first he was even pleased with their stubbornness, as if it were a proof of his own incorruptibility. And he kept exceeding himself in his generosities to them, distributing money frequently to the poor and offering so much help in times of famine that it was said that people looked forward to lean years, since they lived then better than in years of plenty. During the worst famine of his reign Herod stripped the new palace that he had built for himself of all its beauties and treasures, making the rich buy them, to shame their meanness in assisting the sufferers.

In Herod's new palace all the furniture was covered with pure gold, and the rooms were of great height, as if it were a temple. Each room bore the name of an illustrious person: there was one named after Augustus, and one after Agrippa, Augustus's vice-regent in the East. And the great stairway leading up to the Palace was all of polished stone.

For Agrippa, Herod felt admiration as well as friendship; he had the same restlessness to get things done well and quickly, though inspired by no such grand purposes as Herod. Until Agrippa's death in the year 12, Herod paid him frequent visits and was continually helping him. Both felt that if there only were more people like themselves, fearless of hard work, the world would not have got so far behind itself in time. Had it not been for Agrippa, Herod knew, Augustus would never have won at Actium. And then perhaps Antony would not be dead, or Cleopatra . . . or Mariamne.

Herod now looked on Mariamne's death as a natural part of the events of those crucial years, something necessary for the world's tranquillity and his own. And yet he continued to remember her, with a cloudy tenderness in which there was an increasing insincerity: as a man remembers a woman who in his youth rebuffed him, pleased that his life has turned out otherwise than he once desired, yet smiling when he mentions her name, as if there had been some secret love between them. He had kept Mariamne's clothes untouched for many years; and then he gave them to Julia, Agrippa's wife and Augustus's daughter. Julia seemed to him as beautiful as Mariamne, but more clever in her dealings with men. For he had come to think that Mariamne's only fault had been that she was too simple in managing him, and mistakenly frank. Surely, he said to himself, every woman in her heart despises men a little, and every man knows this: yet Mariamne behaved as if the feeling never ceased to shock her and must be scrupulously confessed at every moment, and the world come to an end because of it.

In the year 17 Herod went to Rome to bring away his sons Alexander and Aristobulus, who had been sent there for their education, and in whom Livia, Augustus's wife, had taken a gracious interest. Salome accompanied Herod on this occasion. She had already visited Rome and enjoyed an intimate friendship with Livia; many letters passed between them, full of secret talk about Judean politics, for Salome still regarded Herod as too innocent of the wickedness of his enemies to be entrusted with a full knowledge of his own affairs.

Costobar had been executed shortly after Alexandra's death for intriguing with the aristocratic party, the Sadducees: the accusation had come from Salome herself. Then she had fallen in love with Syllaeus, the vizier of the Nabatean King, when he came to visit Herod at Jerusalem; and he with her. He was an ugly man, lame and scowling. Although the court at Jerusalem laughed at the idea of a marriage between them, Herod favoured it for political reasons: the marriage would improve relations between the two kingdoms. In order to be able to marry Salome, however, Syllaeus would have to become a Jew, which meant that he would have to be circumcised. When Syllaeus learned what would be required of him, he felt that he had been grossly insulted, and left Jerusalem in a rage; and for some time afterwards obscene jokes went round about Salome's love-affair. Salome was highly vexed with Herod, blaming him for her mortification and disappointment, for she would have had no objection to marrying Syllaeus even if he had not become a Jew. But in such matters Herod was always strict, from policy as well as faith; it was only by constant tact and watchfulness that he kept the support of the Pharisees, who would have been shocked if a member of the royal family had committed a violation of the Law.

For a long time, remembering Syllaeus, Salome refused everyone that Herod proposed to her as a husband. Finally, when Herod thought he had found the very man for her, he wrote to Livia and begged her to persuade Salome to consent to the marriage; so Salome at last gave in. This new husband, Alexas, was dull-minded but adoring. He looked upon Salome as the wisest woman in the world and never ceased to be grateful to Herod for conferring on him so great an honour. It was a childless marriage, but she had had four children by Costobar. Soon after Herod's two sons were brought back from Rome, Berenice, Salome's youngest child, was betrothed to the younger, Aristobulus.

For many years all Herod's ambitions seemed slowly on the way to fulfilment. His kingdom was extended by the successful pacification of unruly neighbours, and Rome acknowledged his authority over the new regions. Instances of brigandage still occurred, especially in Galilee, but he made the punishment so severe (to be sold into slavery abroad), and his army was so strong, that no large bands of brigands remained. Indeed, after the year 30 the Roman legion at Jerusalem was withdrawn, Herod finding his own troops sufficient; besides the Jewish troops, and some Romans among the officers, there were Itureans, Nabateans, Thracians, even some Germans and Celts—and the Galatian guard formerly attached to Cleopatra, presented to him by Augustus. He studied ways to improve cultivation, and farmers were urged to plant fruits and grains never before grown in Judaea. Huge works of irrigation and construction were undertaken, whole cities were founded and completed. And in the year 20 the rebuilding of the Temple began; it was finished eighteen months later. The treasuries were filled and the banks busy. Nor were the taxes a burden upon the people, being severe only for the rich. So ably, in fact, did Herod administer the commerce and finances of his country that Augustus made him financial adviser to the procurator of Syria. No need to seek riches in the tomb of David!

Yet as the years passed a feeling grew that if he could not make things happen faster life would slide back into the past again. The more furiously he strained, the more exasperated he became with the slowness of human accomplishments. From the heathen he had more sympathy and encouragement than from his own people—and it was their approval that he most desired, and for their happiness chiefly that he worked. Those among them who approved of the foreign innovations were the aristocrats, who had the least love for him and whose good opinion he valued the least. The common people were suspicious of every new effort, as if it were against the Law in being new, although plainly a thing for their good. Yet when some soothsayer from Galilee or some other district came to Jerusalem with talk of a new prophet or saviour, they thronged the streets in grinning expectation, like ignorant heathen.

Herod tried to learn patience. 'After all,' he said to himself, 'I am not a mere merchant of a king, trading in glory. I must live with more dignity. I must nurse the finer talents in myself and conduct my affairs with so much art and confidence that I will seem to have no need of the applause of the populace : which I shall then undoubtedly win without courting it, as all illustrious men do.' He now demanded a greater punctiliousness in his court and household. His vizier and secretary of state were ordered to increase the number of their attendants and to use more formality in consulting him; his chief huntsman and butler and chamberlain were given close instructions for the perfecting of their offices, and for the dress and behaviour of those under them. And he became somewhat less familiar in manner with his intimates, organizing a new nobility, of four degrees of privilege. In order that the effect of all these regulations should not be too harsh, he increased the pleasures of the court with musical performances, philosophical discourses and literary readings and recitations, bringing to Jerusalem scholars from Alexandria and poets from Greece and Rome. For his own edification he attached to himself a philosopher of Damascus, Nicholaus.

But Herod gradually realized that these refinements provoked fresh antagonism and mockery; it was said that he wished to make a new Rome of Jerusalem, that he demeaned himself by aping Augustus. Could it be true, he asked himself, that he was laughed at abroad for patronizing heathen customs and institutions? For the honour of Jerusalem and to endear the Jews to the world he had paved the whole length of Antioch's principal street with marble. And on a visit to Greece, he had given a large sum of money for the revival of the Olympic games, in order that they might be permanently celebrated. Were Jews and heathen equally ungrateful? What of the many favours and dispensations he had won for Jews—not only the Jews of his own country, but those who were settled abroad in Syrian and Greek cities? Why should everything he did take on a wrong look, as if it were ill done, with poor heart? What was the cause?

Thus, even at the height of his success, a gnawing began in him, in his bowels and in his head. Before everything, he feared the Pharisees, remembering what Antipater had told him before he died, of the oath he had sworn to the old

Alexandra: how she had said that the cold madness would seize him if he broke it, or any of his children after him. There had been an icy stinging in his head after Mariamne's death. Was this the beginning? Had the execution of Mariamne been an offence against the Pharisees? Yet no protest had come from them at the time.

If he had not been such a strict Jew, he might have eased his rancour in the company of gay women. For he had come to regard women in a lighter way than formerly, as beings to whom a man should show his weaknesses without shame. A few years after Mariamne's death he married a Jewish woman of Alexandria, the daughter of a pious scholar of that city—because it seemed to him that she had a bent for foolishness. Her name also was Mariamne, and for this alone Salome hated her. Herod soon found that she was herself all foolish. But he did not divorce her for years. When at last Salome accused her of having plotted against him, he did not inquire into the evidence, gladly using it to be rid of her. By the second Mariamne Herod had one son, whom he called by his own name. After his third marriage he took seven other wives: it was permitted to the Jews to have several wives at once, though by this time considered unseemly. However, Herod never had more than one wife at the Palace, tiring quickly of each in turn but not troubling to divorce them. They were all very young, and he tired of all of them for the same reason: that, as a result of his encouraging them to be gay and care-free, they thought of nothing but amusing themselves and coaxing money and fine presents from him. There was Malthace, a Samaritan woman; and Cleopatra, a Jewish woman of Jerusalem; and Pallas and Phaedra and Elpis, all three from cities outside his dominion; and the elder daughter of his own sister; and a daughter of his brother Joseph. And by all these women he had children, except the last two, his nieces.

Herod grew very weary. His chief interest toward the end

of his life became the marriages and settlement of his children:
this now seemed a way to hurry time forward into the future.
Yet only quarrels and ill-feeling came of his hopes; here too
the same heavy slowness of time. Salome tortured him with
suspicions and accusations: Glaphyra, the sly Cappadocian
princess whom Herod's son Alexander had married, was plotting against Herod, and treating Berenice, her own daughter,
with impudent condescension—Berenice was married to Alexander's brother Aristobulus. And Herod's brother Pheroras,
whom he had hoped to redeem from a scandalous life by
marrying him to Salampsio, his daughter by the first Mariamne,
had preferred to marry a slave-woman.

Herod at last allowed himself to be persuaded by Salome
that Glaphyra was treacherous, and Alexander and Aristobulus
also. He had tried to love these two sons of Mariamne and
had designed them for his heirs, but they both resembled
their mother in appearance and he fancied a constant reproach
in their faces. Moreover, they were very popular in Jerusalem, because of their Asmonean blood: the thought that
the old troubles would begin again sickened him. It was only
in moments of despair that he felt close to Salome; and,
forgetting that her fanatical devotion to him had in the past
brought him only anguish, he took her advice once again.
He called to Jerusalem his son by his first wife, Antipater, and
treated him with marked favour, in order to humiliate the
sons of Mariamne. So began another long period of agony
for Herod, in which Antipater, Salome and Pheroras all
worked upon him to make him hate Alexander and Aristobulus: until, after many changes of heart and sore misgivings,
he had them both strangled.

Now Herod suspected everyone but Salome. Many had
already been killed for implication in the plots of which
Alexander and Aristobulus had been accused: a lust of killing
took hold of him, as if he could thus cleanse the world, and
finally himself. The gnawing disease which was fast tearing

him in pieces, he regarded as caused by the corruptness of his times, and believed that he would be miraculously cured of it when he had punished all the crimes and transgressions about him. He looked upon every misdemeanour, even the breaking of a ritualistic law, as a sin against God and himself, the King of the Jews. 'Herod has had a new attack of piety' was a saying heard in Jerusalem in these days, every time an execution was reported. Of all the crimes of which Alexander and Aristobulus had appeared guilty, he had been most offended by that charged against Alexander—misbehaviour with a eunuch. Had not Moses said that those who made a shame of their manhood must die? 'At least one of my sons,' Herod said, 'had already brought death upon himself, by breaking the laws of God. And surely the other practised some secret sin.'

Herod now had his whole family watched by spies, and also all the important families of the kingdom, wishing to know of any impurity in their ways of life—whether of an adulterous kind or indulgence in the Theban vice, as the shaming of manhood was called. Of his brother Pheroras he had the gravest suspicions, since he had lived carelessly in his youth and had married a woman who was perhaps little better than a whore. Herod had given his daughter Cyprus to Pheroras's son, and he relied on her for reports of his brother's family. She had nothing to tell him, however, except that Pheroras was often in private conference with the artful Antipater. Salome would have made much of this, since she had come to doubt Pheroras's loyalty to Herod; but Herod was less interested in such matters now than in rooting out immoralities, especially from his own family. And he continued busily arranging marriages between the members of his family, to make all pure and orderly among them.

THE NEW ERA

HEROD began to surround himself with sorcerers, of whom there were many always in Jerusalem—star-readers and magicians from the East. For he had persuaded himself that God would provide someone to take over the rule of the kingdom, for among all the members of his family he found no one worthy. The sorcerers encouraged him in this belief, especially three from Ecbatana whom he trusted beyond all the others. These three spoke of an infant, not yet born, whom he would adopt and train in all the virtues proper to the king who would carry on the great works of Herod.

Think, then, how all Herod's family hated this talk of adopting an unknown infant to supplant the rightful heirs. And think also how the hearts of all the women of Judaea about to bear a child fluttered with hopes and dreams. At last the three sorcerers said that the stars had revealed to them that the promised infant was already born. Herod, writhing with sickness and excitement, ran through the Palace crying 'We are saved! The child has been born!' When the calculations revealed that the child would be found in Bethlehem, Herod sent the sorcerers off dressed in courtly clothes and loaded with splendid gifts. And the night before they left, he had paid a visit to the tomb of David. If, in the chest that the sorcerers carried, there were jewels that had lain next the bones of David, was this not a fitting journey for them to be taking?

The pains from which Herod was suffering were sometimes in his bowels and sometimes in his head; and when they were in his bowels he was more content, for he regarded the pains in his head as a sign of God's displeasure. After the sorcerers set off for Bethlehem, the pains moved from his bowels to his head. He awaited their return with anxious misgiving.

Just at this time Bethlehem was crowded with people who had come to enrol themselves in the public register according to the families to which they belonged by lineage. This was because of an order regarding a census that Augustus had issued. Many preferred to journey to the town where the most distinguished branch of their family lived and enrol themselves there. Thus to Bethlehem came hundreds who could count themselves as belonging to the House of David, although they might be unknown to the chief members of the family. Among such as these was a carpenter belonging to a branch of the family that had long been settled in Galilee. His name was Joseph, and his wife bore a boy child while they were in Bethlehem: it was this child that the sorcerers chose, after going from house to house and inn to inn and inquiring into the respectability and lineage of all the parents to whom a boy child had been newly born.

When the sorcerers returned with news that they had found the child, and that he was a perfect infant, beautiful, and of the House of David, Herod felt that the Lord was at last pleased with him. But the icy pains in his head were sharper than ever. 'Perhaps when I see the child they will pass,' he said. For Joseph and his wife Mary had been ordered to bring the child to Jerusalem. Herod was eager to hear everything concerning it: was the mother fair, of what profession was the father? Then he learned that the family was really of Galilee, and that the child had been conceived there. 'Can anything good come out of Galilee?'

The sorcerers fled from Jerusalem, fearing that Herod would have them killed in his anger. And the news spread that the sorcerers had deceived Herod. Hearing this, Joseph and Mary fled with their child and their gifts to Egypt. But they never forgot that he had once been chosen as the coming king;

and when he was older his mother often told him how the three sorcerers had read his fate in the stars and sought him out at Bethlehem with gifts of gold and jewels and frankincense and myrrh.

Herod now lived in a long death-agony. The same old searching for plots went on. And there were plots enough to occupy him. Pheroras's wife conspired with the Pharisees, and Pheroras and his whole family were finally sent out of Judaea. Then, during a terrible seizure, when he thought that he was at last dying, Herod sent for Pheroras; but he refused to come. But some time later, when Herod heard that Pheroras was dying, he went to him, and forgave him: 'Let us take some happiness in reaching an end, for we have had little in living.' Pheroras's funeral was a very fine one, and it seemed that Herod envied him his death. Yet Herod was not ready to die.

Herod appointed Antipater, the son of Doris, to be his heir. But he did not believe that Antipater would really succeed him. Antipater was the cause of the death of his two sons by Mariamne, having lied against them and driven them to desperate behaviour. Herod still saw their faces, and in their faces he saw the face of Mariamne: in which he read that all was not yet over. He knew that when his life was done the face of Mariamne would no longer haunt him. And sometimes he tried not to see it, not to remember it; but when it came to him again he was glad.

An intricate conspiracy was slowly uncovered. Pheroras's wife was involved in it, and it seemed that even Pheroras himself had for a time planned to poison Herod. But most deeply involved was Antipater; he was put in prison on his return from a visit to Rome and kept there until sufficient evidence of his complicity had been gathered. Meanwhile Herod's exasperation with the Pharisees broke loose.

All his life he had courted the Pharisees and been meticulous in every matter of law and piety. But they had remained cold and carping. The cause of his final rage with them was that they inspired a group of students to tear down a golden eagle that he had put up over the great door of the Temple. Herod was sure that he had broken no injunction of God or the prophets: Solomon himself had adorned his temple with such images. The tearing down of the eagle seemed to Herod a symbol of all the misunderstanding and ingratitude from which he had suffered; and so he spoke of it to a crowded assembly at Jericho, before which the culprits were brought.

'I have given you glory and prosperity. And always you have taken it as if I gave you too much. But my own complaint against myself is that I have given too little, done too little. Yet who in these times could have done more? There is no easy way in the bringing down of glory from heaven. The favours of God are not to be won by the will of man. Beware therefore of prophets who ravish the minds of the people with heavenly hopes. Remember the golden eagle!' And many, hearing him speak, thought that he somewhat justified the Pharisees. Yet the two chief culprits were burned alive, at the desire of the assembly. Of which Herod said: 'A worthy compliment to receive on my death-bed!'

This was the end. As he entered the upper city on his return from Jericho he looked from his litter toward the towers of the citadel that he had built there. One was named after his brother Phasaël, whom the Parthians had killed: a good man, who had not lived too long. Another was named after Hippicus, a man who had been humbly faithful to him in the early days of his reign and died at the siege of Jerusalem: he had had no thought for himself, but his name would not be forgotten. The third was Mariamne's tower: this Herod had made the most beautiful. He felt that it looked back at him like a stranger, someone he had never known: at last he could no longer see Mariamne's face.

Antipater was now executed. And Herod waited impatiently for death, not understanding why, when he had come to wish for it, he should live on against his will. To prove to himself that his wish was earnest he cut his throat with a knife. But his physicians mended the wound: even the pace of death would not be fast for him. In March of the year 4 he died.

The kingdom was divided between Archelaus and Antipas, Herod's sons by his fourth wife, Malthace, and Philip, Herod's son by his fifth wife, Cleopatra, a woman of Jerusalem. Archelaus took the name of Herod, and married Glaphyra, the widow of Herod's son Alexander. And Antipas also called himself Herod: he was the shrewdest of these brothers, and ruled over Galilee and Peraea across the Jordan. He was first married to a daughter of the Nabatean King, but he put her away to marry Herodias, the daughter of his half-brother Aristobulus. Herodias was married to Herod's son by the second Mariamne, another Herod; but she left her husband for Antipas, taking with her an infant daughter, called Salome.

And by this time Salome the sister of Herod the Great had died—bequeathing all her property to the Empress Livia.

And by this time a prophet called John had begun preaching in the regions that Antipas governed—denouncing the frivolities of the day and women who went from one husband to another, and telling of strange things soon to befall. Antipas would have ignored him, for there were many fanatical preachers in those parts and he believed that punishment emboldened them. But at Herodias's insistence John was imprisoned; and then she taught her little daughter to reproach her stepfather with kindness to a man who said vile things of her mother. So at last John was beheaded.

Before he was taken by Antipas, John had come to an understanding with another preacher who was going among the people with talk of miraculous happenings. This man was called Jesus, and he came from Nazareth in Galilee. Jesus and John were cousins, John being the elder by six months, but they had not met since they were children. John knew the story of how the three sorcerers had visited Bethlehem by old Herod's command and chosen Jesus to be the next King of the Jews. A stern-minded man, with a loathing of all that was fanciful and extravagant, he had set his heart against Jesus when he heard that he called himself the Messiah—thinking that the story of the sorcerers had turned his head. Moreover, he had heard that Jesus had preached of a time of great bliss soon to come; and his own preachings were grave and even menacing in temper—of the descent of the spirit of the Lord upon earth in extreme judgement. 'Repent, repent!' were the watchwords of John, while Jesus cried 'Hope, hope!' Another cause of John's suspicion of Jesus was that he had stayed for a while in Gadara, still a centre of heathen rhetoric: Joseph had been able to allow his son to lead an unlaborious life.

Then at last John and Jesus met. Jesus talked long with John, answering many questions about himself. The followers of John said that he saw that Jesus would persuade the multitudes to believe in him, because there was a soft charm in his voice and he held out golden promises to them; and that therefore he yielded to him and acknowledged him, feeling that his own truths would be lost if he went on preaching a different gospel. It was after his conversation with John that Jesus began to denounce the Pharisees, and also to stiffen his language against sinners—though he spoke more often in his own beguiling manner than in the manner of John.

Jesus's preaching caused increasing restlessness in Galilee, and Herodias advised her husband to deal with him as he had dealt with John. Antipas said that as John had bequeathed his followers to Jesus, so Jesus would find a greater one to whom to entrust his mission, and thus it was better to take no notice of him, lest the whole country be swept into fanaticism. But Herodias said: 'This man will yield his glory to no one: if you try him and condemn him now, he will tell his followers to remember him as the true Messiah—

and in a little while they will forget him.' Nevertheless, Antipas did nothing. And then it was heard that Jesus was going to Jerusalem. 'Destroy him before he goes to Jerusalem,' Herodias urged, 'for the people there are easily impressed by such talk, and if he makes a disturbance Pilate will be vexed with you for having let him come.' Pontius Pilate was the Roman procurator in Jerusalem at this time.

Antipas was himself going to Jerusalem, to celebrate the Passover; and when he arrived he advised Pilate to have Jesus watched. There was a disturbance, as Herodias had anticipated. Since the man came from Galilee, Pilate would have had Antipas decide what was to be done with him. But Antipas answered that his father Herod in his last years had once, in a wandering mood, thought of conferring his kingdom on this man, then an infant: he preferred not to meddle in the matter, lest it should seem that he was mocking his father's follies.

A little more must come into our story. The life of Herod the Great was a long one, not altogether ending with his death. For all these later things still taste of him—a taste from which Mariamne shrank at the start of her life with Herod and that Herod could not change. Perhaps it is how the world tasted in his time.

In A.D. 37 Herod Agrippa, the grandson of Herod the Great and brother of Herodias, succeeded in getting himself appointed King of the north-eastern regions, over which Herod's son Philip had ruled. Philip had died a few years before—his wife was Salome, Herodias's daughter, who had asked the death of John the Baptist. Archelaus had already been dead for many years, and Judaea and Samaria and Idumaea were now under direct Roman rule. But Antipas still lived, and Herodias.

Herod Agrippa resembled his grandfather Herod in character, but he had more confidence in himself. He was brought up in Rome, in the household of the Caesars. Herodias became jealous of him on her husband's account, fearing that by his influence with the Emperor he would one day gain possession of the whole of her grandfather's kingdom. Therefore she was always urging Antipas to oppose Herod Agrippa in every possible way, and at last persuaded him to go to Rome and complain to Caligula. And the result of this was that Antipas himself was punished, with banishment to Gaul.

Herodias accompanied him into exile. 'I do not feel that these are our troubles,' she said, 'but rather my grandfather's. Let us be glad that we are out of the shadow of Herod, and live now like free people.' Among the possessions she had brought with her was a portrait of her grandmother Mariamne. Studying it, Herodias said : 'I think she must have been free always.' Nor did Antipas blame Herodias for having caused their exile by making him go to Rome with complaints; for he understood the impatience that had driven her, being himself Herod's son.

But Herod Agrippa never escaped from the shadow of Herod. Even his death was not his own : he died of the same gnawing disease. It was he who put to death James the son of Zebedee, a Galilean follower of Jesus who had witnessed his crucifixion—having become as careful of the sensibilities of the Pharisees as his grandfather.

Shortly before his death James went to Spain, preaching in various cities there. Herodias and Antipas heard him, at Cadiz, where they had recently been permitted to move. Antipas was angered by his talk. But Herodias said : 'Let Agrippa tease his head with such things, which we have put far behind us.'

AFTERWORD

THE writing of *Lives of Wives*, first published in 1939, followed close upon the preparation of my *Collected Poems*,
first published in 1938. *A Trojan Ending* had its first publication in 1937; and in 1937 *Epilogue III* was also published
– the final issue of the critical review of literary and human
history of my editorship. In 1938 there was also published
The World And Ourselves, a symposium of my editorship,
a sequel to the *Epilogue* volumes treating of the then–visible
gathering of ominous clouds on the scene of human event.
In this year also, with publisher encouragement, I entered
upon a project-course aimed at introducing into the definition of words principles of meaning-value reflecting rational
principles I had come to see as inhering in the nature of
language itself. These were years, thus, uniting central
importances in my life's concerns: literature and poetry,
human history and destiny, and language as the ground of
human intelligence.

This period was, for me, one of crisis, a crisis of conjunc-
tion of the essential factors of the story of human existence:
its historical reality, the poetic promise, part-implicit, part-
explicit, in it, of a reality transcending the historical identity-
limits of human nature, and the coherencies of language in
relation to this. Yet the sense of crisis mounted in my feelings to a head of serenity. The case of human existence, its
history, and the problematical history-surviving ultimate,
took on, for me, clear-cut outlines. The past had brought
the story through trials of consciousness to the reality of
human existence in a reality of existence to a question-mark:

What do we *do*, having learned the nature of us? The question spoke itself, for me, out of an emptiness of time, time no longer history-shaped, an engulfing void – *or*, an all-livable ultimate.

By the time of my writing of *Lives of Wives* the feel, to me, of the pass to which the entire human circumstance had come was a seasoned one. The serenity I knew was proving to be a durable equanimity of fortitude towards the comprehensive criticality of the question that had spilled itself over from the supposed all-elastic confines of historical human life. At last, one could *judge* the human – look upon it, pronounce upon it, with self-responsible finality! Human sense of the human stood at last poised at the edge of an unignorable question about the human, whether it be of creature make or universal nature. The choice of creaturehood could not be other than an ignoring of the question for a lingering ever of one moment more and more – ultimate denial to the human of any dimension of content or property of being other than an all-self-referent character of humanness. *Lives of Wives* attests to the weightedness of history with the burden of the human problem of choice: how determinedly human were these, those, and these, those, others?

It is evidence of traits of human maturity in the lived human life of the past, mingled with the temporally or locally or otherwise idiosyncratic, that sustains interest in historical narrative, and faith in the integrity of the identity 'human'. But despite confirmation of the continuity of a quasi-permanent achievement of identity-credit under that name, the quality of maturity of the lives of human beings of historied time on time can be seen to have evaporated in the atmosphere of self-sufficiency breathed out and in – each time a claim of human identityhood achieved then, then, again. The record is not of a repeated sense of attainment to an ultimate, in being human, but of repeated stopping the story at a variable something viewable as the humanly comfortable (which has been, and is, variously, doctored to include the uncomfortable). The difference between sense of the human as an essence of history and as an essence of a living universal immediate is a matter of vision: seeing the human past in historical perspective, historical time the movable measure, or in human perspective, the measure a whole reality of conscious being, at once a scale of truth and of the real.

My adopting a view of the human circumstance as of a consummate reality, in the closing years of the decade of the Thirties (the closing years of my own third decade of life) fulfilled the main tendencies of my concerns of thought and work. The spirit of this, manifest in *Lives of Wives*, was an impartiality admitting of proportions of partiality – of partialities presided over by a generous impartiality. The spirit also had presence in the story-book *Progress of Stories*, published in 1935 (it appeared in a new edition in 1986). Someone who had interested herself in my work wrote to me recently, after reading *Lives of Wives* that she thought I must have undertaken such a task from desire to 'discover' what the make-up of the human was. I told her that I could not have written the book without knowledge of what the human was-is. The nature of the form of life we are, as I understand it, is indwelling, knowable only inwardly, not taxonomically: human identity is not distributive, collective, a sum – its detail is its general, its general its detail, it spells not a kind but encompasses the unities of living being. *Lives of Wives* abounds in detail; the general permeates it with due regard for its being, as far as it goes, no more than human story suspended in history.

I recall that I wrote in a copy of the book that I gave to a friend over ten years ago that it was 'something written of the past to make the present, our present, something more than that.' And, also: 'These are supplicitious histories,

327

but the foundations are factual. Fancy, in them, imitates knowledge, and delineation, truth – with some lucky strikes.' But knowledge and truth and time now seem, all, to have been fabricated into a game in which luck is a super-annuated issue – the game, the playing of it, made the life-point, the reality-crux, of the story of us. I hope that the varied complexities of the story that this book presents will not be understood as designed for reading-play; much serious matter is covered in its course, though I might be judged, mistakenly, to have skirted the story of Jesus with an irreverent evasiveness.

Laura (Riding) Jackson
1988

LAURA (RIDING) JACKSON

Born in 1901 in New York City, Laura (Riding) Jackson attended Girls' High School in Brooklyn and Cornell University. Her early poems appeared in several magazines, including *The Fugitive*, published by a group of southern poets, whom she soon joined.

From 1926 to 1939 she lived abroad, in England and Spain. It was in this period that she published most of her prose and poetry: her first book of poems appeared in 1926 simultaneously in England and the United States; *Lives of Wives* was published in 1939.

In 1941 she married Schuyler B. Jackson, poet, critic, and farmer, and begin a long collaboration with him on a book of word-meanings titled *Rational Meaning: A New Foundation for the Definition of Words*. The same year she renounced the writing of poetry, describing poetry as "blocking truth's ultimate verbal harmonies." She and her husband settled in Florida, where she lived until her death in 1991.

Besides the linguistic project she worked on for most of her later years, Jackson published various books, including *The Telling*, *Collected Poems* (a new edition of the 1938 collection), *Progress of Stories* (enlarged edition) and *The Word "Woman" and Other Related Writings*. During these last years she was also the recipient of several awards including a Mark Rothko Appreciation Award (1971), a Guggenheim Fellowship (1973), and the Bollingen Prize (1991) for her lifetime contribution to poetry.

SUN & MOON CLASSICS

This publication was made possible, in part, through an operational grant from the Andrew W. Mellon Foundation and through contributions from the following individuals:

Charles Altieri (Seattle, Washington)
John Arden (Galway, Ireland)
Paul Auster (Brooklyn, New York)
Jesse Huntley Ausubel (New York, New York)
Dennis Barone (West Hartford, Connecticut)
Jonathan Baumbach (Brooklyn, New York)
Guy Bennett (Los Angeles, California)
Bill Berkson (Bolinas, California)
Steve Benson (Berkeley, California)
Charles Bernstein and Susan Bee (New York, New York)
Dorothy Bilik (Silver Spring, Maryland)
Alain Bosquet (Paris, France)
In Memoriam: John Cage
In Memoriam: Camilo José Cela
Bill Corbett (Boston, Massachusetts)
Fielding Dawson (New York, New York)
Robert Crosson (Los Angeles, California)
Tina Darragh and P. Inman (Greenbelt, Maryland)
Christopher Dewdney (Toronto, Canada)
Arkadii Dragomoschenko (St. Petersburg, Russia)
George Economou (Norman, Oklahoma)
Kenward Elmslie (Calais, Vermont)
Elaine Equi and Jerome Sala (New York, New York)
Lawrence Ferlinghetti (San Francisco, California)
Richard Foreman (New York, New York)
Howard N. Fox (Los Angeles, California)
Jerry Fox (Aventura, Florida)
In Memoriam: Rose Fox
Melvyn Freilicher (San Diego, California)
Miro Gavran (Zagreb, Croatia)
Allen Ginsberg (New York, New York)
Peter Glassgold (Brooklyn, New York)
Barbara Guest (New York, New York)
Perla and Amiram V. Karney (Bel Air, California)
Fred Haines (Los Angeles, California)

Václav Havel (Prague, The Czech Republic)
Lyn Hejinian (Berkeley, California)
Fanny Howe (La Jolla, California)
Harold Jaffe (San Diego, California)
Ira S. Jaffe (Albuquerque, New Mexico)
Pierre Joris (Albany, New York)
Alex Katz (New York, New York)
Tom LaFarge (New York, New York)
Mary Jane Lafferty (Los Angeles, California)
Michael Lally (Santa Monica, California)
Norman Lavers (Jonesboro, Arkansas)
Jerome Lawrence (Malibu, California)
Stacey Levine (Seattle, Washington)
Herbert Lust (Greenwich, Connecticut)
Norman MacAffee (New York, New York)
Rosemary Macchiavelli (Washington, DC)
Beatrice Manley (Los Angeles, California)
In Memoriam: Mary McCarthy
Harry Mulisch (Amsterdam, The Netherlands)
Iris Murdoch (Oxford, England)
Martin Nakell (Los Angeles, California)
In Memoriam: bpNichol
Toby Olson (Philadelphia, Pennsylvania)
Maggie O'Sullivan (Hebden Bridge, England)
Rochelle Owens (Norman, Oklahoma)
Marjorie and Joseph Perloff (Pacific Palisades, California)
Dennis Phillips (Los Angeles, California)
Carl Rakosi (San Francisco, California)
Tom Raworth (Cambridge, England)
David Reed (New York, New York)
Ishmael Reed (Oakland, California)
Janet Rodney (Santa Fe, New Mexico)
Joe Ross (Washington, DC)
Jerome and Diane Rothenberg (Encinitas, California)
Dr. Marvin and Ruth Sackner (Miami Beach, Florida)
Floyd Salas (Berkeley, California)
Tom Savage (New York, New York)
Leslie Scalapino (Oakland, California)
James Sherry (New York, New York)
Aaron Shurin (San Francisco, California)
Charles Simic (Strafford, New Hampshire)
Gilbert Sorrentino (Stanford, California)

Catharine R. Stimpson (Staten Island, New York)
John Taggart (Newburg, Pennsylvania)
Nathaniel Tarn (Tesuque, New Mexico)
Fiona Templeton (New York, New York)
Mitch Tuchman (Los Angeles, California)
Hannah Walker and Ceacil Eisner (Orlando, Florida)
Wendy Walker (New York, New York)
Anne Walter (Carnac, France)
Jeffery Weinstein (New York, New York)
Mac Wellman (Brooklyn, New York)
Arnold Wesker (Hay on Wye, England)

If you would like to be a contributor to this series, please send your tax-deductible contribution to The Contemporary Arts Educational Project, Inc., a non-profit corporation, 6026 Wilshire Boulevard, Los Angeles, California 90036.

SUN & MOON CLASSICS

Author   Title

Alferi, Pierre   *Natural Gait* 95 ($10.95)
Antin, David   *Selected Poems: 1963–1973* 10 ($12.95)
Barnes, Djuna   *At the Roots of the Stars: The Short Plays* 53
                                ($12.95)
                                The Book of Repulsive Women 59 ($6.95)
                                Interviews 86 ($13.95)
                                New York 5 ($12.95)
                                Smoke and Other Early Stories 2 ($10.95)
Bernstein, Charles   *Content's Dream: Essays 1975–1984* 49
                                ($14.95)
                                Dark City 48 ($11.95)
                                Rough Trades 14 ($10.95)
Bjørneboe, Jens   *The Bird Lovers* 43 ($9.95)
Breton, André   *Arcanum 17* 51 ($12.95)
                                Earthlight 26 ($12.95)
Bromige, David   *The Harbormaster of Hong Kong* 32   ·
                                ($10.95)
Butts, Mary   *Scenes from the Life of Cleopatra* 72
                                ($13.95)
Cadiot, Olivier   *L'Art Poétique* 98 ($10.95)
Celan, Paul   *Breathturn* 74 ($12.95)
Coolidge, Clark   *The Crystal Text* 99 ($11.95)
                                Own Face 39 ($10.95)
                                The Rova Improvisations 34 ($11.95)
Copioli, Rosita   *The Blazing Lights of the Sun* 84 ($11.95)
de Nerval, Gérard   *Aurélia* 103 ($12.95)
De Angelis, Milo   *Finite Intuition* 65 ($11.95)
DiPalma, Ray   *Numbers and Tempers: Selected Early Poems*
                                24 (11.95)
von Doderer, Heimito   *The Demons* 13 ($29.95)
                                Every Man a Murderer 66 ($14.95)